VICTORIOUS LIVING
By E. Stanley Jones

Living Victoriously

UPDATED
By MaryAnn Moore

xulon PRESS

FORWARD

W hile most all would agree the Christian life may not be an easy life, it most **definitely** should be understood that Christians have received the Victory. Our eternal life and our sins have been paid for by God's very own Son on our behalf! Jesus Christ paid the price so you and I might have the chance to live a victorious life.

Often we find that we are not the new creature Christ created us to be, instead of living victoriously we live defeated, believing a lie instead of living the truth. E. Stanley Jones said it best when he said, "Victorious living does not mean freedom from temptation, nor does it mean freedom from mistakes."

Almost daily some one will ask me about a great devotional book that would help them in their pursuit of Holy victorious living in Christ. MaryAnn Moore has not only captured the heart and vision of E. Stanley Jones in her update of *Victorious Living,* but she has truly captured the heart of Jesus Christ and His desire to have an intimate relationship with us. MaryAnn has helped to protect and preserve the message of Dr. Jones for many, many more years.

It is my prayer that this great book will be read and shared with many so Christ is made much of and we as believers will live victoriously through the power of the Cross.

J. Phillip Martin
Teaching Pastor
First Baptist Concord

June, 2008

INTRODUCTION

In the late summer of 2004 a persistent Inner Urge came to me to update the excellent, inspiring and compelling book by E. Stanley Jones, VICTORIOUS LIVING. The Inner Urge seemed to impress upon me the need for this great book, already inspired by God, through a great godly man, to be updated for our day and time. Some of the words and phrases familiar in the early twentieth century and used by Dr. Jones in the original version would not be familiar and easily understood in the early twenty-first century. This book, which is no longer in print, is just too good and enlightening to be put aside and never shared with our present generation, as we struggle to live life victoriously. Many people today are living morally and spiritually defeated lives, therefore causing us to be inwardly beaten and outwardly ineffective for Christ.

The structure of this book remains the same as the original book, it tries to meet three needs: (1) this is a book of daily devotions. Usually in a devotional book you will find, a book of scattered thoughts, changing from day to day, however these devotions are woven around one theme, LIVING VICTORIOUSLY. (2) These daily studies are gathered into groups of seven, so that the book can be used as a daily devotional for personal, family, or weekly study for Sunday school classes, small groups, and such. (3) The subject material is put in such a continuous whole that <u>it may be read through as an ordinary book</u>. (This is my personal favorite, even though every one of the options has excellent merit).

We start at the lowest point and climb steadily up, step by step, to the highest level of living victoriously. <u>Many people are not able</u>

to live a victorious life because they do not know how to link up with God's power. This book is for you. The first steps have been made very clear.

Do you have an unquenchable thirst to know how and where to start to achieve a life that is evidence of the peace that surpasses understanding, and how to pass it to others, as well? You may have asked yourself, how does the kingdom of God start within my unruly, discontented, selfish, ungrateful, impatient, and sullen self, so I may be a witness to others? In this book you will be given the brushes and colors to use and shown how to use them to live a victorious life.

MaryAnn Moore

This book is dedicated to my five grandchildren, Adam, Janna, Jennifer, Ben and Hannah. And to all young people and older people alike who desire a life with Christ that is wonderfully victorious.

* To receive the most from your daily devotions, PLEASE read scriptures located in upper right hand corner of each day. Your study and learning will not be clear and complete without the daily Word.

My sincere prayer is for all who read and study this book will find through its pages a clear path to a life that is truly victorious.

MaryAnn Moore

THE QUESTION THAT STOPS OUR
PURSUIT OF LIVING VICTORIOUSLY

In the beginning God (Genesis 1:1).

It would be great if, in our pursuit of Living Victoriously, we could all begin with God. It would put a solid foundation of truth beneath our searching feet. It would give meaning and purpose to our whole life. However, many of us cannot begin there. For God is vague and unreal to us. We wish we could feel His presence, for life without the Great Companion has a certain emptiness and meaning-lessness about it. Doubt is not something we want to do, but apparently something we can't get away from. The facts of life are just too much for us – the sorrow, the pain and suffering, the unemployment, the hunger, homelessness, the stress of modern life, the exploitation of the weak and deprived by the strong, and the heartlessness of nature, all these things and more seem to shatter our belief in God. Not that we completely reject belief in Him; it just fades away and becomes unreal. Among all the losses of our modern day we are trying to salvage one thing in the midst of the wreckage, the desire for reality. We want to keep an inner integrity. We detest all unre-ality. That leads us to face the facts –our doubt has gone deeper than our belief in God; we find ourselves questioning life itself. Does life have any meaning? Any goal? Any purpose? Is the flame of life within us different from the flame that leaps from the logs that burn in a fireplace – both destined to die down into a final ash? If life has no ultimate meaning, has it any meaning now as we live it from day to day?

Prayer for today: O God, our Father, if we may call You Father, as we begin our search we are haunted with fears and doubts. Help us to face them all and come out living victoriously. Amen

January 2   Ecclesiastes 4:1-2; 9:2-3; John 10:10

SHALL WE FOLLOW A LIFE "NO" OR A LIFE "YES"?

Philosophies of life may change but the end result remains the same.

Philosophies have changed since the early 1930's when E. Stanley Jones wrote, "there are just two elemental philosophies of life: that of Buddha and that of Christ. The rest are compromises between." Today we would have to say that Buddha is not the other main philosophy of life beside that of Christ. However, any philosophy you choose to live by except that of Christ, will not give you victorious life – so whatever philosophy you choose, if not that of Christ, you have chosen to live – Life Denial – a life "NO".

Christ – Life-Affirmation, other philosophies – Life-Denial. It actually comes down to two basic philosophies – Belief and Unbelief. Two completely opposite views of life. When we look at the same facts of life from belief and then from unbelief we come to two opposite conclusions – one to a final "yes" and the other a final "no".

Speaking of Buddha, he taught that existence and evil are one. And the only way to get out of evil is to get out of existence. Is that so different than what unbelief teaches us today: Does everything seem to be under the process of ruin? The beautiful baby girl, the happy child, the blushing bride – and then the withered old woman shriveling to fit her final burial dress. We grasp the lurid colors of the sunset and find that we have grasp the darkness – first beauty, then the blackness. A final "NO" to life.

Prayer for today: O God, our Father, help us not to be confused and dismayed. Let us not be compelled to adopt the soul of a pessimist. We know there is a better way of life, Father, help us to find it. Amen.

January 3   Ecclesiastes 1:1-9; 2 Corinthians 5:1-4

IS LIFE A BUBBLE OR IS LIFE AN EGG?

In the early part of the twentieth century, there were many followers of Buddha and some were unaware that they were driven there by the hard facts of life. They worshiped at the shrine of the"stupa." (The stupa is a large mound of earth or a dome-shaped building made to hold relics of Buddha.)

Standing in the midst of a Buddhist ruin, an Indian guide was asked why the stupa was always oval shaped. "Because Buddhism believes that life is a bubble, therefore the stupa is shaped like one," he replied. Life is a bubble – "nothingness" - look at it again, is it shaped like a bubble or is it shaped like an egg? Is it a bubble with nothing in it, or is it an egg filled with infinite possibilities – possibilities of growth and development and perfection? I vote for the egg view of life. We know that even an egg, if badly handled, can turn rotten, just as life can turn rotten if we handle it badly. Nevertheless, we have to vote on one side or the other, let's follow a man who saw more deeply into the sorrow and misery of life, than any human in the past, present, or future has ever seen or will ever see, and that man "Jesus" came out at the other end and affirmed His faith in Life. *"I am come that they might have life, and that they might have it more abundantly."* (John 10:10 KJV). Jesus affirmed that life was not a bubble, but an egg. Was He right? ABSOLUTELY!

Prayer for today: O God, our Father, light shines bright on our darkened horizon as we listen to you. Help us not to drown in the sea of despair. Amen.

January 4   1 Corinthians 15:19-26

THE ALTERNATIVES

Is life a bubble or an egg? We must make a choice. One side tells us that the universe is slowly running down and that one day it will end in ash, carrying with it all things and all life to its final doom. Death shall reign. The other side tells us that the universe is being renewed by a silent and saving bombardment of life-giving rays, so that the last word is NOT being spoken by death but by life. Life shall reign. One says the universe is an empty bubble, the other says it is an egg with substance.

One side tells us that we are made up of elements which can be found in a chemist lab, so life is only mucus and misery. On the other side we are told that we are made in the image of the Divine, that we have infinite possibilities of growth and development before us. One says we are a bundle of futilities, the other says we are a bundle of possibilities.

One side says that we are just a composite of responses to stimuli from environment, mechanically determined and with no real power of choice. The other side tells us that we have sufficient freedom to determine our destiny and that our soul shapes its environment as well as being shaped by it. One says that human freedom is a bubble; the other says it is an egg.

Some say that prayer is an autosuggestion of oneself into an illusionary state of mind, that nothing comes back except the echo of ones own voice. Others say that in prayer actual communication takes place, that we link ourselves with the resources of God, so that our powers and facilities are heightened and life is strengthened and purified at it center. One says prayer is futile, the other says it is fertile. WHAT DO YOU SAY?

Prayer for today: O God, our Father, we want life, true life. Show us the way and help us to choose it. Amen.

January 5   Psalm 42:1-5; 53:1

LOOKING AT ALTERNATIVES – (Continued)

On one hand, there are those who tell us that God is an unnecessary assumption, that science can explain everything, that the spaces and gaps of the universe into which we used to put the working of God are slowly but surely filled up by science, so that the universe is self-sufficient, law abiding, and predictable. On the other hand, there are those who tell us that God is not to be found in the gaps and spaces and on occasion breaking into the process, but He is the process itself, the life of its life; that the universe is dependable because God is dependable; that it works according to law because God's mind is an orderly mind, not whimsical and notional, that since intelligence comes out of the universe and meets our intelligence it must have gone into it, so that according to some "the universe is more like a thought than a machine"; since the universe seems to work toward purposeful ends, we must either equip "matter" with intelligent purposes (in which case it would not be mere matter), or we must put a creative Intelligence in and around the process; that since the universe from the smallest atom to the farthest star is mathematical, we must either believe that God is a pure mathematician; it would seem that the purposeful matter-hypothesis takes more sheer gullibility to believe than to believe that there is an Infinite Spirit, called God, who is within the process working toward intelligent moral ends, inviting our limited spirits to work with Him toward intelligent, redemptive purposes.

One says the idea of God is a bubble, the other says it is an egg. We must make a choice. What choice do you make?

Prayer for today: O God, our Father, shall I rule You out and vote for a dead universe – dead because its final goal is death? Or shall I vote for a living universe with You as its beginning, with You as its perpetual Creator and with You as its goal and end? Clarify my mind, my heart, that I may not lose myself and You among the maze of things. Amen.

January 6   2 Corinthians 13:3-4; 2 Timothy 2-8;
                                        Hebrews 1:1-3

CONTINUING TO LOOK AT THE ALTERNATIVES

There are those who tell us that Christ is a spent force in humanity; that His day is over because He spoke to a simple age, but now we face a complicated scientific age; that Christ was good, but not good enough - for us.

Then there are those who feel that Christ day is just beginning; that what has failed has been a miserable exaggeration and not the real thing; that even the partial application of His teaching and spirit has been one thing that has kept the soul of humanity alive; that He has been and is the trustee and creator of the finest and best in humanity; that when we have Him in our heart we have the key to God, to the meaning of the universe and to our own lives; that when we expose ourselves to Him in simplicity and obedience, life is changed, lifted, renewed, that He is truly the one unspent force in religion – He faces us as the Great Contemporary and our Judge. One says that dependence upon Jesus is a bubble, a crutch, a weakness; the other says it is an egg with untold redemptive possibilities.

There are those who say conversion is an adolescent phenomenon; or that it is the result of group-suggestion, easily induced and quickly fades away. On the other hand, many affirm that this change called conversion is far from being group-suggestion; it helps them cut across the purpose of both the group and self when they are wrong. One says that conversion, (being born again) is a bubble; the other says it is an egg. What say you?

Prayer for today: O God, our Father, hold us steady as we face the complex issues of our time, may there be no eluding, no turning to irrelevancies, and no excuses. Save us to be real. Amen.

January 7   Joshua 24:15; Matthew 4:17-22

WE MUST MAKE A CHOICE – WHICH IS IT?

The issues of life are before me, I must vote for or against a view of life which has worth, purpose, and goal. If I vote that the universe has no meaning, then I vote that my own life has none. However, if my life has no meaning and therefore no purpose, it will go to pieces, for psychology tells us that without a strong controlling purpose, which co-ordinates life, the personality disintegrates through its own inner turmoil – no purpose, no personality. But that purpose must be high enough to lift me out of myself. If my purpose ends with me, again I disintegrate. My purpose in life must include God, who gives firm foundation and everlasting meaning to my purpose. If I lose God, I lose myself, my world, I lose everything! Someone has said, and they are right, "If there is no God, we will have to invent one to keep us sane."

If I let go of Christ, then God becomes distant, vague and unreal. In Christ I find "the near side of God." In Him God speaks to me in a language I can understand, a human language. And as I listen to that language my universe seems to become a face-tender, strong, forgiving, and redemptive. Law becomes Love.

If I do not sincerely get in touch with Him through the written Word, I neglect the greatest and most redemptive fact of history and I pay the penalty of being unfed at the place of my deepest need. If I do not pray I will become cynical and shallow. If I do pray, I will have nerve and courage, a sense of adequacy, power over wayward desires and passions. If I undergo a moral and spiritual change called conversion, I will be unified, morally straight, and spiritually adjusted. If I do not I will become a stunted soul. If I must vote, and I must —I vote for life!!

Prayer for today: O God, our Father, I make the choice; I do choose life with all its fullest, deepest implications. Help me to find life and live it - victoriously. Amen.

January 8   Matthew 5:48; Romans 8:18-23

WHY ARE WE RELIGIOUS?

There are many various definitions of religion. One says it is "what we do with our solitude"; another that it is "how we integrate ourselves socially"; another that "the root of religion is fear," and so on.

The reason that religion is so difficult to define is because life is difficult to define. When we define religion in terms of its various outward appearances, we get partial, sometimes contradictory definitions. Religion having many forms has <u>one root</u>. That root is the urge that drives us to pursue a fuller life. In everything, from the lowest cell, to the highest person, there is an urge toward completion, toward perfection. The religious urge is found in the urge for a more complete life. It is that urge turned toward higher, more noble ends. We feel that we cannot be complete unless this urge for life is fastened onto the highest life - God. Religion is the urge for life turned to quality living. It is not satisfied with life apart from quality. Life urge makes us want to be better not bigger. The quality life and moral life emerge.

We are religious because we cannot help it. We want to live in the highest, fullest sense, and **quality expression of life is called religion**. So true religion is not something we can put on or off; it is identified with life itself. We are all incurably religious. Even unbelievers are deeply religious. They are striving for a better social life, right or wrong in their method of getting it, but the very desire for better social standard is religious. <u>For religion is a cry for life</u>.

Prayer for today: O God, our Father, who planted this urge for completion within us, let not this urge be for nothing. You have inspired it. It will only be satisfied with You. Amen.

January 9   John 1:9-18

THE DIVINE INITIATIVE

Yesterday we said we are religious because it is the giving vent to the life-urge, the quality expression of the life-urge. This upward movement of our spirit alone would not account for our religious spirit.

The other side of the truth is that we seem to be urged on from above. We do not merely aspire, we are inspired. We feel we are being invaded by a Higher Power. This pressure from above awakens us, makes us discontented with a divine discontent; makes us pray – sometimes with longings, but no words; makes us inwardly and sometimes outwardly revolt, against things as they are and against what we are. This is divine initiative – the cosmic Lover wooing His creation to Himself and in the same way to its own perfection.

This is dual movement in religion – the going up of one and coming down of another. We move toward God and God moves toward us. The Old Testament is our search for God, and the New Testament is God's search for us. This is generally true, but not entirely true, for there would have been no search for God in the Old Testament and in the various religions had not God inspired and initiated that search. So when we began to seek for God, we <u>will</u> find Him!

Impossible? Too good to be true? Not if we study the nature of life. Life not only wants more life, but it wants to share life. The creative urge is within us. God being the perfect life, therefore, the divine initiative. We are religious because we crave and because Christ loves. He creates, we crave.

Prayer for today: My Father, if this is true, then I am not far from You and You are not far from me. Perhaps this very longing in my heart is the presence of Your being. My heart craves for You, for I want to find You. Amen.

January 10   John 1:14; 1 John 1:1-4

DEFINITION OF RELIGION

Yesterday we said that religion resulted from a dual movement of our aspirations and God's inspirations. God's life has an effect on our life at every point. The result? When something disturbs us, we desire peace about it; we pray for that peace, we protest within concerning that which disturbs us. Christ is the meeting place of this upward and downward movement. Christ is man ascending and God descending – The Son of man, the Son of God. Since He is the meeting place of the two sides of religion He becomes its definition— CHRIST. This is not a spelled-out, but a lived-out definition. Some things cannot be said, they have to be shown. So – it has been shown to us what constitutes religion - His spirit of life, His relationships with God and humanity, His purity, His love, His mastery of environment of humanity and things, His care for the sinner, the underprivileged, His redemptive purposes for us and society, His sympathy, His final willingness to take all our pain, all our sorrow, all our defeat, all our sin into His own heart and die for us, and His offer to us for a new way of life – the Kingdom of God on earth – all this, and His transparent Spirit of Victory in the middle of it all constitutes religion. Never was there such a definition of religion as He gives in His own life. It cleanses away all relevancies, all magic, all superstition, all controversies about particular form of ceremony and superiorities and turns us to the serious business of learning how to live and to live victoriously. When in our churches we are confronted by this rite and that ceremony, this order of worship, that church government – we should simply remember– it's marginal – not the central interest and we have seen the Center. We know who defines religion – by His own life!

Prayer for today: O God, we have seen what we should be, what we must be, if we are to really live. Help us this day to give ourselves over to it with our whole-hearted devotion until it becomes a fact within us. Amen.

January 11   Matthew 4:23; Luke 17:20-21; 21:27-28

THE MAIN EMPHASIS IN THE DEFINITION

There is one point in this definition of religion that needs emphasis – the Kingdom of God on earth. We need to emphasize it because Christ emphasized it. It is the one thing around which all else revolves. *"And Jesus went about all Galilee, teaching in their synagogues, and preaching the gospel of the kingdom."* (Matthew 4:23 KJV). Just what was the Kingdom? E. Stanley Jones wrote in one of his earlier books that the Kingdom of God is a Higher Order founded on the Fatherly love of God, redemption, justice, fellowship, and standing near by – the lower order founded on greed, selfishness, exploitation, not supporting others. This Higher Order breaks into, cleanses, renews, and redeems the lower order, both within the individual will and the collective will. And there is still more to this truth – it is all around us, yet it is within us—*"The Kingdom of God is within you,"* (Luke 17:21b KJV). This Kingdom has been "built from the foundation of the world." Did Christ mean that this Kingdom has been built within the very foundation of the world and within the very structure of our mental and moral make-up? Yes, He meant just that and more – it is "all around us" and we will see what that means later. But it does mean that the Kingdom is written, not merely in sacred books, but in the very structure and make-up of the world and of us and society. When we study the laws deeply embedded in the universe, in our own mental, moral and physical being, the laws that constitute true sociological living, we discover the laws of the Kingdom. Not fully, but nevertheless, real and actual. This is important, for when we start with this business of living victoriously; we are starting with the solid facts of the laws written within our own being, within the structure of society and the world around us.

Prayer for today: Our Father, You are all around us. Your will has been worked within the texture of things. Help us discover Your kingdom and obey it. You are our foundation. Amen.

January 12   Jeremiah 31:33; Romans 2:14-16;
2 Corinthians 3:1-3

THE KINGDOM WRITTEN WITHIN

Yesterday we saw that we do not begin with something imposed on life when we are beginning with the Kingdom, but begin with life itself – its laws and its ways of fulfillment.

Moral laws are deeply embedded in the constitution of things – we do not break them, they break us. Many have demanded freedom to do as they like, (we've all heard it, "if it feels good, do it"), many rebel against morality, they want to express themselves as they so desire. The result? Those who try this become sad and disillusioned. The fact is this lifestyle is not a natural lifestyle, but a style imposed on life.

The first law of mental health is to be direct and honest in ALL relationships, but especially with ourselves. The universe and all humanity are built for truth; the universe will not back a lie. Lies sooner or later come apart when the facts show up. Since the Kingdom stands for absolute truth and our own mental make-up demands the same, then it certainly appears that the laws of the Kingdom are written within us!

"The right thing is always the healthy thing." Conversely, you could say, "the wrong thing is always the unhealthy thing." Therefore we cannot function at our best unless we discover the right and obey it. Isn't it true that sin is not only bad, but unhealthy and crippling to our lives? Does this not sober you?

Prayer for today: O God, our Father, the moral law written within us makes us tremble. But are these laws redemptive: Teach us and help us to listen. Amen.

January 13   John 1:4; 11:25; 14:6; 17:3; 20:31

THE KINGDOM AND LIFE

We learned that the only way life will work, as it is designed to work, is God's way. When we find God's Kingdom within us, we find ourselves.

Jesus said the same – He made the Kingdom and life synonymous, *"it is better for you to enter into <u>life</u> maimed"*... *"It is better for you to enter <u>the Kingdom of God</u> with one eye"*... (Mark 9:43, 47). Here He used the terms "<u>the Kingdom of God</u>" and "<u>life</u>" interchangeably. To Him they are one.

Life to Jesus had to be spelled with an upper case "L" to express what He meant. It is true that this life and its laws are within us and the universe. But there is more. If that had been all, it would have been naturalism. Not that we condemn it when we call it naturalism, for nature, human and nonhuman, is God's handiwork. While God wrote the elemental laws of the Kingdom "within us" He did not stop there. The Kingdom is "within us" but also "all around us" and to spell life with an uppercase "L" we must be prepared to let life natural and life supernatural meet and when they touch – the white light of Life results!

The Kingdom then is life-plus. It is the grafting of a higher Life upon the tree trunk of the lower life. The trunk will still be there; its roots going deep in the soil of the natural, but we will bud, bloom and bear fruit with great new possibilities. It is up to each one of us to decide – will you live life with a lowercase "l" or an uppercase "L"?

Prayer for today: O God, our Father, we talk of the Kingdom. You are the Kingdom; You are at our heart's door. We put our trembling hand to the door knob and let You in, we know that we have let in Life with an uppercase "L". Amen.

January 14   1 Corinthians 1:21-31; 2:15

ARE CHRISTIANS UNNATURAL AND STRANGE?

Sometimes the Christian may seem unnatural and strange. This makes many honest people hesitate, for they do not want to appear strange. Many feel that Christians try to bend human nature into an impossible position, something that makes us unnatural and disconnected. Someone asked, "Is Christianity natural?" We usually fear the unnatural. On the other hand, someone said, "the <u>soul</u> is naturally Christian." I think we can say this statement is true. When we obey Christ, we feel natural; we fill at home, completely adjusted. When we disobey Him, we feel orphaned, estranged, disconnected with ourselves and the world. <u>We just seem to be made for Christ and His Kingdom</u>. It is true that when we obey God we have to break with society in many ways. That makes us seem strange and impossible. But it may be that society, at those places, is strange and impossible. We call a person strange when they are peculiar –"off center." Isn't society, insanely bent on its own destruction through its selfishness, its conflicts and immoralities, peculiarities – "off center?" The center of life is Christ; when we are adjusted to Him, life catches its rhythm, its harmony. When life revolves around something else, it is peculiar, and consequently self-destructive and society-destructive.

Was Christ strange? Many people of His day thought He was. We now see that His was the only sanity. He moves through those Biblical scenes, poised and masterful, at home in the huts of the poor and in the houses of the rich – **the one sane One, to whom we must turn to or lose our sanity, and ourselves**.

Prayer for today: O God, our Father, we have become so used to the insanities of life around us that we look on the sane as the insane. Give us a clear mind and heart that we may turn from the insanities of selfishness and greed to the sanities of Your way. In Jesus' name we pray. Amen.

WORKING IN THE DARK

We must be perfectly clear whether Christianity will work before we can go on to "Living Victoriously." As long as we have suspicion and doubt lurking in our minds that we are about something that cannot be done, that the universe won't back it, then we are paralyzed at the center of our thinking. On the other hand, if we are sure that <u>we</u> are completely behind our actions, then we will be determined to do the impossible.

The disciples were laboriously rowing in the dark and getting nowhere. The winds and the waves were against them and the whole process was futile. Then Jesus came! They cried out in fear thinking He was a ghost. Finally they took Him into the boat and, "Immediately the ship was at the shore where they were going." The entire situation ends in futility – a laboriously rowing and getting nowhere. We feel a sense of striving meaninglessly. Everything looks dark. Life is just too much for us. Then Jesus comes and we are afraid of Him – He is ghostly, unnatural, and will demand from us the unnatural and impossible. This is our first reaction. But finally we <u>let Him in</u> – and "now," we find ourselves at the very place we were striving to reach! This is the way it works.

Are you afraid of Jesus? When Herod heard that Jesus had come he *"was troubled, and all Jerusalem with him."* (Matthew 2:3). Troubled at the coming of the Deliverer! Should the flower be afraid of the sunshine? Should the heart be afraid at the coming of love? Should life be afraid of the coming of Life?

Prayer for today: Help me, gentle, redeeming, impressionable God, not to keep You at a distance through fear. Help me to take You into my little troubled boat. Amen.

January 16   2 Corinthians 2:14-16; Galatians 2:20; 6:14

THE INSTINCT OF SELF-EXPRESSION

We saw in yesterday's study that we labor in vain until Jesus comes into our lives. Consider the natural things within us; those things which are a part of our physical being, can these natural instincts be fulfilled, can they reach their goal apart from Christ?

Consider the instinct of self-expression. The "self" instinct is extremely strong. Therefore, self-expression is natural and normal. We strive to reach the goal of self-expression. We all do. We have seen a small child display their self-expression and at times may have laughed thinking it was cute. However, in polite society we do not laugh at sophisticated attempts – we get irritated. Place a dozen people in one situation, all wanting to express themselves, and you have the stage set for disagreement, confusion and jealousy. The result is strife, stress and struggle. The whole thing ends in futility. We prevent each other from accomplishing a thing. We are laboriously rowing and it is getting darker and darker. Then across the troubled waters Jesus comes to us. We cry out in fear of Him, for we suspect what He will ask of us. He will ask that we stop all this and forget about ourselves. But as we labor on in our futilities He keeps coming back, until we finally <u>let Him in</u>. Then we lose ourselves in His will and purpose. We forget about our self-expression. And **now**, we are at the shore where we were rowing laboriously to reach. We are never more ourselves than when we are completely His. We have found ourselves. We have arrived. We have obeyed the deepest law of the universe: *"For whoever wants to save his life will lose it, but whoever loses his life for me and for the gospel will save it."* (Mark 8:35). IT WORKS, IT REALLY DOES WORK!!

Prayer for today: O Christ, when we were drowning we were afraid of the life-line – forgive us. But the very fact that You rescued us is Your forgiveness. We thank You. Amen.

January 17   Matthew 5:43-48; Romans 12:19-21

HOW TO ELIMINATE OUR ENEMIES

Another natural instinct: wanting to eliminate our enemies. Those who oppose us, who hurt our feelings, who do us harm, become our enemies. We strive to get to the place where we have no enemies. Sometime we might try going through fist-city; sometime thinking it more "sophisticated," we try to cut their heads off with our sharp tongue, or socially kill them. Or if possible we'll take them to court hoping to make them bend, if not break. Or collectively we go to war waving banners with hurtful, untrue gossip, and words that will kill. In all these attempts, and many more, we strive to eliminate our enemies. But soon we are rowing laboriously and getting absolutely nowhere. We are not eliminating our enemies, we are multiplying them.

We learn that harsh words produce harsh words, and sharp tongues have a way of sharpening other tongues. "Cutting others to pieces" results in isolating ourselves. Court cases produce court cases. And as for as eliminating our enemies, we find it only produces them and hard fists shaken at the world turns our world into a mirror from which hard fists shake back at us. We get nowhere.

Then Jesus comes to us across our troubled waters. We are afraid, because we suspect He will ask us to <u>love</u> our enemies. And we do not want to love them, we want to eliminate them. But He keeps coming back until finally we <u>let Him in</u>. Then as we accept His way we find a desire, even a craving, to do good to others, yes, even to our enemies. And **now** we are at the place where we were going. Our enemies are eliminated. We are free of them in the only way possible – we turned them into friends. Even if they do not respond, our animosity has gone and therefore our enemies are gone. We arrived.

Prayer for today: O Christ, help us to accept Your way, even toward our enemies. Help us to live in such a way that we have no enemies. Amen.

January 18   Mark 9:33-35; 10:35-45

HOW CAN WE BECOME GREAT?

Another phase of the "self" instinct: how to become great. We all want to be great. No matter our station in life, we all want to achieve greatness.

Many women wear expensive designer clothes and jewelry trying to "out-do" their co-workers and friends. Many men, by acting "macho" try to be forceful and impressive. What about the fancy cars we buy each year, when we don't need them, bigger and nicer homes? And never let us forget those who smoke, drink, do drugs, sex, "whatever" because they think it makes them appear great in the eyes of their peers. We must keep up appearances, if we are going to appear great.

But it does not work. It all ends in futility. We grow small trying to be great. We labor in rowing, striving to get to the place of greatness, and end nowhere. Then Jesus comes. Again we fear Him, for we fear He will ask us to be servant of all in order for us to be great. We do not want to serve, we want to be served. But He's still there. Then we let Him in. We forget greatness as we submit with Him to serve others. And "now" as we submit our will to His we rise, the servant of all becomes the greatest of all. We arrived.

Prayer for today: O Christ, You who came not to be served but to serve, please help me to be more like You. Amen.

January 19   Acts 5:41; Galatians 5:22-23;
                                    Philippians 3:1

HOW DO WE ARRIVE AT HAPPINESS?

We all want to be happy, and rightly so. This is a deep rooted instinct. God must have planted it there. The God who made sunsets, painted the rose, put play into the kitten and the smile on a baby's face and laughter in our heart, is surely not happy when we are unhappy.

So we start out to find the place of happiness. We declare that the world will show us a good time. However, for some reason happiness eludes us. It slips through our fingers as we grasp for it. The most miserable people are those who are fed-up with life and are determined to be happy no matter the cost. They jump from one thing to the other trying to avoid being bored to tears with themselves. Try as hard as we may to enjoy ourselves, to be totally satisfied and happy, it doesn't happen. The soul weeps within us and doesn't know how to enjoy itself. It has missed the way. It is dark, very dark within us. The place of happiness is not in sight. Then we see a Figure across the waters! We are afraid! We cry out in fear. But His patient insistence overcomes us and we <u>let Him in.</u>

We now forget our happiness as we begin to think of the happiness of others. We walk with Him into others sad situations and strive to lift that sadness, and "now" our heart sings with a new song – a deep, fundamental and abiding song of joy and happiness. We arrived.

Prayer for today: O Christ, we have misunderstood You. We thought because Your symbol was a cross that You were therefore Christ the Sad. Forgive us. We now see that You are Christ the Glad. One touch of Your gladness and our hearts sing forever. We thank You. Amen.

29

January 20   Matthew 5:27-30; 19:3-6; Galatians 5:19-21

HOW DO WE ARRIVE AT SEXUAL FULFILLMENT?

Sex is an integral part of human nature and is therefore God-given and in itself is not unclean. It is as natural as the appetite for food.

Through this strange power being female can turn to motherhood and being male can turn to fatherhood. When this happens a home is formed with a child as part of the union. Love binds all three. There is nothing on earth more beautiful than a loving family. Heaven touches this earthly thing and makes it a heavenly thing.

But while sex, under the guidance and restraint of pure love, can be a heavenly thing, sex, used in the wrong way can be turned into hell on earth. Sex has produced more happiness and unhappiness than any other single thing in life. It all depends on what you do with it. Many try to get sexual fulfillment through unrestrained sexual freedom. They say they have a right to experience life anyway they choose, including any form of sexual experience, apart from morality. And they do so. They are soon laboriously rowing in a black sea of despair. It is dark and getting darker. The promised heaven turns to present hell. They are getting nowhere except into deeper "self-disgust." Then Jesus comes. They are afraid of Him. He is unnatural and strict. But they get nowhere without Him, they <u>let Him in.</u> And "now" they are at the shore on the other side. Inside the marriage relationship – restraint and dedication create a beautiful end. Outside marriage – the taking of this power of sex and turning its driving force to create a "no limits" attitude even on levels of music, art, books, poetry, movies, religion, etc, serves only the weak and evil-minded. In either case we have arrived at sexual-fulfillment.

Prayer for today: O Christ, close to us the lesser gates of life that You might open the larger life gates. Help us to thank You when You will not let us be deplorable people. For You want to make us men and women after Your own image – Help us rise and follow You. Amen.

January 21   Matthew 6:22; Ephesians 4:1-6 James 4:8

HOW DO WE ARRIVE AT INNER UNITY?

If we have no inward unity we can have no personal happiness and our life will not be effective. Jesus said, *"Every kingdom divided against itself will be ruined…"* (Matthew 12:25). That simple statement has within it all the wisdom that modern psychology has discovered from their study of the facts of inner life. Divided personality - inward conflict, these are the things that bring human personality to ruin. People will say to a person who is deeply depressed, "Pull yourself together." Useless advice when there are several opposing forces within us. They won't pull together. Experience taught Old Testament lawmakers the senselessness of trying to plow with an ox and a donkey together. It was forbidden. Experience forbids us from pulling ourselves together when there are conflicting selves. "Exercise your will" advised another. But suppose the will, which expresses your acting personality, is itself divided. Again useless advice. The Psychoanalyst, after discovering the disturbed place in a disordered life, and after relating it to the rest of life, says that for a life to be orderly and hold together there must be something upon which you can fasten your affections. This will lift you out of yourself and hold you together. But often the psychologist has nothing to offer a patient in terms of a solution. So we row laboriously, trying to get to the place of inward unity. We are tossed by many winds and waves, doused by many storms. And it grows very dark. Then Jesus quietly comes. This time, we more easily <u>let Him in,</u> for there seems to be no other alternative. The soul seems to instinctively feel, "the Master has come." He gathers up the inward conflict and unifies our life around Himself. We have arrived!

Prayer for today: O Christ, we need a Master, someone to command us. You are that Someone. For Your commandments are our freedom. Help us to accept Your way, so that we may find our own. Amen.

January 22   Acts 17:22-28

HOW CAN I FIND GOD?

We have seen that life will only work one way, God's way. The statement of Saint Augustine is often repeated because it is so often confirmed: "<u>You have made us for Yourself, and we are restless until we rest in You</u>." Let that fact burn into our mind. Let it save us from wasting our time ignoring the obvious and get on with the business of finding God and His purpose for our life.

In our search for God let us look at a few preliminary things. **Keep in mind that the purpose of your very being, your very creation is to find God and live for Him according to His purpose**. As the eye is fashioned for light, so we are fashioned for God.

Have you ever wondered why you were created? Ask yourself this: Why does a parent create? Doesn't a parent create because of the impulse of love – the impulse that would have an object upon which they can lavish their love and to whom they can give themselves in the development and growth of that child? Is parenthood different in God?

Could God being love, done otherwise than create objects of that love? And having created us, will He not give Himself to us? With that thought in mind we can be full of hope and expectancy. Our lover is at our hearts door. Let Him in!

Prayer for today: Father, You have come a long way through creation to the very door of my heart. I let You in. Welcome, Lover of my soul, Welcome! Amen.

(Please read next page)

LET HIM IN

Will you let Jesus in?
He wants to be your savior and friend.

His great love, His mercy, His care,
This and more, He longs to share.

Let Him dwell in your life complete,
For you will find perfect rest at Jesus feet.

Are we truly afraid of Jesus?
Afraid of how He really sees us?

Remember, He knows our heart and every thought,
He still loves us, we are who He bought.

Let Him in your heart and life today,
Do not continue to send Him away.

Experience joy, understanding, wisdom, and peace,
And love overflowing, that will never cease.

LET HIM IN.

By-MaryAnn Moore
    August, 1982

January 23   Matthew 25:34-40; 2 Corinthians 5:2

THE RISK GOD TOOK

Yesterday we were speaking about God's creative love creating us in order to give Himself to us and to find that love fulfilled in our growth and development in his own image.

But, was it not risky for God to create us as He did, with the awful power of choice and with the possibility of us going astray and breaking His heart and ours? Yes, very risky indeed. He could have made us without the power of choice, or with the power to choose only good. But this would not be choice, for to be able to choose you must be able to choose in two directions, not one. Besides, if we are able to choose only good, then it isn't good for us. Our direction would be determined for us. The very possibility of goodness is in freedom. So where there is no will there is no goodness, no badness—in fact, no personality. There was no other way to create personalities except to give them freedom. Risky? Absolutely! Parents take that same risk when they bring a child into the world. That child may go astray and crush the parent's lives and their lives as well. But, parents assume that risk. Why? Because they determine that whatever happens they will do their best for that child – they will enter into that very life, until the child's troubles are their troubles, the child's growth and happiness is theirs. This will mean a cross! Absolutely! But parenthood accepts that cross because it cannot do otherwise. Same with God, our creation meant that He would enter into our very lives – our troubles – His troubles, our sins – His sins, our joy – His joy. So creation then means a cross for God? Yes. But He took it. Love could not do otherwise.

Prayer for today: God, we stand awed by Your courage. But You did create us – it might be – it just might be, to re-create us. That is our hope. We hold that near to our hearts. Amen.

January 24   Luke 15:1-10; John 3:16

GOD'S SEARCH FOR ME

If what we learned yesterday is true, then we must accept that God searches for us persistently and redemptively. It seems too good to be true. It is too good **NOT** to be true.

Read in the New Testament the astonishing parables of the 15th chapter of Luke: the lost sheep, the lost coin, and the lost son. What wonderful truth is found in these parables!

Someone once said, "The author of the universe is hard to find. In finding God you must have as much patience as someone who sits by the ocean and undertakes to empty it with a straw." But in these parables we see Jesus open the curtains and we take a look at the God of the shepherd-heart who seeks and seeks the lost sheep until he finds it. Then the woman who sweeps the house for the lost coin – just as, God will sweep the universe with His redeeming grace, until He finds that lost soul, lost as it may be among the dust of degradation. It is true that the father did not go into the far country searching for his son, but wasn't the father's love there with him and wasn't that love the connection the son felt as he made his way back to his father's house? This son held on to his father's outreaching love and let it lead him back to his father. God relentlessly pursues us with His outreaching love. Will we let that love lead us back to Him?

Prayer for today: O God, I dare not close my heart to You. You found me with Your persistence. But how happy, oh, how happy I am to be found! I thank You. Amen.

January 25   1 John 4:16-21

FINDING GOD – (Continued)

We have learned one true fact – God is reaching out for us. But there is a question in some minds: "Isn't it easier for those who are emotionally inclined to find God compared to those who are not?

If by "emotionally inclined" we mean that some people are more emotionally sensitive than others, then yes, this may be true. However, God does not come to us <u>only</u> through <u>emotions</u>. He comes to us through the <u>mind</u> and through the <u>will</u> as well – His approach to us, for our life, includes all three. So if your active side is more developed than your emotional side, you can receive Christ through your will. This is also true with the mind – if you lean toward the intellectual, then you can receive Christ through the mind. However, if He comes into your life in any of these three ways, He will possess the whole person – your emotions, your mind, and your will.

The center of the whole relationship will be love, whether the emphasis is on emotional love, intellectual love, or your willing- ness to love. Everyone has a capacity to love God. Everyone who is willing to pay the price of searching can find God. Remember this: no one is constitutionally incapable of finding God. If we do not find God, the cause is not in our constitution, but in our consent.

Prayer for today: O God, You made us, made us for Your entrance into our lives. The doors of our lives may be low, but Your cross bent so low that You can enter the very lowest doors. Come into my heart, Lord Jesus, come in today, and come in to stay. Amen.

January 26 Luke 11:9-13

WHO CAN FIND GOD?

Two other things we must look at before we can grasp finding God: Many feel that, since Jesus called His disciples away from their ordinary occupations, we must leave so-called secular life to find God. This is a mistaken idea. Jesus did ask His disciples to leave their occupations and follow Him, but did He not in the very act of calling them approve their occupation by filling their boat with fish? And did not one hundred and twenty disciples wait in the upper room for the Holy Spirit, perhaps only twelve of whom had left their occupations?

A young person might ask, "Can I be both a student and a Christian?" There should not be a conflict; if you have found Christ, then you should be a better student. Now, you can study and pray your way through to being the kind of student you want to be. **Any "legitimate" occupation can be lifted into an order that is holy**.

There are those who feel only the older adult can find God. But Christ way is different. Even a small child learns early in life, through Sunday school, Vacation Bible School, youth camps, and other Christian teaching, that God can live in their heart. It does work for a child, for to find the Kingdom we must catch the child-like attitude of open frankness and willingness to follow.

Prayer for today: O Christ, You did make holy every worthy occupation and You did open the life gates to a little child. In Your Father's house there is the sound of the carpenter and the laughter of little children as well as the quiet place for prayer. We thank You. Amen.

January 27   Luke 11:33-36

FACING THE ISSUES

Any obstacles to finding God are our obstacles not God's. Since He is seeking us, then the problem is not our finding God, but our permitting Him to find us. We must remove the obstacles so we can be found. Some of us are not doing the removing; there are definite obstacles in our way.

Some obstacles are intellectual. People do have honest doubts, but the problem is usually deeper. Not always, but usually. For instance, you may be puzzled about the Trinity, but the emphasis in Christianity is not about the Trinity, it is about the incarnation – (the doctrine that the second person of the Trinity assumed human form in the person of Jesus Christ).

The adolescent life is the simplest life; but as we come up the scale of existence we find a more complex life emerging, so when we become adults we find a very highly complex being made up of mind, body and spirit – you are a trinity. I am a trinity. The movement of life moves from the simple to the complex. When we get to the highest level of life - "God" – we should expect to find complexity rather than simplicity – the Trinity is therefore the natural highest level. In the middle of that complexity as life moves upward it moves toward unity. We are a trinity but we are also a unity. So if you were puzzled concerning the Trinity hopefully this explanation has helped you. If not, then ask yourself if your life is pure before God? You want your trouble to be honest doubt, not dishonest sin.

Prayer for today: O God, hold us steady at this point. Help us to be absolutely honest, and then as the obstacles are removed Your presence will strangely warm our heart. In Jesus' name. Amen.

January 28   Matthew 5:8; 2 Corinthians 13:5-8;
                              1 Thessalonians 5:21-22;
                              1 John 3:3

APPLYING THE TEST

Yesterday's study showed us that being morally wrong causes intellectual blindness. It is easier to live ourselves into right thinking than to think ourselves into right living. In a moral world a moral response comes from deep knowledge. Without that knowledge we are blind, no matter how much we think. So we must look at the moral obstacles. They are not the only obstacles, but we cannot go on unless we remove them. Think of someone whose moral and spiritual influence is powerful and penetrating. The secret is in their relentlessness toward themselves. They continuously examine their lives in the quietness before God, in absolute realism in which there is no pretense. Do you want to try it? Ask yourself these five questions, **once a week**, in the quietness before God, with honesty and no pretense.

1. Am I truthful? Are there any conditions under which I will or do tell a lie? Can I be depended on to tell the truth – no matter the cost? Yes or No?
2. Am I honest? Can I absolutely be trusted in money matters? In my work? In school? With other people's reputations? Yes or No?
3. Am I pure? In my relationships with the opposite sex? In my habits? In my thought life? Yes or No?
4. Am I easily offended or am I loving? Do I lose my temper? Am I quick to get my feelings hurt? Or am I developing the attitude of love which refuses to be offended? Yes or No?
5. Am I selfish or am I dedicated? Am I living for – myself, my own position, money, fame, power? Or is all my energy at the disposal of human need? At the disposal of the Kingdom? Again I ask, am I living for - myself or others?

As we finish today's study let's look at our self. The bravest moment of our life is the moment we can look at our self objectively without flinching, without excuses.

Prayer for today: O Christ, it is said that You know what is in every one of us. We do not even know what is in our self. For we have never looked "honestly" at our self. Help us to do it today. In Your name we pray. Amen.

January 29   Acts 5: 1-11; Colossians 3:9-10;
                              Hebrews 6:17-18

AM I TRUTHFUL?

One of the test questions of our character is: Will I lie? And yet how easy it is to lie – even for religious people: the willingness to twist the truth to gain acceptance with someone, a lack of complete truth if it benefits us financially or otherwise, misrepresenting ourselves, etc. Is the basis of this looseness with the truth, the fact that we think a lie is justifiable? When several students were asked if a lie is ever justifiable, these were their answers: (1) Yes, in business. (2) In politics. (3) To save a life. (4) In war. (5) They weren't sure about a big lie. They thought to be able to lie well was an asset to their character. They did not see that the ability to lie is a liability and not an asset.

Learn and keep these two principles:

First, God cannot lie (Hebrews 6:18). Second, He cannot delegate to you the privilege of lying for Him.

The early Christians, standing before tribunals their very lives before them, could tell a "little lie" and their lives would be spared. They refused. They could die, but not lie. Christians never lie. When we lie, we are not Christian. The scripture is unequivocal at this point. *"Do not lie to each other, since you have put on the new self, which is being renewed in knowledge in the image of its creator."* (Colossians 3:9-10). If we lie no matter how religious we may be, it is still sin.

Prayer for today: Our Father, from this moment make me crystal clear, with nothing covered up, nothing which I must hide from myself or others. Help me to be truthful in everything I say and do. I will do my part. Amen.

January 30   1 Corinthians 6:8-11;
                                               2 Corinthians 6:3; 8:20-21

AM I HONEST?

The second question: Am I honest?
It is a little hard to be completely honest with ourselves because of our tendency to rationalize. This means we are seldom objective in our attitude concerning ourselves. We set our minds to work not on things as they are, but on inventing reasons for our conduct. The man in the parable who was negligent with his talent laid the blame on the toughness of his master. (Matthew 25:24-25). That is rationalizing. A person allows themselves to fall in love with another person's spouse, and then proceeds to rationalize the whole affair by telling themselves about the sacredness of this feeling of love, until black looks white. Their mind has played a trick on them, they are self-deceived. We need objectivity and honesty as in the example of the young adult who confided: "I cannot keep my degree. When I look at it I am reminded of my dishonesty. I cheated on my final exam. I'm going to send it back to the University." He did. The vice-chancellor replied, "The end of education is to produce honest character. You now seem to be an honest man. We hope you will keep your degree." But will not God forgive the sin of dishonesty without this restitution? How can he? He can forgive the sin of the act only as we are willing to restore the truth. Because of circumstances, we may not be able to restore all at once or completely, however, we must be <u>willing</u> to make restitution. God sometimes has to take us on faith. But He knows our heart. Are we willing to cut out of our life every dishonest thing no matter how deep the humiliation may be?

Prayer for today: O Father, the relentless pursuer of our souls, You are not content to leave us half-well; You have Your finger on our sickness. Help us not to beg off from Your surgeon's knife. Cut, O Christ, deeply if need be. But make us completely well. Amen.

January 31   Matthew 5:27-28; 1 Corinthians 6:15-20

AM I PURE?

This question of purity is basic. The battle of life will probably not rise above the sex battle. If life declines at that place, it's probably declining in all other areas of your life as well.

Obviously, the first thing to do in this matter of purity is to acknowledge the fact of sex. To act as though there is no such thing as a sexual desire in us is to repress it, and in doing this we set up disorder that can lead to a mental breakdown. Every normal person has sexual desire. There is no shame in this. It is a part of our God-given make-up. So – <u>the question is not whether we have sexual desire, but whether sexual desire has us</u>. As a <u>servant</u> - of the higher purposes of life it is a wonderful servant giving drive and beauty to the rest of life. As a <u>master</u> - it is hell.

Do we have victory or defeat at this place? We, who have come under the influence of Jesus Christ, have no excuses for not being pure! *"You have heard that it was said, 'Do not commit adultery.' But I tell you that anyone who looks at a woman lustfully has already committed adultery with her in his heart."* (Matthew 5:27-28).

Am I committing adultery in act or in thought? If so will I surrender it? <u>NOW</u>? Or will I pray the prayer of the unrepentant person, "Make me pure, but not now."

Prayer for today: O Christ of the pure mind, the pure habit, the pure act, cleanse the open wounds of my heart and make me from this hour a person of purity. I consent to have it done. Amen

February 1   Ephesians 4:31-32; Colossians 3:12-14

AM I EASILY OFFENDED OR AM I LOVING?

Yesterday we put ourselves through the test concerning sins of the flesh. Today we will test our lives concerning sins of our attitude. In the parable of the prodigal son (Luke 15:11-32), the younger son sinned in his flesh, in his lusts and wild living. The older brother sinned in his attitude, in his bad temper, in his lack of love, in his smallness of soul, in his unwillingness to forgive. Now, the sins of the flesh are despised by us. They are not respectable. But the sins of the attitude are sometimes highly respectable. If a person commits the sin of sexual immorality in the flesh, we look down on them and with our pious attitude condemn them and make them feel unwelcome in "our" church. However, if one sins in their attitude – if they have an ugly temper, they are selfish, and gossipy, etc. we want to make them a member. And yet it is quite possible that the sins of the attitude does much more harm to the Kingdom of God as the sins of the flesh. Bad tempered, touchy and quarrelsome "religious" people do as much harm, maybe more to the Kingdom of God as drug addicts or those who are sexually immoral. Suppose the younger brother had met the older brother on the road to their father's house? One look at the older brother and the younger one would have turned back to the far country, driven back by a bad spirit. Question: How many people have we met on the road searching for Christian love and our "not so Christian" attitude caused them to turn and run back to the far country? Think about it! Two major obstacles are fear and anger. They form the basis for most of our unhappiness. They are impossible to integrate into a healthy personality. Am I prepared to face the fact of my ugly temper and my irritability and consent to have it removed – even if it means major surgery?

Prayer for today: O Christ, You who stood poised and unruffled among the most gross insults and provocations, give me that loving, disciplined spirit. In Your name I pray. Amen.

February 2   Philippians 2:4-8; 1 Timothy 6:6-10;
                              2 Timothy 4:9-10

AM I SELFISH OR AM I DEDICATED?

The last test goes to the root of the matter. In the final analysis, what really controls my actions – self-interest or Christ-interest? In the deepest recesses of my spirit who gives the final word? Do I or Christ? The answer depends on whether or not I am a Christian.

And what is the issue? It is this: If I control my life, it will disintegrate. I will lose it. If Christ controls my life, I will find it – It will be integrated, happy and useful.

Life teaches us: If my desires control me, I will drown in my own desires. I will have my own way and then I will detest my way. If self is on the throne, its inner being is unhappy, disagreeable. That self may be a very refined self, it may be a very religious self, it may be even an apparently servant self, but if it is on the throne and makes final decisions, then, unavoidably, I will lose my life. My life needs a master, but self is not the master it needs.

Quiet your heart and ask yourself this question: Who has the ultimate say in my life – I or Christ? Am I self-directed or am I Christ-directed?

Prayer for today: O Christ, I know in my heart that when my hand is on the steering wheel of life that my life careens out of control. I cannot manage without You. Take my life and steer it in the direction You want it to go. Amen.

February 3   Luke 12:2-9; James 5:13-16

IS CONFESSION NECESSARY?

After having faced these five questions - <u>Am I truthful</u>, <u>Am I honest</u>, <u>Am I pure</u>, <u>Am I easily offended or am I loving</u>, <u>Am I selfish or am I dedicated</u>? How did you rate? Repeat them to yourself, slowly one by one, and give an honest answer. Your self will want to excuse, rationalize, to go off to something irrelevant – don't let that happen. Hold yourself to the issues and answer truthfully.

If you fail at any or all of these, confess it honestly and directly. Confess it? Yes. When our conscience condemns us for wrong actions, and the feeling of guilt results, there are three possible modes of conduct open to our conscious mind. (1) The consciousness may do nothing whatsoever about our feelings of guilt, (2) It may repress the feeling; (3) It may get free of the depressing sensation by spiritual purging, through confession. Obviously the first two methods are unsatisfactory, and more than that they are disastrous. To know we are wrong and do nothing about it is to condemn ourselves to a life of disrespect, even to ourselves. To repress that feeling of guilt is even worse than doing nothing about it. To drive such a feeling as guilt and fear into the subconscious and close the door on it is not the way to be free of it. There it becomes infected and causes irritation. The life is unhappy, ill at ease, nervous, bitter, and it scarcely knows why. It is the result of this repression.

Jesus teaches: *"If we confess our sins, he is faithful and just and will forgive us our sins and purify us from all unrighteousness."* (1 John 1:9). There is no other way.

Prayer for today: O Christ, we take a deep breath, for this confession means humiliation to our inmost self. We would gladly hide our wounds. But we dare not. We open them to You and we do it now. Amen.

February 4   Psalm 32:6; Luke 18:9-14;
                                              Acts 19:18-19; 1 John 1:9-10

TO WHOM MUST I CONFESS?

We left our study yesterday believing that if we are to be free of the guilt that has occupied within and about our lives, we must confess it openly. But – to whom? Obviously, it must be to the one or ones against whom we wronged, we sin against ourselves, against God, and against others.

First, we sin against ourselves. We have not been true to ourselves, we have betrayed our ideals, and we have sinned against our better nature. We must then admit it to ourselves. Until you first admit it to yourself you cannot admit it to God or others. Do you actually confess to yourself? Yes, completely and without question. Confessing to yourself, completely, is very important, for you will try to compromise with half-confessions, half-repentances.

Second, we must confess it to God. We have not only broken His law, we have broken His heart. You must tell Him so. The approach to God has been made easy through Jesus. His purity condemned sinners, yet invited them. His purity is not forbidding, but forgiving. Do you dare expose your heart to that Heart? You must –to get relief. But, again, it must be whole-hearted and without anything held back, for **one thing held back ruins it all - cancels the rest.**

Third, we must confess it to those we have wronged. We do not need to broadcast our sins to everybody. There are some things God deals with in His private office. But when we have wronged others or others have wronged us, we must both ask forgiveness and offer it.

Prayer for today: O Christ, I cringe and yet I consent for You to remove the sins of my life leaving no roots behind. I not only want to be a better person, I want to be completely well. Amen.

February 5   Matthew 5:9-16; 5:23-26; Romans 12:18

STREIGHTENING OUT OUR LIVES

Yesterday we said we must confess any wrong done to others or forgive any wrong done to us. That cuts deep.

For instance, suppose we have been dishonest. No matter the effect it may have on our position in life, we must confess it. Then restoration can begin.

Take resentment. Whether you have wronged someone or someone has sinned against you, in either case you are to go and be reconciled. Whether sinned against or sinning, the Christian is obligated to take the initiative in settling the dispute. (Matthew 5:23-24).

But you say, "I can't forgive." Then you can never, ever be forgiven. *"For if you forgive men when they sin against you, your heavenly Father will also forgive you. But if you do not forgive men their sins, your Father will not forgive your sins."* (Matthew 6:14-15).

Remember the Lord's Prayer – *"Forgive us our debts, as we forgive our debtors."* (Matthew 6:12). So, if you do not forgive, you are asking not to be forgiven. In refusing to forgive others you break down the bridge of forgiveness over which you yourself must cross.

When we hold resentment against others, the resentment grows deep. It is not easy to confess resentment, especially to the one or ones we resent. But it must be done before we can find release. When release is found then our life will be radiant and spiritually contagious. You can do it! By God's grace, you will, won't you?

Prayer for today: O Christ, You who hung on the cross, tortured in every nerve of Your body, yet You prayed for Your enemies – *"Father forgive them."* Help me today, right now, to forgive those who have wronged me in a much smaller way. In Your name I pray. Amen.

February 6   Matthew 18:23-35

STREIGHTENING OUT OUR LIVES – (Continuing)

We left yesterday's study in the process of freeing ourselves of resentments. We must dig out the last root.

You say, "Well I'll forgive, but I won't forget." You don't really mean that, do you? See how that looks as you pray. "Father, forgive me as I forgive others, I do forgive that other person, but I won't forget it. You forgive me in the same way: forgive me, but don't forget my sins, and when I do something wrong bring the whole thing up again." God cannot and does not forgive that way. He blots it out of His book of remembrance. So must you.

But again you say, "Okay, I'll forgive, but I will have nothing more to do with that person." Now, pray that prayer again, "Father, forgive me as I forgive others. I forgive that person, but from now on I'll have nothing to do with them. You forgive me in the same way: forgive me, but have nothing more to do with me." You see how absurd this is, don't you?

Don't try to forget it, don't try to smooth it over, and don't drive it into your subconscious mind. Get it completely out of your system. Anger and resentment are literal poison. They will poison us physically, mentally and spiritually. Dig it up, throw it out, and then know what peace is all about!

Prayer for today: O Father, You did forgive those who spat in Your face, help me to open my heart to the healing of Your forgiveness and help me to give forgiveness as You give forgiveness to me. Amen.

February 7   Mark 6:17-23

WE ARE STILL STRAIGHTENING OUT OUR LIVES

It is not enough to hate our sin, or even pray about it – we must give it up. We call the master-sin "it," because we may not mind giving up what we call smaller sins, but giving up the master-sin is much harder for us. For there is usually a master-sin, a key sin in the accumulation of sins, and unless that key sin is removed there is no release, therefore, no peace. Remember Herod? He was probably sincere in his search for a new life; he was fascinated by the good. But John, one day, put his finger on the master-sin in Herod's life: *"It is not lawful for you to have your brother's wife."* (Mark 6:18). Herod must have turned pale. A life struggle was on. The outcome? The Bible tells us, *"When Herod heard John, he was greatly puzzled; yet he liked to listen to him."* (Mark 6:20b). Herod may have liked to listen to John, but he was not willing to listen to the fact that he should give up his brother's wife, Herodias. He was willing to give up this thing, that thing, and the other thing, but not the woman. That sin was the key sin, the master-sin, in the accumulation of sins. Herod was willing to give up other sins in his life, but not this one. There was no release, no peace. A little girl took a piece of candy that belonged to another and told her first lie. The broken hearted mother put the little girl on her lap and explained to her what it all meant. The little girl cried bitter tears and seemed truly sorry, so the mother said, "I am glad you are sincerely sorry. Now take the candy out of your mouth – and throw it away to show you are sorry." She looked at her mother through her tears, clamped her teeth tight and said, "No." She hated the sin, she cried over it, she did everything except one thing – give it up –surrender it!

Prayer for today: O Christ, You drive me into a corner. I would escape but You will not let me. Actually, I do not really want to escape from You, because I know that would be an escape from life, and I want to live. Please take anything from my heart that will keep me from You and from a victorious life. Amen.

February 8   Acts 2:37-42

I SURRENDER

I have now come to the place in my search for Living Victoriously where I realize I cannot go on until I make a great decision. I must remove every obstacle that stands between God and me – and I must hold nothing back. I must not only remove every obstacle, I must remove myself from the director's chair. I need a director – a master.

I know that I will be directed by one thing or the other. In my heart I know that I will bend to something. I may bow before myself and take orders from me, so that self is my master. Or I may bow before my peers and let them dominate me. Or - I can let Christ by my Master – to me this seems the best alternative. The decision is mine and mine alone, as to who will have the final say in my life. I deliberately and joyfully make that decision: <u>Christ will be my Master</u>. My heart, my will, and my life I give to Him. It is done!

You cannot really see Christ until you kneel at His feet, look up into His radiant face and see Him looking back at you with his outstretched arms waiting for your surrender.

Prayer for today: O Christ, at last my heart has said, be my Master, I'll be the servant. I hold in my trembling hand this will of mine, giving you title to my life for time and eternity, all that I am and will ever be. I surrender all! You are mine and I am Yours. And I am so glad! Amen.

February 9   Matthew 7:21; Mark 5:24-34

TOUCHING JESUS

As Jesus was walking along a crowd followed and pressed around Him. A woman in great need of healing came timidly through the crowd and touched His garment. *"Who touched me?" asked Jesus as He realized that power had gone from Him. "You see the people crowding against you," His disciples answered, "And yet you can ask, 'who touched me?'"* (Mark 5:30-31). Those who come <u>near</u> to Jesus gain little; those who <u>touch</u> Jesus gain everything. In our day many people in the world are drawing <u>near</u> to Jesus. There is great interest in Him. So many other ways of life are breaking down and we turn longingly to Him. Yet, there seems to be so many who draw <u>near</u> to Jesus but never <u>touch</u> Him. Inspiring? Yes, but complete life, no. Sunday after Sunday the crowds go to church and listen. Their thoughts draw them <u>near</u> to Jesus, but how many of those really <u>touch</u> Him – connect with Him, and live for Him? How many <u>touch</u> Him and go away well, not just feeling better. Some go a lifetime following Jesus at a <u>near</u> distance, but never really <u>touch</u> Him! Oh, what a difference! If you ever <u>really touch Him</u>, <u>really touch Him</u>, you will know it and `so will others. You will never be the same. You said yesterday you would surrender to Him. That's good. But now that you have surrendered to Him, touch Him – touch Him for forgiveness, for power over temptations, over fears, over anxieties, over absolutely everything that stands in your way of Living Victoriously. As He threw His life open then so that anyone who had need might touch Him, provided they did so in faith, so He is today, His life is open – take what you need. **Stop following Him <u>only closely</u> – touch Him. Really touch Him!**

Prayer for today: O Christ, I cease my reluctant attitude, I move up from following You closely to boldly touching You. By the touch of faith I receive into my inmost being my salvation and health. Amen.

February 10   Matthew 9:27-29; Mark 6:5-6; Hebrews 11:1

WHAT DOES FAITH REALLY MEAN?

We talked about touching Jesus by faith. What does faith really mean? This woman thought Jesus Power was in His garments, and that by touching them she would be well. Jesus corrected this when he said, *"Daughter, your faith has healed you. Go in peace and be freed from your suffering."* (Mark 5:34). What did Christ mean by faith? Certainly, faith is not an intellectual assent to a fixed belief. We never want to denounce belief, for anyone who thinks has to have something which they believe. Even so, our beliefs are never final, for they are our present conceptions of the truth which always seems beyond us. Our beliefs therefore must be open to correction as we continue to learn more truth. But it is possible to have intellectual belief in everything the churches teach and not have faith. **Faith is an adventure of the spirit, the whole inner life moving forward in response to something we believe to be supremely worth while.** It is believing - **not** just hoping. It is **not** discussion, it is decision. You really don't believe in a thing unless you act on it. You don't really believe in Christ unless you are prepared to risk all to follow Him. **That's faith**.

Jesus made an amazing instrument when He made faith the conditioning instrument, for faith is trust in another, and yet it is an adventure and attitude of our own. It therefore develops self-reliance and Christ-reliance at the same time. If faith were mere passiveness, it would not develop self-reliance; if it were mere activity, it would not develop Christ-reliance. It is both activity and receptivity. *"According to your faith it will be done to you."* (Matthew 9:29). You have faith and Christ responds. You do it and He does it. You are not stymied, and He is Savior.

Prayer for today: O Amazing Christ, as You save us from ourselves You save us. You ask for our faith, and that very faith not only heals us, but makes us. We follow You and find You – and ourselves. We thank You. Amen.

53

February 11   Mark 3:1-6; Luke 17:11-19

MUST I UNDERSTAND EVERYTHING BEFORE I FOLLOW?

Yesterday we said faith was an adventure. A very small amount of faith is enough to start on, for as we act on it, it grows. The ten lepers had only Christ word, *"Go show yourselves to the priest."* (Luke 17:14). They had His word and their leprosy. Then that word grew in them until it possessed them. But they started with very little. Don't wait until you think you understand everything about Christ to follow Him. Some of us do not fully understand electricity. But even so, we aren't going to sit in the dark until we do. We do know two things about electricity: we know we need light and electricity supplies that need. That is enough to start with. We may not know all about the digestive system – how food turns into blood and bone and tissue, but we aren't going to sit and starve until we do. There are many things we do not understand about Christ, but one thing we should know: when we expose our soul to Him in trust and obedience, He meets our deepest need. That is enough, at least to begin with.

Jesus asked the man with the shriveled hand to stretch it out – the one thing the man couldn't do. He must have looked at Jesus with helpless astonishment at such a demand – and yet, the man responded with the little faith he had, and put his all into raising that arm – and, in the very process of obedience the strength came. His arm was well!

As you step out to follow Christ, you will think you are stepping out into a void, but that void will turn to rock beneath your feet. You step out – Christ steps in – into your battles, your temptations, your tasks, and then you begin life on the co-operative plan. Faith seals the deal.

Prayer for today: O Christ, I do not see everything, but I do see You. Let that be enough. I will take the first steps. I will supply the willingness. You will have to supply the power. Amen.

February 12   Luke 19:1-10; John 1:35-42

FIRST STEPS INTO LIFE WITH CHRIST

We ended our last study, "acting on what little faith we had and learning it would grow in the process." Question: What do you believe? How far along are you in what you believe about Christ? Do you believe Christ was a good man, even the best, who ever lived? Then let us begin there. If Christ was best, then He should be our ideal. Are you prepared to act according to that ideal? Are you willing to remove everything from your life that Christ would not approve of? You say, "That is not so easy." No one said Christ way is easy. Again, are you prepared to let go of everything in your life that Christ would not approve? If your honest answer is: "I must and I will." Then, <u>whoever</u> Christ turns out to be, the best man ever, or more than that, you will be stronger and better with Him living with you, in you, all the time. Of course you do know your life will be wonderfully different? Will you let Him into your life? If you think you do not know how, let me help you. You can receive Christ right now, by faith, through prayer. God knows your heart and is not as concerned with your words as He is with the sincere attitude of your heart. You can pray the following prayer or a similar one of your own: **O Christ thank You for dying for me. I open my heart to You and ask You to forgive me of my sins and come into my life, I receive You as my Savior and Lord. Thank You for forgiving my sins and giving me eternal life. Take complete control of my life and make me the kind of person You want me to be. Amen.** If you <u>sincerely</u> prayed this prayer or a similar prayer of your own words, then you know that Christ is now in your life because according to His promise in (Revelation 3:20) Christ said that He would come into your life. He will not mislead you. So know that God has answered your prayer because God is trustworthy, His word is true and by faith you believe. God Bless You!

Prayer for today: Father, Thank You for taking my doubts and fears and for courage to take the first steps into a new life. Amen.

February 13   Acts 2:37-38; 3:19; Romans 8:1-2

WHAT IS BEING BORN AGAIN?

If you have undergone the change in your life that is called "being born again," then what does that mean? Today in many, possibly most, of our churches being born again is not emphasized. However, psychology has re-emphasized it. Not in the language of the church and often not the same belief in God attached to it. Psychology tells us that the subconscious mind is the place of our driving instincts which has come down from a long racial history. These driving instincts think only of our fulfillment, apart from any moral considerations. The conscious mind is built with "the reality principle," or a conscious life-purpose. A conflict between the subconscious and the conscious minds result. The division at the very center of our life brings disturbance, unhappiness. This conflict can be resolved in two ways: (1) either the subconscious mind with its driving instincts, is given full control – in which case the personality would be without variation – or (2) the subconscious mind is placed in a lower position in our mind where it doesn't have full control but is made to contribute to the purposeful side of life. This second process is called sublimation, (converting something to a solid, purified, supreme, outstanding form). This second process unifies our life. The first alternative is impossible for us, if we take it, it is where our driving-instincts rule our lives and the conflict will continue. The second is the only way to freedom. The process by which this is done is called, "re-orientation to reality"; "re-education"; "re-adaptation"; and "reintegration." When Jesus puts within our life the content of the moral and spiritual as well as the psychological, it is called "being born again". All of these are headed toward the same goal, the unifying of the personality and bringing peace into the center of life. We must undergo this change.

Prayer for today: O Christ, We must be born again and born differently. Help us to know the change through living the experience of it. Amen

February 14   John 3:1-11

OUR STUDY OF "BEING BORN AGAIN" – (Continuing)

Jesus said, "I tell you the truth, no one can see the Kingdom of God unless he is born again." (John 3:3). What does Jesus mean by "being born again?" When Nicodemus asked Jesus about entering into his Mother's womb to be born the second time – Jesus answer to Nicodemus suggest that even if that was possible, it would not be the answer, because the "plant" will always be of the nature of the "seed" that produces it – like produces like. The Kingdom of God is spiritual and holy; and that which is born of the spirit resembles the spirit; so it is with the flesh, (continuing in John 3:6), Jesus explained, *"Flesh gives birth to flesh, but the spirit gives birth to spirit."* Therefore, spiritual regeneration is essentially necessary, to prepare the soul for a holy and spiritual kingdom.

The choice is ours. In the quietness of your heart you must make a choice. Someone may say, "I have no quietness of heart." And they are right, they will never have quietness of heart in the deepest and fullest sense until they decide to be "born again" – born of the spirit of God.

But if you experienced that new birth in our study a few days back then you have that quietness of heart, and you know that you have been "born again".

Prayer for today: O Father, we open our heart to Your Kingdom and to You. We cannot go back, we must go forward. Amen.

February 15   Matthew 12:43-45; Luke 13:6-9

EMPTY

It may be that some of you do not feel the need for change because the pressing of natural instincts do not drive you to Jesus feet. The natural born storms of life for you is not a Great Struggle, but a Great Emptiness. Your difficulty is not your inborn nature, but the emptiness within you. Jesus has a word for that type of person. He told of a house that was swept clean, decorated – and empty. Modern civilization is "swept." For the most part, modern civilization has banished superstitions which its forefathers held. It is swept – it is freed from believing in magic and superstitions and such. It is also "decorated" – decorated with intellectual facts and technological inventions. Look at our achievements in medical science, electronic technology, culture, and comfort! Our stores and shops are crammed with the latest computer games, electronic toys, etcetera, and we are urged to buy them for they are sure to bring us happiness. Yes, civilization is "swept" and "decorated." But – and this is the point – it is **EMPTY**, empty of any constructive purpose of life. We are all dressed up and don't know where to go! We look with distain on the past generations, we point with pride to our decorated civilization and its great achievements, and yet modern civilization is empty – and it knows it! May not admit it, nevertheless knows it! When we say our modern civilization is empty, we bring it closer home – and just perhaps we are empty. We need to be reborn just to know what life really is. This emptiness will not last long for we will fill it with one thing or the other. Modern civilization is drawing unto itself the seven devils of unrest, of sinful pleasure, of crime to fill the emptiness. Nature and the soul both detest emptiness. To fill that emptiness we must choose between Christ and these or some other seven devils.

Prayer for today: O Christ, I choose You. My soul is empty. I cannot fill it with other than You. I hate emptiness and I fear devils—but I do trust You. Amen.

February 15 (continued)

THE THREE BEARS

By-MaryAnn Moore
(Year-1999)

Once upon a time there were three bears, a Papa Bear, a Mama Bear, and a Baby Bear. They cleaned and decorated their house until it was beautiful. They scrubbed, they swept, and they painted, until the place was spotless. <u>Then,</u> they went for a walk in the woods. They left their house empty and forgot to close the door behind them. An unclean spirit looking for a place to rest, slithered in and brought with it seven more, more wicked than itself – Mr. Liar, Bad Attitude, Ms. Gossip, Old Jealousy, Killer of Reputations, the Mad Hate-er, and Master Thief. What a dreadful bunch.

(Sometime if we forget to be careful and we let our guard relax while our mind is out to lunch, we may find something has entered that we did not intend to let in.)...Back to the three Bears...When they came home Papa Bear said, "Someone has entered our house."

Mama Bear asked, "Who could have made such a mess?" Baby Bear remembered the house had been left open and EMPTY. Papa Bear with his love and wisdom sweetly said, "We learn from our mistakes, we will sweep it clean once more and this time we will NOT leave it EMPTY.

Prayer for today: O Christ, I choose You. My inner house is empty; I cannot fill it with any other than You. I detest emptiness and I fear devils – but I know I can trust You, and I do. Amen.

February 16   1 Corinthians 5:9-11; Galatians 5:16-17

IS BEING BORN AGAIN AN EXPRESSION OF THE SEX-URGE?

There are people who trace almost everything to the sex-instinct, including the phenomenon called "being born again". They point out that mostly this experience takes place in adolescence, and as this is the period of awakening of the sex-instinct this religious experience is caused by it and is founded on it.

The answer is obvious. <u>Adolescence is</u> not only the period of awakening of the sex-instinct, it is the period of <u>the awakening of the total personality</u>. The <u>self-instinct,</u> its restlessness with, and revolt against authority, and the <u>group-instinct</u>, with its tendency to join a group are also awakening along with other instincts. It is the awakening of the whole life.

Now, religion, as we learned, is a cry for life – a life with more quality, a complete life, a fuller, happy life. It is therefore not strange that youth feeling the awakening of life should turn to religion to guide, complete and satisfy that urge. Interest in religion often leads to accepting Christ into our life. <u>It does not come out of the sex-urge, but out of life-urge</u>. Religion holds the sex-urge in restraint, how then could it be identified with it? If religion were an expression of the sex-urge, then when life matures into old age and the sex-urge dims, we should expect the religious side to dim as well. But does it? NO, just the opposite. Youth and old age are the most religious periods of life. Why? In youth we want fuller life – in old age we want lasting life – in each it is a cry for life.

Prayer for today: O Christ, You are creative life moving upon lesser life and awakening it. Make me into a new person, with a new goal and new power to move forward to that goal. Amen.

February 17   Matthew 18:3; 1 Corinthians 12:4-11

ARE ALL EXPERIENCES ALIKE WHEN ACCEPTING
CHRIST INTO OUR LIFE?

This has been confusing to a great many people, because they may have been greatly moved by the dramatic difference they see in someone who has given their life to Christ, and yet, because they cannot find that exact same thing for themselves they are dissatisfied. This is a big mistake. No two experiences are alike. No two persons are brought up under the exact same circumstances. After God made you He broke the mold. You are unique. Your experience with Christ will also be unique.

Nevertheless, accepting Christ into your life does fall into two great categories – gradual and sudden, with shades between. After a survey was done by a group of Christian workers in several countries, it was found that the majority of experiences are gradual.

The gradual type usually come from homes, were from childhood, they were taught to know and love Christ. They may not be able to tell when or where their being born again took place, because Christian life has always surrounded them. They have opened like a flower to the sun. When they began to belong to Christ they are not sure. But their lives are different than life around them. They belong to Christ there is no doubt.

Then there are the others – to whom the experience came all of a sudden. You may have been brought up in church, had a religious background, but like some sermons we've heard – it didn't sink in. Or you may have had no religious background, whatsoever, but you started listening, either way there came a Great Change in your life, and suddenly nothing after that was the same, forever caught by love that would not let go.

Which of these is the valid type? Either one. Not the facts that surround your accepting Christ into your life but the facts that underlie the experience and fruits that come from it make it valid.

Prayer for today: O Christ, You who do call to Your child in its innocence and to the older ones in their sins, we both come to You. To whom else could we go, for only You have the words to eternal life. We find You so satisfying because of Your saving grace. Amen.

February 18   Matthew 11:29-30; 23:10;
                                         John 13:13-14; Romans 14:4

THE CONTROLLING FACTOR IN OUR NEW LIFE

There is a master-emotion around which life is organized. It may attach itself to one of the instinctive urges: self, sex, or group. If the master-emotion is attached to the self-urge, the life is egotistical and self-controlled. Or it may attach itself to the sex-urge and the entire life becomes sex-controlled. Or it may attach itself to a peer group and life will be lived out under the dominance of what people will say and do – fear of the group will be the deciding factor. Life is group-controlled. There could be a mixture of all three, but in the end the master-emotion decides and dominates. In treating a patient with inward conflict or complex issues it is necessary to have the patient transfer their emotion (feelings) from themselves to someone else. This is called transference. The patient in this way is released from themselves and their problem by the expulsive power of a new affection.

Now, the controlling factor in accepting Christ into our life is also transference. While this involves breaking with this sin, that habit, this relationship, that attitude, yet all of these things are the negative side. The real thing that happens is the transference of the master-emotion from self to Christ. It is the conversion of the master-emotion. Life is no longer self-centered, sex-centered, or group-centered, but Christ-centered. Christ is now the master of the master-emotion. Jesus quietly said to the men of long ago, "*Follow me.*" Not follow a set of doctrines, however true; not a formal ceremony, however helpful; or an organization, however beneficial; but He said, "*FOLLOW ME.*" They did. The transference was made. A new word came to their lips, "Savior," for He was saving them from their complex selves. Being born again was a fact, made so by the conversion of the master-emotion.

Prayer for today: O Christ, You have our master-emotion. We give our love completely to You. Take our love and us. Amen.

February 19   Matthew 24:35; Romans 10:17;
                                               1 Thessalonians 1:5; 1 John 2:14

THE BASIS OF ASSURANCE

We all need assurance that we are a child of God. He assures us in a number of ways, these will be our study for the next few days. Our assurance of God's acceptance is made stronger when it comes from a number of ways, rather than only one way.

<u>First God assures us through His Word</u>. Nothing could be more explicit than Christ received sinners. No one should wait to be good enough to come to Him, because coming to Him makes us good. However, just being good is not good enough. We realize from the study of God's Word that we come to Christ as sinners, no matter how bad we are or have been. If we should wait until we feel we have clean hands, talk sensibly, and living a just and honorable life, we are still sinners and the process is the same – (Acts 3:19) says – *"Repent, then, and turn to God, so your sins may be wiped out, that times of refreshing may come from the Lord."* He calls us to bind up our wounds, to heal our weary souls with the wholeness of faith, and give us peace with His presence. Assurance? I think so.

Prayer for today: O Christ, You have always received sinners, and You will not reject me now. I may have dragged my soul through hell and back, but You will wash it and make it clean even now. I thank You. Amen.

February 20   1 Peter 1:23-25; 1 John 3:19-24; 5:11-12

ASSURANCE THROUGH GOD'S WORD

We learned yesterday that the Word of God assures us that we are accepted by Him. There are promises in God's Word that can not be more explicit: *"Come to me, all you who are weary and burdened, and I will give you rest." (Matthew 11:28).* *"If we confess our sins he is faithful and just and will forgive us our sins and purify us from all unrighteousness."* (1 John 1:9). Is it "neither cool nor politically correct" to quote scripture to heal our present need? To some it may seem so. But to those who have seen raw human need know that we need the simple assurance that we are restored to God. Not knowing for sure gives us a mortal hurt. The assurance that the grace of God in Christ banishes separation and restores us to God is the most precious thing that ever sank into guilty human hearts.

Christ also assures us through the revelation of an act. He asked an adulterous woman <u>who</u> had condemned her, *"No one, Sir,"* she said. *"Then neither do I condemn you,"* Jesus declared. *"Go now and leave your life of sin."* (John 8:1). Jesus says to a hard, money-loving publican, *"Today salvation has come to this house,..."* (Luke 19:9). This is the eternal Word of God speaking through the language of an act. Grasp this thought: The love of God shining through those specific acts will not deal differently with us. He forgave and restored them, He forgives and restores me.

Prayer for today: O Father, who's very healing was so revealing, You who make timeless truths speak through facts of today, do speak to my heart – *"Your sins are forgiven you."* I accept, for Your very character is behind those words, and You do not change. Amen

February 21   Acts 1:8; 2:32-33; 5:32; Hebrews 12:1

ASSURANCE OF WITNESSES

God assures us through His Word. And that Word, speaking specifically and completely through words and deeds in the pages of the New Testament, keeps on speaking. The Acts of the Apostles was not completed. It is still going on. Through the ages the timeless Word speaks the language of time. That Word, "Christ," <u>still</u> speaks through Christian witnesses today.

When you were seeking God, did someone ask to counsel and pray with you? They might have quietly and loving said, "God so loved "you" that He gave His only Son, that if "you" will believe in Him, "you" will not parish but have everlasting life." Did that Christian have a right to assure you? Yes, it was the church whispering its witness in your ear.

Sometimes the <u>assurance may come from any number of God appointed witnesses</u>. Men, women, and children in every walk of life, from the lowest social rank to the highest, from every stage of human development, from the extremely wise, to the ransomed sinner, have heard the message of Christ from at least one or more who have experienced Christ and tells about Him. That is a witness. I give you my assurance and I know of many who would give you their assurance with me. That is collective witness. <u>We have tried Jesus and we know He is REAL</u>!!

Prayer for today: O Christ, we thank You that there are millions whose hearts You have touched and illuminated and who gratefully witness unashamedly for You and to others. We joyfully join their service to You. Amen.

February 22   Psalm 32:1-2; Romans 8:1-9,10;
                                  1 John 3:9-14; 5:4-5

ASSURANCE THROUGH POWER OVER SIN

We have studied two basis of assurance by which we can be sure that we have received God's free gift of salvation: <u>His Word</u> and <u>His Many Witnesses</u>. Another assurance – <u>Moral Power over Sin.</u> God shows Himself within us in our increased moral power. After, by faith, you took Christ into your life, did you feel a change immediately or was it the next time you found yourself in your old surroundings, around the old temptations, and to your astonishment you found you had no more interest in them? You then realized there was a new Power in your life. Christ was there! That new Power over sin was a sign of His presence.

Take someone with a bad temper for instance. Before when anyone crossed you, you would easily fly into a rage. But now when someone does you wrong, instead of anger you feel pity. It is Christ within you.

When we began to show the fruit – "love, joy, peace, patience, kindness, goodness, faithfulness, gentleness, and self-control," then we know we are connected to Christ. This new life is at work within us. In the beginning of our new life with Christ these things may not be fully matured, but they are within you. Let that fact assure you. The bud comes before the flower.

Prayer for today: O Christ, I thank You that I can already feel within my heart the stirrings of new life. I know at first I will make unsure steps, as I begin this walk with You that will take me through my remaining years. Even though, I start out weakly, as I continue to walk with You I will grow stronger and the new moral power within me will grow into perfect strength. I thank You. Amen.

February 23   Psalm 51:13; Acts 5:20; 8:4; 13:1-3

ANOTHER ASSURANCE – THE DESIRE TO SHARE CHRIST

Another source of assurance that we have been Born Again and Christ has taken up residence in our heart and life is when we have <u>a strong desire to share Christ with others.</u>

Our new Life not only desires more of Christ for ourselves, but also wants others to experience the wonderful life we have found. Christian religion is a cry for life – it also is a cry for life for others.

There are two sides of Christian religion: Love to God, and love to others. The moment we sincerely love God is the moment we sincerely begin to love others. Therefore, if we are not completely sure of our love for God, we can be assured of it, if we find our love for others increasing.

When we have surrendered our lives to Christ, we want to share it with everybody. There is almost an irresistible desire to share it. We want everyone to feel Christ presence and experience Him in a new life. It may be that you have no such overwhelming desire; it may be just now rising to the surface of your still partly frozen heart, and yet it is there. Go on, act on it. Some people may reject your new experience with Christ, but stand firm it will only help you grow stronger and deeper. Truly it is the very life of God within you when you have a desire to share. That is also assurance that Christ is living within you.

Prayer for today: O Christ, Your love is conquering me – help me to show others that same love. Let my love flame so bright that others cannot help but be drawn to it. Amen.

February 24   Romans 8:16; 2 Corinthians 1:21-22;
                               1 John 3:24; 5:11-12

THE ULTIMATE ASSURANCE – GOD'S SPIRIT

We may think that all of these assurances, that assure us that we have been Born Again, are wonderful, but can I know Him intimately (personally)? **Absolutely yes**! God would not make known His presence by giving us good gifts, and then withhold Himself. If you are a parent would you do that to your child? Did your parents do it to you? Sad to say this is known to happen with earthly parents and their children, occasionally, but God did not plan it to be that way. Listen to this from (Matthew 7:11) – *"If you, then, though you are evil, know how to give good gifts to your children, how much more will Your Father in heaven give good gifts to those who ask Him!"* Being love, it would hurt Him as much as it would hurt us for Christ to withhold Himself from us. Listen to these words: *"The Spirit himself testifies with our spirit that we are God's children."* (Romans 8:16). His Spirit-our spirit. They come together with nothing between. Quiet! He speaks so quietly, so intimately: "My child I came seeking you through a cross. But that is gone now. You have removed the obstacles. That is what I have waited for. Now remove any lingering doubt and fear. It is I. Do not be afraid. Ask me for what you need. My resources are sufficient and inexhaustible. Tell me all about your troubles, even the small ones, and I will tell you some of mine. We will share together. And as we share together you will grow, and someday, my child, I want you to be like Jesus. I can think of nothing better for you and I wish nothing less. You know that by my coming into your life all your sins are forgiven. They are removed from my memory forever and you must forget them, too."

Prayer for today: O God, my Father, I bow before You in speechless adoration. I am fully Yours. I love You! I feel Your love enfolding me to Your heart. I thank You. Amen.

February 25   2 Corinthians 5:4-5; Philippians 1:9-11;
                           Colossians 2:6-7

IS ASSURANCE BASED ON FEELINGS?

We now have five strands of assurance wrapped around our heart.

1. The assurance of the Word
2. The assurance of Witnesses
3. The assurance through Power over Sin
4. The assurance of our Desire to Share Christ
5. The ultimate assurance – God's Spirit

Surely these five should give us strong assurance that we are now living a new life through Christ. That we have been Born Again. The assurances give us both spiritual and intellectual certainty. We are experiencing facts that work in our new life – facts that bring satisfaction and wholeness. Does all of this depend on how I feel about the change in my life? If my feelings change then what?

We should not be afraid of our emotions; they are an essential part of life. Feelings give driving force to the soul. Feelings may change, according to your physical health as well as many other things. The spiritual life must use them, but is not established on feelings. Our will must be the center of our spiritual life.

We have made a permanent choice to follow Christ. It is one of those choices that we do not have to make over and over again everyday. The less important choices of life fit into this central permanent spiritual choice, not the other way around. Our central permanent spiritual choice continues to be the permanent remaining fact among the flow and change of feeling. Whether your life is made rough by the storms of life or flows smooth and calm, life flows on. When you have made a permanent life-choice, don't raise the issue again and again every time your feelings change.

Prayer for today: O Christ, You do not change, no matter how my feelings change. You live in my heart whether I feel Your presence or not. I thank You for that. As I make my permanent choice to live for You, You will take up permanent residence in my life. Amen.

February 26   Matthew 17:20; Acts 9:17-22;
                               Galatians 5:7; Philippians 1: 6

THE BEGINNING

The first days of adjustment after you have made your deci-sion to live your life for Christ are the most difficult. The infant mortality rate in the Kingdom of God is very devastating. The thing to remember is this, casualties in the beginning of your new life, are preventable! However, it is a fact that the first few days and weeks are the crucial days. It takes twice the power to break with the old life as it does to live the new life after new habits have formed.

This should not frighten you. In (Mark 16:3-4) it says, *"Who will roll away the stone from the entrance of the tomb?" "But when they looked up, they saw the very large stone had been rolled away."* We see large difficulties before us, and as we get to them one by one, they are rolled away. Remember our silent Partner is at work within us and He is practiced at rolling away stones.

First of all, let us remember that there are certain laws of our spiritual life just as sure as there are laws that form the foundation of physical life. This does not mean that we are handed a set of rules to obey. The Christian life is not mechanically and minutely obeying a set of rules. **It is a love affair**. And lovers do not sit down and look at the rules to see what is to be done next. Nevertheless, even in a love affair there are foundational laws of friendship which must be obeyed or else there will be a train-wreck. One reason why so many casualties take place, in our early days and weeks of our new life with Christ, is because we do not stop to plan and organize our new life, we are disorganized. And if **our life is disorganized, we will not be happy.**

Prayer for today: O Christ of the disciplined desires, teach me to live life according to Your way. I came to You stumbling, but I came. I am firmly set to obey; teach me. Amen

February 27   1 Kings 18:21; Luke 19:1-10; John 9:25

COMMIT YOURSELF

One of the first things to do after giving your life to Christ is to commit yourself to Him. The Christian life is the beginning of a life as different from the ordinary human as the ordinary human is different from the animal. You are different so you act differently. <u>Keep in mind we are talking about commitment</u>. The temptation will be for you to sit quietly and raise no issues, to upset no lifestyles, to take on protectiveness of your environment and to settle down, hoping that somehow your new life will show itself. It won't. You must decide it will.

In regard to your decision to follow Christ – when once the decision has been made, let yourself be "irreversibly" committed. Put yourself in the position to do more, to do everything God ask you to do. Note that word "irreversibly". Leave no door open behind you. Your mind in a fearful moment might be tempted to take that way of escape. You are no longer a person of escape mentality.

Don't be ashamed or afraid to be recognized as a true Christian. Come out of the dark corners of your mind where you hide behind fears of ridicule. Stand before the world open and unashamed and decisive. Be ashamed of nothing except sin. **COMMIT YOURSELF!**

Prayer for today: O Christ, help me to commit every aspect of my life to You. Give me courage to take the first bold steps. And help me take them now. Amen.

February 28

Mark 9:49; 1 Corinthians 9:27;
1 Timothy 4:7,8,16;
2 Timothy 1:7

DISCIPLINE YOURSELF

The word "discipline" and the word "disciple" are closely related. In fact they are one – no discipline, no disciple.

One of the greatest needs of today is putting discipline back into our lives. We have reacted so strongly against the imposed authority and taboos of the past that we have swung into an excessive freedom from the normal and thought it was liberty. We are now finding out that it is not liberating at all. Some educators, parents, psychologist, politicians, and such decided that the child should be left to guide itself, which basically means, those psychology minded ones did not want to take on the responsibility of the guidance and discipline a child desperately needs to grow into a responsible adult. Some adults are actually afraid to involve themselves in the younger ones discipline, afraid of the child and their response to discipline. At this point, both the adult and the child need discipline. Otherwise we will all arrive at the same conclusion of Henri Fredic Amiel, "What a strange creature I am!" Let me tell you about Henri Fredic Amiel – He spent his life dissecting and exposing his own moods. In his study of himself it says in his journal, he cried out, "What a strange creature I am!".

In Christ you will not have discipline imposed upon you. You will want to choose God's discipline as He guides your life into Living Victoriously. Discipline is usually gained after much prayer and Bible study. It is not handed to you. In your quiet time with God, ask Him in thought and prayer, for guidance and spiritual discipline. As you accept discipline, you become a disciple.

Prayer for today: O Christ, Let Your discipline be my desire as I follow You to finding my purpose in life. Amen.

February 29   Psalm 5:3; Luke 11:1-13; Acts 3:1;
                               Ephesians 6:18; Colossians 4:2

ESTABLISH THE HABIT OF PRAYER

Yesterday it was suggested that we discipline ourselves spiritually, not merely for the sake of discipline, but because this discipline gathers up our scattered ways and focuses them on the business of Living Victoriously.

The first discipline must be to establish the habit of prayer. Our prayer time is so important because it is a time of quiet communication between you and God alone. Take time to listen as well as talk to God. Set a time everyday that you give entirely to prayer. When our prayer life is neglected we become weak from not drawing from our life source, just as when our prayer life is consistent we become stronger from the flow of the life source. Any outstanding Christian will tell you they became stronger by staying close to God through prayer.

Don't try to fool yourself into thinking that you do not need a particular time and place even though you can find God all the time and everywhere. If you are to find God all the time, then you must find Him sometime; and if you are going to find Him everywhere, then you must fine Him somewhere. That sometime and somewhere will be the special prayer time and special prayer place. Find that time and place. And as you do, it will put your life on the road that will lead you to Living Victoriously.

Prayer for today: O Christ, teach me to pray, to make time to form the habit of prayer, that I may find the habit of victory. Help me to start today in a quiet, unhurried talk with You. Amen.

March 1   Psalm 119:11; Isaiah 55:2; Matthew 4:4;
                           Luke 4:16; John 6:27

ABSORB THE LIVING WORD

Along with our prayer time we need God's Word. Take a Bible, paper and pen as you study. If you will write down inspiration and understanding that comes to you, later when you go back and read what you recorded, it will seem to have been written by someone else and will seem fresh and new. The Bible is our instruction Manual. The more we study it the more we learn and understand about our new life and how to live it according to the way it is meant to be lived.

The story is told of a young man who traveled to another country with no reason to live. His mother had given him a New Testament which he put in the bottom of his luggage. One day, sick and discouraged, he remembered the Book, dug it out of his luggage, opened it and the first word his eyes fell on was the word "Redeemed". That one word turned his life from moral defeat and discouragement to victory and a new life. What a wonderful word! "Redeemed". You will find such words in the Bible and they will meet your need just when you need them. God is in these words. Remember to tell Him; how grateful you are, even though your words may seem so inadequate.

Sometimes God's Word seems so personal – almost if your own name is called through it. At times when we are alone and discouraged verses such as, "*...and surely, I am with you always, to the very end of the age.*" (Matthew 28:20b), and again in (Hebrews 12:5b), "*Never will I leave you; never will I forsake you.*" It is often just that personal.

At the close of your devotional time always remember to thank Him.

Prayer for today: O Christ, In Your Word we find the bread of life and we feed upon it. We thank You for this food. Amen.

March 2   2 Kings 5:3; Matthew 10:8;
                           Mark 5:18-20; 1 John 1:3

THE HABIT OF SHARING CHRIST

We have talked about discipline of prayer and of absorbing the Word of God. Out of these two disciplines will naturally and necessarily come the third: the discipline of sharing Christ and our Christian experiences. Think about this – if the first two <u>flow into</u> our life, the third will be an <u>outflow</u>. <u>There can be no outflow without an inflow, and the inflow will stop</u> – <u>if there is no outflow</u>. This can be called the discipline of sharing. We should discipline ourselves to share our experiences as we pray and study the Bible. If we do not share, how will the Good News spread? Many do not share. They are sincere and faithful in their quiet time, but have never disciplined themselves to share. If something happens in a conversation that bumps them and jolts it out of them, well fine and good. But sharing seems to depend on accident rather than choice. Sharing should be a natural out-flowing of our communion with God. A doctor found a little dog beside the road with a broken leg took it home and cared for it until it was well. The doctor felt terribly sad when one day he discovered the little dog had disappeared. But the next day the little dog was back and had brought with him another injured dog. The impulse in that little dog's heart was natural and right. Has not Christ healed us? Isn't it the natural and normal thing for us to find someone else who needs healing also? As Christians we should say by our walk and by our talk, "**<u>I recommend my Savior to you</u>**." - There is no better definition of a Christian. Can you define your Christian life in those terms? If so, put the discipline of sharing deep into your life purpose.

Prayer for today: O Christ, Your healing is upon our heart. Let us carry Your healing help within our hands. Help us today to find someone with a broken human spirit and lead them to You. Amen.

March 3
Mark 4:30-32; 2 Timothy 2:15;
1 Corinthians 9:24-27; 10:31

THE CHRISTIAN LIFE AND THE SOCIAL LIFE

We must <u>not</u> relate Christian life to our social life. Rather, relate our social life to our Christian life. Our social life must not be the center of our life and Christian life fitted into it. If we try that our Christian life will die. Let's check over our social life and see what part of it can contribute to or take away from our Christian life. Our social life should minister to our total fitness of life. Some social activities do not refresh us – they exhaust us. They leave us morally and spiritually flabby and unfit. We should give them up or so control them that they really do refresh us. We may find after seeing some movies that we are inspired and uplifted. But often a movie will leave us with the feeling of being inwardly violated. Our very spirit seems to have been invaded and trampled on. We feel depressed. We should never expose ourselves to such – not if we value higher values. It is like running over a skunk with our car. IT STINKS! The same can be said for many books. Reading books that leaves us with exhausted nerves and emotions is to handicap us spiritually. The idea that we must read everything that is written in order to understand life is absolutely false. Does a doctor have to take cancer germs into his body to understand cancer? Do you have to roll in a mud hold to understand what it means to be dirty? Only cleanliness can understand dirtiness. To spend long and exhausting hours doing <u>anything</u> that arouses our emotions and yet has no constructive outlet is to leave a person spiritually weaker. Ask yourself if particular activities bring you to better and more victorious living, or if they lead you to spiritual weakness.

Go over your whole life and ask yourself what part exhausts you, and what part refreshes you.

Prayer for today: O Christ of the fit body and soul, make me fit in every part of my being and may my social life contribute to my well being. Amen.

March 4   Acts 2:43-47; Hebrews 10:25

"TOGETHERNESS"

Do you think it is necessary to belong to a Church after accepting Jesus? Yes, you will want and need that fellowship, that, "togetherness". The spiritual life cannot be lived in isolation. Life is intensely social; it is also intensely personal and we cannot separate the two. If the Church should be wiped out today, tomorrow you would have to put something in its place, for there must be a social expression of the spiritual life as well as the individual life expression. To separate the social life and the personal life would not be right, for the social life is the personal life in its larger relationships. Is it our duty to support the Church? The Church is not a duty imposed on us from without. It is founded on the facts of life. Those facts being that our very inner nature demands it. As a Christian if we separate ourselves from the Church we will see how fast our spiritual life dies. That is why it is so important for young Christians to have the corporate fellowship of the Church to hold them up. We rejoice with them, we encourage them, we strengthen them when they become weak, and when they fall we gather around them lifting them up with our prayers and love, without blame or disapproval until they are back on their feet again. The stupidities, the superficiality, the irrelevancies and the formalities of the Church – Yes, we've seen them all. Nevertheless, the Church is the Mother of our Spirit, and we love our Mother in spite of her weakness and wrinkles. So – do as the scripture says, *"Let us not give up meeting together, as some are in the habit of doing, but let us encourage one another..."* (Hebrews 10:25). As you begin your new life in Christ begin it as a member of the Family of God, in a Bible based Church.

Prayer for today: O Christ,, who gathers us together into a Family which You are the Older Brother and God is the Father, we thank You that You invite us into Your Family circle, the Family of God. Amen.

TOGETHERNESS

By – MaryAnn Moore

"It's time to go," announced, father Crow.
"God where?" asked, Baby Hare.
"In from the storm," declared the animals from the farm.
"It is getting chilly," bay-ed, the goat, Billy.
"No cause for alarm, it's safe and warm in the big red barn,"
Snorted, the bull with the crooked horn.
"There is room for all," nay-ed, the mare, so sleek and tall.
"I'm getting awfully cold," fretted her shivering foal.
"Me, too," echoed the spider, hanging close beside her.
"Then why are we standing here?" inquired the pretty deer.
"Is everyone awake?" hissed the slithery snake.
"We are all alert, as can be," barked the squirrel in the tree.
"Then let's be off," hooted, the owl from the barn loft.
"Hooray, we are on our way now," moo-ed, a relieved brown cow.
"It sure will be nice," squeaked, the tiny mice.
"Yes," agreed, Mr. Rooster, with the red tail feather,
"Especially in this frightful weather."

—AND SO—

The animals marched into the big red barn,
Where there was delicious hay and corn.
Protection from the approaching storm,
And best of all "TOGETHERNESS".
It can't get any better than this," oink-ed, the beautiful piggy
    princess.
They were just settling in,
When from the top of the corn bin,
Fluttering miss red hen,
Cackled, with a wide grin, "We will all go out again,
When spring time comes, that's when.

March 5   Acts 19:1, 2, 6, 20; 1 Corinthians 3:1-4

LIVING VICTORIOUSLY IN THE CHRISTIAN WORLD

We might want to go straight from the beginning of our new life in Christ into trying to figure out how our new life will fit into our old life. But not yet.

If we try at first to figure out how our new life will relate to the old life, we would bypass the lessons to be learned about Living Victoriously as a Christian among "Christians" – those living for Christ completely, those partly living for Him, and those not in any way living for Christ, for inside the Church we have all three. Even the most enthusiastic person in the church would not claim that the characteristic of all its members is Living Victoriously. Here and there you see it, but in looking at the Christian World in general, you see a lack of "Christians" Living Victoriously.

Spiritually we seem to have turned gray. The vitality, the sparkle, the spontaneity, the joy, the radiance which should characterize people called Christians seems to have faded. We seem to have no moral power; we seem to have a paralysis that makes us limp and helpless in the face of rampant wrong. We may protest against wrong, but we seem to have little power to change things.

There is nothing-absolutely nothing needed so much among Christians today as the discovery of the secret of Living Victoriously. If we can find that then anything can happen. Without it nothing will happen – except staleness, tastelessness, and bitter disappointment with our new life and Christian religion in general.

Prayer for today: O Father, You are putting Your finger on our need. Help us not to rest until we know this secret, and use it in our life. Amen.

March 6   Matthew 9:2; Mark 4:40; Luke 18:8

THE SPIRIT OF EXPECTING "NOTHING"

Yesterday we said that the main characteristic of modern Christianity is not living a victorious life. This would not be so serious if we expected something else – like if we were pushing at the gates of abundant life to have them open. But many have settled down to a spirit of expecting nothing. They do not expect anything from their spiritual life except to muddle through. This is serious! The awful power of fatalism can devastate an entire civilization. Fatalism is the acceptance that everything and all events have been predetermined and no matter what you do or how you live your life it will not make any difference. So, why expect anything to be different. Hence – expect nothing. Helpless resignation. Across our land this danger lurks at our hearts door. When it slowly creeps into a heart, we are then resigned to moral and spiritual defeat. A doctor, who, for years, worked with people who were troubled in body and soul, said these astonishing words: "Most Christians do not expect their religion to do them any great or immediate good." However, when someone tells these same people that this condition of moral and spiritual defeat does not need to last even a single hour, that victory, joy, and peace can be found in living, they look at you as if you are trying to teach them a strange new doctrine. For they have become conformed in defeat. Do you think being spiritually straight and upstanding is something strange and unnatural? As Christians let's have a spirit of expectancy – not one of non-expectancy. God wants us to have faith enough to expect miracles. And we should.

Prayer for today: O Father, speak to our dead desires and direct them to rise. We know we cannot live without a desire to live. We do desire to live – to live fully and completely. Your presence awakens us, our eyes are opened. Amen.

March 7   Romans 6:1-7

IS FORGIVENESS THE BEST WE CAN EXPECT?

Many Christians do not expect anything beyond repeated forgiveness for constantly repeated sins. This kind of thinking turns Christianity, namely the forgiving grace of God, into something most destructive, for it actually turns out to be something that encourages evil. Think what a cross that must put on the heart of God! Also what a travesty it is on our Christian faith!

This expecting constant forgiveness of constantly repeated sins is weakening to character, and is one reason for so much weak character within the Christian Church. Under this idea life turns weak.

A cheap easy forgiveness of sins does not represent the true gospel of Jesus Christ. Christ teaching <u>does</u> offer forgiveness of sins, and as a part of that forgiveness, we are also offered **POWER OVER THOSE FORGIVEN SINS. FORGIVENESS AND POWER** <u>are</u> <u>parts of the grace of God that cannot be separated</u>. We cannot have one without the other. If we should try to have forgiveness without power to combat those sins then moral weakness would remain in us, and if we should try to have power without forgiveness, then moral guilt would remain. So we must receive both or neither. God does not give one without the other. And we must have both to have victorious life. Our Choice – both or neither!

Prayer for today: O Father, we thank You for redemption. This redemption that comes from the cross that we have twisted and made into more of a cross for You. Forgive us – we need POWER to be used of You. Amen.

CHRISTIAN GUARANTEE

God's Grace and Power go hand in hand,
Teaching forgiveness and strength,
To every believing child, woman and man.

God's Grace forgives our sin,
His Power keeps us free,
This is our "Christian Guarantee"

Grace heals our sorrow,
Power dulls the pain,
When in our life Christ does reign.

Power wins the battles,
Grace helps us to firmly stand,
When we hold to God's unchanging hand.

God's Grace and Power is unequaled,
It endures to the end,
When we let Him abide deep within.

March 8   Mark 5:15; Romans 7:24-25; 8:1-2;
                           1 John 1:7-10

WHAT DOES THE GOSPEL OF CHRIST OFFER?

At this point in our study there are two dangers we need to look at. One is to set our standard of living too low, the other is to set our standard too high. In either situation we may hesitate to act – because one demands no change, the other demands such change that we feel helpless before we even start. We must avoid both dangers.

You might find it interesting that both psychology and the gospel agree in being pessimistic about humanity. They both say that "we are not as perfect as we might be; that there are great possibilities for idealistic progress which we universally reject." But while they are both pessimistic about us, they are both amazingly optimistic. Both psychology and gospel teaching agree in saying that this divided state must not continue, we and our ideals must come together if human happiness is to result. Sin is not a necessary part of our make-up. Sin is an intrusion in our being. Sin is no more necessary to give spice to life than sand in the eye is necessary to see. So—the first thing to remember, then, is this: The Gospel of Christ offers freedom and release from every sin. There is no compromise at this point, for compromise would be deadly! The Gospel of Christ sweeps over us and says, "Sin shall no longer have control over me." (Romans 8:2) says, "*Because through Christ Jesus the law of the Spirit of life set me free from the law of sin and death.*" If you have repeated these words from (Romans 8:2) until they are threadbare, restring them with a thicker thread, because they are not threadbare words; they are the astonishing offer of God to give us release from the Power of evil.

Prayer for today: O Father, we thank You for what this means to us. It is an open door, the one open door out of our inner divisions, our inner turmoil, strife and confusion to happiness, to just what we want. We thank You. Amen

March 9   Luke 22:28; 1 Corinthians 10:13;
                                       Hebrews 2:17-18; James 1:2-4

WHAT THE VICTORIOUS LIFE IS <u>NOT</u>

In order for us to see what the victorious life <u>is</u> we must first see what it <u>is not</u>. It <u>is not</u> freedom from temptation. Sin can result from using a good thing in a wrong way. Just as dirt is misplaced matter, sin can be a misplaced good. Sex is natural and right – adultery is sin; so is sex outside marriage. Self-respect pushed too far becomes pride, hence – sin. Self-love is normal; taken beyond limits it becomes selfishness. The group instinct is right, but when against our ideals, and we follow the crowd, it is sin. (James 1:13-14) says, *"When tempted, no one should say, 'God is tempting me.' For God cannot be tempted by evil, nor does he tempt anyone; but each one is tempted when, by his own evil desire, is dragged away and enticed."* Note the phrase "<u>dragged away</u>" – the natural is dragged away— dragged too far away into sin. Now the natural self is always with us. It is constantly pressing upon the boundaries we set for it; therefore, we are constantly being tempted. But, temptation is no sin. It is only when we give into or let ourselves be "dragged away" by that temptation that it becomes sin. We've all heard it said, **"You can't keep the birds from flying over your head, but you can keep them from building a nest in your hair." You cannot keep the suggestion of evil from coming to your mind, but you can keep from letting it dwell there and allowing it to rest in your mind until it hatches its brood. Dismissed at once it leaves no stain. Thoughts of evil only become evil thoughts when we invite them in, offer them a chair and then entertain them.** Temptation <u>can be</u> the ladder to higher living.

Prayer for today: O Father of the wilderness temptation, we thank You that You are with us in our temptations, lifting, saving, and turning our battles around. Go with me today as I turn temptation into character. I thank You. Amen.

March 10   Galatians 2:11; 6:1; Philippians 3:12-15

WHAT THE VICTORIOUS LIFE IS **NOT** (Continued)

Yesterday we learned that Living Victoriously does not mean we are free from temptation.

Also, Living Victoriously does not mean we are free from making mistakes. We are all personalities in the making, limited and struggling with things too big for us. Obviously, at our very best, we will still make many mistakes. However, these mistakes need not be sins. Our actions are the result of our intentions and if our intelligence is limited, in a particular area, our actions may turn out to be a mistake – not necessarily a sin. Therefore the action carries a sense of incompleteness and frustration, but not guilt. Sin comes out of a wrong intention. Living victoriously does not mean perfect living without a flaw, and that can be consistent with many mistakes.

Living victoriously does not mean maturity. **Living victoriously does mean clearing away things that keeps us from growing spiritually**. In addition to the many mistakes we will make in our Christian life, there will also be many immaturities. Purity does not mean maturity.

Also, the victorious life does not keep us from an occasional fall into a wrong act, which may be called a sin. At that point we may have lost a fight, but we can still win the battle. We may even lose a few battles and still win the war. One difference in a sheep and a hog is when a sheep falls into a mud hole it bleats to get out, while a hog loves it and wallows in it. In saying that an occasional fall is consistent with Living Victoriously, hopefully, will not open the door to cause such falls. This is dangerous and weakening to our new Christian life. We must not dwell on such thoughts. We must be absolute about the whole thing. Nevertheless, you can Live Victoriously with occasional failure.

Prayer for today: O Father, we thank You that You know our heart. Therefore You know that we are longing for a heart like Yours. Amen.

March 11   Acts 15:37-41; Romans 12:18;
                            Philippians 4:2-3

WHAT THE VICTORIOUS LIFE IS **NOT** (Continued)

Living victoriously does not mean you will have the ability to get along with everybody. There are certain people whose outlook and interest are so different from ours that when we are in their company, we find it almost impossible to get along with them. They may be very good people. Nevertheless, we are very incompatible with them. However, we can use those "thorns in the flesh" to make us better, more patient, a victorious person.

As a Christian when we find we are incompatible with someone, talk the situation over calmly and honestly with them and we may find what we thought was incompatibilities are misunderstandings. We will be able to see the other person's point of view, and seeing it we may sympathize with it. It is not at all necessary to agree with another person to get along with them. Some of the greatest fellowships come out of the most opposite dispositions.

Very often our incompatibilities are not rooted in our real nature, but in complex issues, in hidden sin, in wrong attitudes, in misunderstanding one another, not taking time to really know a person, etc., and when brought out and corrected leads to an amazing deep fellowship. There are some real incompatibilities – but they are very, very few.

Prayer for today: O Father of the patient heart, we thank You for the possibility of bridging gaps through love. Teach us to love even those who we find hardest to love and help us to live victoriously in all our relationships. Amen.

March 12   Ephesians 4:11-13; 1 Thessalonians 5:23-24

WHAT **IS** VICTORIOUS LIVING?

Now that we have seen what the victorious life is not, let's see what it is: It is the life of Christ reigning victoriously in every intricate part of our being and in every one of our relationships.

First let's consider every part of our being. There are many Christians who have certain areas of their lives in which Christ acts, weakly perhaps, but there is some action. However, we may withhold some areas from Him completely. These are reserved areas in the community of our soul. Over these reserved areas we rule, we make the decisions there. This is a double principle of control in our life. Anytime we try to compete with God, as to who is in control, we lose. Yet many Christians wonder why their spiritual life is so unsatisfactory. It will continue to be unsatisfactory as long as there is inner division. Our soul must be unified. We must make our choice: either we must dismiss Christ completely from our life and forget Him, and take over control, in which case our whole life will be unified under <u>OUR control</u>, or we must make a complete surrender of every area we are withholding from Christ control, in which case our life will be <u>CHRIST-controlled</u> and therefore unified.

There is no third way, even though many are trying to develop a third way – that being a way of compromise. It will not work. We have just enough of the love of Christ in our heart to make us miserable, when we try to compromise with ideas we know are wrong. This sets up a conflict in our life and we live with that turmoil and call it Christian. As pure unadulterated heathen we might be happy. "Might be": - the attempt has so far not succeeded. But as compromised Christians we <u>cannot</u> be happy.

Prayer for today: O Father, forgive us for making You a half-King, leaving other half-gods in our heart. We cannot bow to two, You are our only God. Amen.

March 13   Amos 5:21-24; 8:4-6; Matthew 6:24

WHAT **IS** LIVING VICTORIOUSLY? – (Continuing)

Yesterday we learned that Christ must reign victoriously in every part of our being, and today we will look at the second part. Christ must reign in every one of our relationships.

Double entity cannot be introduced into the soul without disaster. There is another point where double entity is just as disastrous – it is the point between the individual and society. If double entity is introduced at this point, there will also be defeat. <u>Christ must reign in every one of our relationships</u>!

This is where many try to introduce double entity into their lives – Christ will be allowed control in their personal lives, but the social and economic life is something else again. That is where we want to apply our own control.

An amazing amount of unhappiness comes from inner division, the division which applies to Christ ruling on the outside – especially our money. This is where present-day civilization is divided against itself, and it cannot stand. With this double entity at its heart our present life is unhappy and at a stand still.

This is bad psychology. This division between the personal life and the social life is artificial. It is not rooted in facts. The personal life exists in relationships with others. Our relationships with others are just as much a part of our personal life as our so-called inner life. <u>Think about how much of your life is made up with relationships to others, and how much is made up of relationships with yourself alone, and you see at once that they cannot be divided. It is all personal</u>.

Living victoriously must include both, our personal life and our social life.

Personal + Social = Victorious.

Prayer for today: O Father, we thank You for claiming our whole life, for we can tolerate no longer these paralyzing divisions. Help us to end them by bringing everything under <u>Your</u> control. Amen.

March 14   Galatians 5:16-24

DOES ACCEPTING CHRIST INTO OUR LIFE GIVE US
VICTORIOUS LIFE?

Now that we have our definition of Living Victoriously, let's take a few steps back. Does the victorious life began at the time we give our life to Christ or are there other turning points or events necessary to bring about <u>complete</u> life with Christ?

Giving our life to Christ is certainly the beginning of Living Victoriously. Life is lifted to a permanently higher level at that time. Things are changed. We may feel strangely new when new life is introduced within us. Life is forever changed, but not completely changed.

Most of us experience a rapid climb to a new high with this new life, but soon after there follows a time of alternate defeat and victory. It is up and down. And when we find ourselves on this roller coaster of life, victory-defeat, victory-defeat, we feel disappointed and troubled. We expected more. This wonderful experience introduced new life within us, but not complete life. As the first rush of new life declines a little we find things within us we did not dream could have survived the inrush of the new life. Yet they did survive. The old self has been cut down, but roots have remained. We are not comfortable with old roots beside our new life, and we want compete deliverance.

Prayer for today: O Father, You have started a new work within me, will You complete it? The very fact that I am uncomfortable is a sign of Your redemptive love at work, gently pointing out that I need healing here and there. Heal me where I need healing, and heal me completely. Amen.

March 15   Romans 7:14-2

THE INNER CONFLICT

Usually after we have invited Christ into our life a strange conflict will follow. For a time we may feel life is one happy, unified, glorious day. Then one day we may be surprised to find, we are ill-tempered and even sullen and gloomy, impatient, and you can't understand it because you've never been more sincere about your love for Christ and He has never been more precious to you. You dislike this feeling of inner conflict and division within. Let's look at what may have happened. Psychology tells us that down in our subconscious the instincts hold within them our hereditary habits and tendencies. These instincts have gathered up within themselves the hereditary experience running back through a long history. Therefore, they, have certain inclinations, certain drives, when unrestrained they bend toward evil. If this sounds like the almost forgotten doctrine of original sin, <u>it is</u>. These instincts control the conscious mind in very large degree. It is true that the mind builds up a higher standard of principles which try to hold the natural instincts under control. When we have Christ in our life there is a cleansing of the conscious mind of everything that conflicts with the love of Christ. For a time no conflict may occur, the new life reigns supreme. These instincts in the subconscious are frightened – frightened, but not transformed. They soon demand recognition and attention. They knock at the door of the conscious. We are startled and alarmed that there are voices in the basement. These surprised instincts are like old stories of pirates who hid in the lower level of a ship and then when the ship was well on its journey, the pirates would rise up and try to capture the ship. And a fight followed. When Christ introduces new life into our old life a conflict begins between our new life and the old life natural instincts. We will be divided – **but hang on** …

Prayer for today: O Father, I open it all to You! Cleanse me in the secret places, the hidden depths. I wish to be unified. Amen.

March 16   Romans 7:24-25; 8:1-2; 2 Corinthians 7:1

CAN THE SUBCONSCIOUS BE TRANSFORMED?

The question has been asked: "Is salvation possible for the subconscious mind?" This is a great question for a person seeking the victorious life. This is a very important issue.

Our natural instincts cannot be eradicated. From the book (Psychology and Life): "The instinctive forces cannot, by any known process, be eradicated, and the method of evasion and pretense simply means that these forces function at the depths of the personality at which they cannot be controlled." We cannot eradicate them.

And we must not suppress them. If they are suppressed then they are driven below and form what is called a complex. "A complex is a system of emotionally charged ideas surrounding one central idea." Suppressed instincts in the subconscious mind are dangerous.

So—if they cannot be eradicated, and they must not be suppressed – in the interest of our new life we cannot allow them to be expressed, is there a way out? Yes-yes-yes! They can be refined, purified, exalted, and turned into expression in a higher form. In the language of Christian religion they can be TRANSFORMED!

We cannot put our natural instincts out, we can't put them under, but we can put them behind the central purpose of our life and they can become the driving force. Our former inner enemies now become the allies of our new life. The wild horses are now tamed and harnessed and working for the Kingdom of Christ.

YES – Our natural instincts can be transformed and dedicated.

Prayer for today: O Father, we thank You that in Your life every Power, conscious and subconscious was dedicated to the Kingdom. We want that oneness within us. Amen.

March 17   Luke 24:48-4; Acts 1:8; 2:4 & 33

MUST WE FACE ANOTHER SPIRITUAL EVENT?

We will face many spiritual events along the way, and our spiritual life grows from each event. But will we have another decisive turning point like the first? Since it happened to the disciples <u>then</u>, why not to His disciples <u>now</u>? We cannot go on changed in our conscious mind and unchanged in our subconscious mine. It is absolutely necessary to bring our self-instincts and our whole life in line with the will of God. While "being born again" starts the process, another event in some form or another is necessary to bring everything under God's control. <u>Until we are driven to a deeper walk with Christ we will not find victory, we will only be a moderate Christian – serving Christ, but not being like Him</u>. We will develop tempers and bad attitudes and become a working compromise between Christ and our old self-instincts. (Does this not describe Peter before Pentecost?) The disciples an example: (Read again Acts 1:8). Jesus' final words to His disciples gave them a promise of power, the only resource they really needed to succeed in the work He had spent three years educating, and developing them to do. Then He supplied what they needed to accomplish the task He had given them. Only when He knew they could handle the resources did Jesus supply them with the power they needed to accomplish their given task. He knew giving them the power before they knew what to do with it or how to use it would be setting them up for failure, but now they were prepared to succeed. This spiritual event has been called the second work of grace, sanctification, being filled with the Holy Spirit, among other things. Call it whatever you wish or don't call it anything – just do it. **It simply means in the language of Christianity – consecrate, devote, dedicate, commit yourself completely to God and the purpose He has for your life. When you pursue a lifestyle of holding nothing back, giving your all to Him, He will give you Power to do His perfect and pleasing will.**

Prayer for today: Father, equip us for our life's purpose. Amen

March 18   Luke 9:18-25

OLD LIFE AND NEW LIFE SIDE BY SIDE

The fact of the old life and new life side by side and unrelated to each other can be seen in the circumstance of the disciples. As we study them we may see ourselves. (Read carefully Luke 9:18-62).

Jesus took the disciples to Caesarea Philippi, where there was a white rock with a cave-like structure and temple where the image of Caesar was worshiped as God in the flesh. He brought them here to ask them the great question: Who am I? Here is where their mind needed to be perfectly clear. Is Caesar, God made evident in the flesh? Is <u>power</u> the final word? Or is Jesus, God made evident in the flesh? Is <u>love</u> the final word?

When Jesus asked the question, "*Who do you say I am?*" Peter's lips must have trembled with the great confession: "*The Christ of God.*" (Luke 9:20). At last the great revelation had dawned. It was a wonderful moment. We would have thought from that moment on everything in their lives would have been agreeable and powerful as they organized themselves around it. On the contrary, they did nothing else right in the rest of the chapter. Everything seemed out of order. Jesus did nothing in the remainder of the chapter except correct their mistakes. What is wrong? Had they not seen the glorious fact of Christ, the Son of the Living God? Yes, the conscious mind accepted that fact, but the subconscious mind had not. Particularly the instinct of SELF. It was there at the place of the self-instinct that the conflict had to be fought and won if they were to be Christian. Jesus immediately took the job in hand. He says to them, "*If anyone would come after me, he <u>must deny himself</u>...*" (Luke 9:23). He launched a missile straight at the <u>SELF</u>.

Prayer for today: O Father, we come to You. You have your finger on our problem – it is our inmost self. Heal us there and we will be healed everywhere. Amen.

March 19   Luke 9:28-45

THE PRINCIPLE DIFFICULTY REVEALED

Yesterday we learned that the principle problem in the lives of the disciples before Pentecost was their un-surrendered natural instincts, <u>particularly the self-instinct</u>. Jesus showed them themselves. First He showed them that He was going to the cross to lay down <u>Himself</u>, but that self would rise again. And He taught them that they must do the same – <u>they must go through spiritually what He was going through physically</u>. The most important thing in their being Sons of God must be losing "self". But in losing themselves they would find themselves. The disciples did not understand this deepest of spiritual lessons. So He took them to the mountain to show them the same thing in a kindergarten way. As Jesus looked out toward the cross and talked with Moses and Elijah about His death His face began to shine. The lesson was this: <u>Life will only shine as it faces its cross</u>. <u>The self will shine brighter as it surrenders to God</u>. The disciples did not understand. At the foot of the mountain they were not successful in their attempt to heal the boy with the evil spirit. Divided in inner loyalty, they were defeated in outer attempts. Jesus cast out the evil spirit with a word. *"And they were all amazed at the greatness of God."* (Luke 9:43). *While everyone* was marveling at *what Jesus did, He said to His* disciples, *"Listen carefully at what I am about to tell you: The Son of man is going to be betrayed into the hands of men."* (Luke 9:44). **You may think Christ "greatness" is in performing miracles of healing, but His "greatness" lies in the miracle of losing Himself. That is the principle thing we must do– lose our self in Christ.** They did not understand Jesus when He told them He was going to be betrayed into the hands of men because they did not understand this kind of attitude. We think more with our emotions than with our minds, and emotions fasten themselves around "SELF". The emotions were not surrendered.

Prayer for today: O Father, We <u>will</u> follow You. Amen.

March 20   Luke 9:45-48: 1 Corinthians 3:3

THE CONSEQUENCES OF THIS "SELF" ATTITUDE

This attitude of the unchanged **self**-instinct starts to show itself in social settings. The conflicts begin where there is a group of people who have **not** surrendered **self**, the stage is set for conflict and confusion. If **self** is reigning supreme within, you can be sure, self is reigning supreme without. It may try to accomplish this in subtle, refined, even "religious" ways, The conflicts begin; *"An argument started among them as to which of them would be the greatest." (Luke 9:46)*. Here we have Christian disciple causing conflict with Christian disciple. Not only were they causing conflict with the Master, they were inwardly struggling with themselves. The conscious mind surely must have been ashamed, but the unrepentant **self-instinct** demanded that "number one" be looked after. Of course they all fought for the "principle" of the thing. For **self** soon learns that it cannot get its way in the presence of religious principles unless its assertions are clothed with religious principles. Each disciple convinced himself that in the interest of the Kingdom he should be first. "I am the oldest," said Peter, "and besides, I made the great confession of His Messiah-ship – the interest of the Kingdom demands that age and insight be first." "But remember who brought you here, first here, first in authority," demanded Andrew. "Wait just a minute, I belong to the best family," replied John, "After all if we are going to influence these important people for the Kingdom, I must lead, for I am known to the high priest." "The Kingdom depends on solid financial sense, and I am the treasurer and therefore first," said Judas with an air of finality. (It **could** have happened something like that). The Kingdom was in their words, but "**self**" was in their intentions. **Most all difficulties in Christian service come from conflicts between Christian workers, and most of these conflicts come from the unrepentant self-instinct of otherwise "born again" people.**

Prayer for today: O Father, I must be reborn deeper. Amen

March 21   Luke 9:49-50; 1 Corinthians 1:10-13;
                                           Ephesians 4: 1-3

CONQUENCES OF "SELF" ATTITUDE WITHIN A GROUP

We are still talking about the attitude of the unchanged self-instinct. Yesterday we saw that the first conflict was the conflict between individuals. The conflicts have just begun, because the unrepentant self-instinct when dropped into human relationships sends out waves of conflict in ever widening circles to the far shores of society. As Jesus dealt with His disciples over this selfish situation, John felt the sting of it and brought up another; *"Master, we saw a man driving out demons in your name and we tried to stop him, because he is not one of us."* (Luke 9:49). Here is the second conflict – one group of Christian workers against another group of Christian workers. The unrepentant self-instinct may want to fight with individual members of its own group for place and power, but it is quite ready to band together with them in standing against those trying to encroach on their territory. For "self" sees this group as trespassing and threatening to "self". We are ready to stand and fight – for "principle" of course! The interest of the Kingdom is in danger. Who are these unauthorized people? They are dangerous. They are not one of us. They do not believe as we do. They do not speak the correct words for casting out demons. The unrepentant self-instinct is backing the religious party spirit, and it causes most denominations to refuse to unite with other Christians. There was a church that divided over the issue of how to use a gift of <u>four thousand</u> dollars. <u>They spent two hundred thousand dollars</u> in court cases for the right to manage the <u>four thousand dollars</u>. Think about it! One <u>concerned</u> leader on one side said, "We must defend the faith." Anyone could plainly see that the defense of the faith meant only that "self" was defending and asserting itself into power through group authority. That faith was in the gutter.

Prayer for today: Our Father, how our narrow mindedness and prejudices must crucify you, we want a heart like yours. Amen.

March 22 Luke 9:51-55; Galatians 3:27-28

RACIAL CONSEQUENCES OF THIS "SELF" ATTITUDE

Conflicts and arguments do not end with groups, as in our last study.

Jesus sent His disciples to a Samaritan village to prepare for His arrival. The Samaritans refused to allow Jesus to come to their village because His destination was Jerusalem, not Samaria. James and John were furious, "*Lord, do you want us to call fire down from heaven to destroy them?*" (Luke 9:54). The "self" is ready to assert itself through one race against another race. Again, it does this in the name of religion. "*Lord...from heaven...to destroy them.*" But underneath all the religious wording was the dark grim fact, the inner Jewish self hated Samaritans, for they were in a struggle for position and power. We dress our prejudices in religious garments to try and hide the naked truth beneath.

These race prejudices are not born within us. Self learns it from social heredity. People born and brought up with another race grow up and know no prejudices. Deep and lasting friendships are formed. If later, they absorb race prejudice, it is from their surroundings, it is not inherited. With all of us those prejudice ideas are dropped into our subconscious and the self-instinct absorbs them there. We wonder why we are critical of other races, easily find fault with them and are happy in their weaknesses – the reason is that the subconscious mind has absorbed the prejudices, and the subconscious mind is still unrepentant. The self-instinct has never bowed to Jesus Christ.

Prayer for today: O Father, You who made every person of every race, forgive me for not loving everyone of every race. I cannot do it unless this "self" within me bows its head and accepts You completely, allowing Your complete control of my life. Help me do it. Amen.

March 23   Ephesians 2:14-18; Colossians 1:17

THE CONTRAST

We have seen how the unchanged self-instinct is at the base of most all difficulties with ourselves and others. The unpurified ego stands in the way of our individual attainment of a happy well adjusted life. Remember these disciples were changed men in a big way. Most of their conscious mind was controlled by Christ, but most of their subconscious mind was not. Now note these contrasts: We see in (Luke 9) that the recognition of Christ as the Son of God solved very few of their spiritual problems. It left the problems of inner adjustment, adjustment of individual with individual, of group with group, and of race with race, untouched. But later those four problems were solved so easily and majestically that we hardly noticed. Now look at (Acts 2:46): *"They broke bread in their homes and ate together with glad and sincere hearts, praising God and enjoying the favor of all people."* That solved problem number one – they were no longer at war with themselves in their inner life. Now (Acts 2:14): *"Peter stood up with the eleven."* Their attitude had changed – they stood together. That solved problem number two – they were no longer competitive, they were co-operative. Look at (Acts 2:44): *"All the believers were together and had everything in common."* This brought together all groups of believers and made them a living fellowship, where they rejoiced in each others accomplishments. That solved problem number three – there was no longer suspicion among groups of believers. Now look at (Acts 8:14-17): *"Then Peter and John placed their hands on them (the Samaritans), and they received the Holy Spirit."* Instead of calling down fire from heaven to consume Samaritans they tenderly lay hands on their heads, that they might receive the Holy Spirit. That beautifully solved problem number four – their race prejudices had vanished.

Those four problems had been solved. How? **The Holy Spirit!**

Prayer for today: O God, we thank You that You have provided for us healing at the depths of our being. We thank You! Amen.

March 24   Romans 8:13; 2 Corinthians 3:17;
                                  Galatians 5:25; Ephesians 3:16-21

THE SECRET

Yesterday we talked about the Holy Spirit coming into the lives of the disciples and how it solved their problems. Most of the Christian world agrees with the disciples and confesses that Jesus Christ is the Son of God, but is appalled and disappointed that this does not solve their spiritual problems. They still have most of their problems. To recognize Jesus Christ as the Son of God is more or less an "outer" thing, a matter of our perceived intelligence, a matter of our conscious mind. This may not touch our subconscious mind at all. But the Holy Spirit does.

The work of the Holy Spirit is in both the subconscious and the conscious mind. This is important because it brings salvation where we need it. The subconscious mind can be cleansed, converted, controlled, and united with the purposes of the conscious mind by, and only by, the Holy Spirit. Following Christ as example will not solve our problems this is more or less following on the surface. It has to be deeply and permanently inward.

Even seeing the Holy Spirit as an influence now and again in a life will not solve our problems. The Holy Spirit as a Living Person must permanently live in the depths of our being, having full control, cleansing, directing, and coordinating the powers of our instincts to the purposes of the Kingdom of God. The disciples after Pentecost were not automatically trying to imitate Christ in their actions; they were joyously expressing a new life that bubbled up from within. **The Christian life is not forced by a pump, it is an artesian well.**

Therefore their lives were not automatically and suddenly trying to follow an Example, they were rhythmically and agreeably giving out from their inner life. Nothing, absolutely nothing, was left out of Christ control. Therefore they were no longer doubled-minded, conscious and subconscious arguing against each other—they were single-minded because they were single-controlled. They were spirit-filled men.

This is exactly what Christ wants and expects for us today. This is how we fulfill His purpose for our life. This is pure inner peace and joy in the service of our God.

Prayer for today: O God our Father, we thank You that we do not have to go through life with an inner contradiction. You can bring everything under Your control. Amen.

March 25   Hebrews 5:11-14; 6:1-3

STUNTED LIVES

Spiritual freedom is not a characteristic of present-day Christianity. We are stiff, conceited, inwardly bound Christians. Unified spontaneity is not what we think about when we think of ourselves. Should we talk about God only at our churches and close the door on Him when we leave? Normal Christianity is God as thought of our thought, joy of our joy, the will of our will, and life of our life – and if this is not our experience then we must have closed the door on Him and left Him at church.

There is a way to stunt forest trees so they never grow higher than two feet. They become potted plants, instead of giants in the forest. This is done by binding the taproot, so that the tree lives off the surface roots. It remains a stunted tree.

Many of our lives are like that. We live off the surface not from the depths. The surface roots go out into the cultural, the educational, the economic, the social, the political, perhaps even into thin religious life of our churches, and they draw "some" growth from these, but it leaves life stunted, for the taproot has not been allowed to grow deep into **God**. <u>Only as the taproot is loosened and grows deep into Christ and draws every moment the nourishment from those depths do we completely and truly live</u>. Are you a stunted spiritual being?

Prayer for today: O Father, Who came to give us life and to give it abundantly, we ask that You help us to put our taproot into Your vast resources and draw power and life and victory from You. Amen.

March 26   Luke 12:16-21; 1 Corinthians 6:7-11;
                            Ephesians 5:3; 5:5

STUNTED GROWTH

Is there anything sadder than a child who never grows up? The body is that of a man or woman, the mind is that of a child.

We are deeply touched by such, but are we as deeply moved by the sight of people who grow up in mind and body and remain absolutely undeveloped in their soul? They are morally and spiritually stunted human beings. What are some of the things that inwardly bind the taproot and stop growth as spiritual human beings? First of all we measure success by the amount of possessions we can accumulate. It has been said, the order of life is: gain fortune, fame and power, this is truly the outlook of many. The first is to gain possessions – fortune. Fortune comes from having an abundance of possessions – wealth. Fame in some circles of society comes from having a fortune. In order to have power we once were compelled to be honorable, for to be honorable we must be honest – to be honest we must make peace with God and our souls – souls now so stunted that we can hardly find them among the accumulations of fame and fortune..

We have become so intent on putting our surface roots into the economic life around us that we forget that they are just that –surface roots. True, the surface roots are necessary roots and are quietly in place **if** the taproot goes deeper. But life fed upon surface roots alone becomes very shallow and weak. When Jesus said, "*A man's life does not consist in the abundance of his possessions.*" (Luke 12:15b), He was not moralizing, but announcing a simple fact. We speak of "frozen assets". <u>The most real frozen assets are the neglected spiritual resources, the real sources of power in our life</u>. Even if we gain it all outward, we have lost the greater – the inward. Often possessiveness turns into powerlessness. The taproot is bound.

Prayer for today: O God our Father, Save us from the secondary. Unloose our spiritual lives. Amen.

March 27   Jeremiah 30:5; Matthew 25:25;
                            Luke 21:6; Hebrews 2:15

BOUND BY FEAR

Is there anything quiet like being paralyzed by fear? Of course there is fear that is biological and functions effectively when necessary. Like when surprising a deer feeding in the woods, it will jump with huge leaps away from you – it was seized with great fear. But it was a necessary fear, a fear of survival.

Do you have a fear of hurting your inner spiritual life by being careless? We may also have a fear of disappointing people spiritually. So when a temptation is before us, it is all right to say: "I am afraid to do that – I would be disappointing others. Also what would it do to my Christian witness?" This is a fear taking care of spiritual survival and fitness.

But there are fears that paralyze. Some of our fears may be things of the world which surround us and make us afraid, or they may be vague inner fears of poverty, sickness, death, failure, or of what people will say about us, afraid at attempting anything new, of certain people, of being laughed at – all these and many more have our inner life bound tight.

We will learn later how to deal with these fears, but for now we will simply note that unless we can unbind the cords of fear from the taproot of our lives, we will remain stunted human beings.

Prayer for today: O God our Father, fear is a disease to our inner life and keeps us small. Release us from them. And help us to stand unafraid because Your hand is on the center of our lives. Amen.

March 28   Psalm 44:15; Proverbs 16:18;
                                       Isaiah 24:10; John 8:32

BOUND BY "MENTAL" PRIDE

The activities of the world leave their influence on our inner life. Scientific progress, in all categories, has captured the minds of many and has left their inner life bound. We have come to terms with the world and with nature's law to such an extent that we have become naturalized in nature. We are afraid that there are no other roots of life except these surface roots which are natural and normal. Is there a taproot and is there Deeper Soil?

We are afraid to unbind the taproot completely and let it grow into God, for fear of appearing to be unscientific or technologically inadequate. We sure don't want that, we do not want to appear mentally out of style. However, we know it is socially accepted to live and live abundantly. Even though many great and wonderful discoveries have been made through the years, we usually only consider the outer life things. Let's now turn our attention to great and wonderful inner life discoveries. Modern religious liberal thinking has gained great heights; it must now find its depths. Much of modern religious thinking is shallow, feeding on the surface roots of modern civilization. It cannot go further until it goes deeper. It will be a turn-around for some of us to lay down our "mental" pride and confess to deeper needs spiritually, but we must do it if the inner life is to be freed. Laying down the pride of our mind will be the symbol of laying down our "self". We must crucify our "mental pride" in order to attain resurrection of our spiritual life. In doing so you will find an inner release that will astonish you. You will then know that you are truly alive – alive with Christ and Him at the center of your life.

Prayer for today: O Father, You have said that we should know the truth and the truth would make us free. Help us to lay down our mental pride and gain life. Amen.

March 29   Psalm 19:12; Galatians 5: 13, 19-21 &
                            24; 1 Timothy 1:19

BOUND BY MORAL DEFEAT

It would be nice, more respectable; to say we are bound by mental difficulties, rather than moral defeat. Respectable or not, this is where many of us will have to pay attention if we get release. <u>For many of us the problem is just plain sin.</u>

It is not easy to confess this fact to ourselves, especially if we consider ourselves a Christian. It is easier to keep pretending. Easier – and more deadly. **Suppose we gossip about others, tear their reputations to pieces (doing it of course in the interest of Christ), suppose we are jealous and make unfavorable remarks about the ability and work of a peer, suppose we hold resentment in our heart, suppose impure thoughts are allowed to gather in our mind, suppose we exaggerate until it becomes lying, and we twist the truth until it is untrue, will it help us at all to pretend that we are inwardly free? <u>We know that we are not free – and others know it as well.</u>**

The first thing to do is acknowledge to ourselves just what we really are. If we have been Bible-quoting-dishonest-jealous-gossip type of Christian, then we must admit it to our self, and then to others, if necessary. We must "rid" our self of our "rottenness". To publicly publish that we have been circulating falsely will not be easy, but it will unbind the cords that have our inner life bound. Then we will be free. Our taproot is now circulating in God and free to grow strong.

Prayer for today: O Father, help me not to squirm or make excuses, but in Your sight confess my need and have the cords of defeat cut from my inner life. I want to be free. Amen.

March 30   Jeremiah 1:6; Luke 1:74;
                                         2 Timothy 1:3, 7, 8

BOUND BY SHYNESS AN SELF-CONSCIOUSNESS

The spiritual life should be contagious. It should be sweet and winning. But many find it impossible to share Christ with others because of being shy and self-conscious. Actually being shy is a form of being self-conscious. When it binds our inner life and stops us from being natural Christian, it must be looked on as bondage, or as a stronghold.

Being shy and self-conscious means when an issue is brought up, we immediately direct it to ourselves – and this means that we are in a constant state of self-centeredness. This is hard to say, but it must be said. If you will think deeply about this and study on it you will see that it is true. We must look on being shy and self-conscious as a stronghold from which we must find freedom.

The speaker who becomes conscious of themselves and what they are saying will probably stumble and not have their audience complete attention. Only as they forget themselves, become lost in their message, will their words come with power and effect. Lose yourself in the message – don't become conscious or self-conscious and the words will flow. Being self-conscious binds the flow of thoughts and words. Don't concentrate on your gestures, lose yourself in the message. **When the center of life is shifted from ones self to Christ, this stronghold of being shy drops away**. Instead of constantly thinking of your interest, think of Christ best interest. Instead of asking, "How will this affect me?" The question will be, "How will this affect Christ and His Kingdom?" We are then set free from those inner cords that bind. The taproot grows into God.

Prayer for today: O Father, we thank You that we can be set free from being shy and self-conscious – this is a freedom we sorely need. Amen.

March 31   Psalm 102:4; Matthew 13:6; Luke 11:6, 13:6

BOUND BY EMPTINESS

Many of us are bound by emptiness; we lack anything spiritual to give. The cords that bind our inner life are just at a surface level and we have nothing to contribute.

In our society, usually after we greet someone with, "hello," out of sheer habit we follow that greeting with, "how are you?" And the almost sure response is: "fine." After that comes the real truth of what sometimes are amazing problems, troubles, disappointments, sorrow, etc., after the preliminary words and phrases, what are the real facts? What is at the center of our problems? Often a central emptiness is at the center.

Around this emptiness we build up lots of activities to try and fill that central void. But life cannot come to definite and sincere decisions surrounded by emptiness.

No amount of mere stirring of our emotions by sermons will do. To stir emptiness is futile. A little girl, having been given tea by her Mother, began to stir it. She alternately stirred and sipped her tea. Finally, with tears of disappointment in her eyes, she said, "Mama, it won't come sweet." Her Mother said with a smile, "I'm sorry, I must have forgotten the sugar." No amount of stirring will ever make it sweet until the sugar is in it!

Our lives do not need stirring – they need filling. If Christ is not in the depths of our being, no amount of stirring will make our life sweet and victorious. With Him it does so, naturally and inevitably.

Prayer for today: O Father, You have come to give us life and to give it abundantly. We need that "abundantly." Life is not enough – we need our life to be full of You. Amen.

April 1   Romans 6:6-7; 12:2-3; 13:14

RESULTS OF LIVING VICTORIOUSLY

We have now seen some of the things that inwardly bind us. We must now look at some of the positive fruit that result from the Christ-centered-Victorious Life.

The <u>first</u> thing we will be released from will <u>be our "self" and our own problems</u>. We are constantly bound by them. When an occasion arises where we could be of help to someone, there is this place deep down inside us that says, "But what about me?" I'm shy, I might fail, I might be laughed at, etc, etc. It's always about "ME", that stops dead the process of our helping others. We do not have release from our self and our own difficulties.

We must first realize it is not about 'ME". It is about God and the purpose He has for our life. Many of us have our strength and attention drained by our badly functioning inner life. Our heart is not at rest from ourselves therefore we can't enjoy God's creation and to sooth and sympathize with others. At the end of the day we are worn out with "our self". And when life presents opportunities for service to others, our mind is still in too much of a whirl around our "self" to meet the needs of others.

Living life victoriously will release us from our problems and from our own "self".

Just keep saying to your self – **"it is not about me, it is all about God and His purpose for my life."**

Prayer for today: O Father, Your own problems never stopped You from helping the needy who crowded around You. You have always been free, full, and available. Make me like that. Amen.

April 2   Matthew 6:25&34; Acts 14:19-20

A RELAXED HEART

Yesterday we said that many people are absorbed with themselves and their own problems. They do not have a heart that is relaxed. But some people have. Jesus had a relaxed heart. He was never in a hurry, never running, was never complaining, never worried, and was always busy – so much so often there was no time to eat. But He always had time for the next person or that next need. At the end of the day He was fresh and efficient.

Many of Jesus follows have found that same secret. You have probably known someone whose life was busy and contained the average problems of daily life; however they never seemed ruffled, never angry and always relaxed. They always have time for others. Always inwardly adjusted to the will of God. And that will functioned as peace, power, poise, and proficiency.

We can become so interested and absorbed in other people's souls that we almost forget our own. Is that healthy? It seems much healthier than so much of our modern spiritual advice which keeps us too absorbed with ourselves. It is certainly true that from time to time we need to look at ourselves with one long, searching self-examination which may result in a complete adjustment – and then dismiss our self from the focus of attention, and get back to the work at hand. That will bring us a relaxed heart.

Prayer for today: O Father of the adjusted will, give us that inner adjustment, that we too may move quietly through our work with our heads held high, our hearts proficient, and our hands full. Amen.

April 3   Acts 14:21-22; 26:29; Philippians 1:12-14

THE POWER TO LIVE IN SPITE OF – "WHATEVER"

The <u>second</u> thing we will recognize in living victoriously will be "<u>the power to live in spite of – whatever</u>. Many of us know the power to live "because of"—, but not "in spite of"—. When our surroundings are favorable and life is good, we live on. But life is not always easy. It often turns rough. And that is when we are tested to the depths. If our faith is <u>real</u> it will speak from the depths of our inner being. Before finding how to live victoriously, the disciples were at the mercy of many of their circumstances. Afterward they were the masters of them. They learned how to mold life instead of being molded by it. There are three types of Christians: <u>the rowboat type</u>, <u>the sailboat type</u>, and <u>the motorboat type</u>. <u>The rowboat type</u> is the type that is humanistic, self-dependant, trying to get along with its own resources. But as the resources are limited, the progress is limited. <u>The sailboat type</u> depends on the winds. These are the people who are dependant on circumstances. If the winds are favorable, if people are constantly complimenting and encouraging them, they sail on. But if the praise stops, they stop. They are conditioned by circumstances, not very dependable Christians. Then there is <u>the motorboat type</u> those who have power from within, and they go on whether winds or favorable or unfavorable, wind or no wind they travel on. They have "inner fuel". They are not self-dependant, or circumstance-dependant, but Christ dependant. They are dependable.

This power to go on when life is completely against us is the deepest necessity of our lives. In living victoriously this power is a working fact, it is <u>fuel</u> for the soul.

Prayer for today: O Father, You who did go on when life turned so rough, that it meant a cross, help us to find that same power and continue on –in spite of – "whatever." Amen

April 4   John 14:1; 19:8-10; Philippians 4:7;
                                     Colossians 1:11

THE STRESS OF LIFE REMOVED

The <u>third</u> result of living victoriously is – <u>the stress removed</u> <u>from</u> <u>our lives</u>. Many Christians live stressed spiritual lives. They are trying, trying hard to do the right thing. Their fists are clenched, heads held high, their back straight – they are fighting with all <u>their</u> strength. It is all very sincere, but not very inviting, for this type of devotion to God produces stress. And a stressed devotion to God is not contagious. It is also wearing on the person concerned. Stress drains us. We are so inwardly screwed up, wound so tight that we snap under such stress. When you want to bend or shape a piece of glass or metal you must subject these pieces to extreme heat. The inner strain is taken out of the pieces by that intense heat. By this process the molecules are so harmonized that the glass or metal can now be bent or shaped without breaking. Without this fiery process the pieces would break, not bend.

Do you think we may need something like this to take place within our soul – a fiery baptism that will put every molecule of our soul in such right relationship with each other and with God, that when the stress comes we may bend, but not break? Jesus bent in Gethsemane; the weight on Him was very, very heavy! Why? Because of <u>the prayer,</u> (<u>the prayer that never fails</u>), "*Not my will, but yours be done*." (Luke 22:42). That prayer set every fiber of His spirit in right relationship with the will of the Father. Afterward life might bend, but it would not break, for there was no inner stress. When life is broken from within, living victoriously takes away the inner stress, and makes life so harmonious that it can stand anything that can outwardly happen to it.

Prayer for today: O Father, We thank You that You did not break! For had You broken we would have broken also. Put us through Your fiery baptism until all stress is removed! We consent to the fire because we know it means freedom. Amen.

April 5   Romans 5:20-21; 6:6-14

POWER OVER SIN

A mistaken idea that we often use as an excuse in regard to our own personal sin: "**I couldn't help it, after all I am only human.**" That very human expression shows guilt and estrangement from God. The implication is that sin is an essential part of our being human. In (Romans 5:12-21) Paul carefully presents the extreme difference between our human dilemma and God's divine resolution. Before Jesus came, the depths of the radical innovation God had in mind were impossible for the human mind to comprehend. **The dynamic changes that Jesus Christ brought – <u>transformed death into life, transgression into grace</u>, <u>condemnation into justification</u> <u>and sin into righteousness</u>**. In (Romans 6:1-23) Paul challenges us – to realize what Jesus has done for us, acknowledge it in our lives, and offer ourselves to God as transformed people, dead to sin, alive to Christ. A mere <u>surface</u> acceptance of Christ will not do **– we must understand and grasp the idea that sin is unnatural, an invasion, an intruder, and sin <u>is not</u> a necessary part of being human**. There are unnatural things which have invaded life: **<u>Sin</u> is the unnatural evil of the soul, <u>error</u> is the unnatural evil of the mind**, and **<u>disease</u> is the unnatural evil of the body.** Jesus said that salvation is health. Wherever He uses the term "Be saved" it can literally be translated "Be whole". **The health of the soul is goodness, the health of the mind is truth, and the health of the body is freedom from disease.** Is a mind more of a mind when it has error in it? Is a person more of a person when they have evil in them? Every sin can be conquered. Our mind must not admit to any exception. *"Clothe yourself with the Lord Jesus Christ, and do not think about how to gratify the desires of the sinful nature."* (Romans 13-14). In other words, think about victory; do not think about failure. We must have an attitude of absolute power over sin.

Prayer for today: O Father, thank you for a complete offer of complete release from all sin. Help us accept that freedom. Amen.

116

April 6   Luke 10:41-42; Acts 4:13; 2 Corinthians 1:2; 11:3

SIMPLE AND STRAIGHT

People who are seeking Christ want to hear it simple and straight. Living victoriously should and does reduce life to inward unity, and therefore, to outward simplicity and straightforwardness.

We need to be cleansed from all double purposes in word and attitude. Our speech should become pure and simple in expressing anything.

See what the Holy Spirit did for Peter when it came into his life. Note the contrast: **As Peter denied Christ he says,** *"I don't know what you are talking about."* (Matthew 26:70). Here was Peter double-minded and with fork-ed-tongue. **Later when Peter was filled with the Holy Spirit, Pete said to them,** *"Rulers and Elders of the people! If we are being called to account today for an act of kindness shown to a cripple and are asked how he was healed, then know this, you and all the people of Israel: It is by the name of Jesus Christ of Nazareth, whom you crucified but God raised from the dead, that this man stands before you healed. Christ is 'the stone you builders rejected, which has become the capstone.' Salvation is found in no one else, for there is no other name under heaven given to men by which we must be saved."* (Acts 4:8-12). Note the straightforwardness, the directness, the pure simplicity of Peter's words. **The Holy Spirit who is the Spirit of Truth – the Spirit of Simplicity and Directness, brought this revelation into Peter's life.**

He will bring it into ours. Misleading words and indirect attitudes will cease and we will now speak with words that flow in simplicity out of the depths of our unified life.

Prayer for today: O Father of the simple speech and direct attitude, give us that likeness. We too want to be saved from complex attitudes, fork-ed-tongues and double-meanings. Amen.

April 7   John 7:37-39; 15; 1 Thessalonians 1:8

A SPIRITUAL CREATIVE LIFE

The last thing we will mention as being a sign of Living
Victoriously is the fact that life now becomes spiritually creative.
Living a victorious life is life organized around LOVE. But just as
love is creative, life is now also creative.

When we possess divine love it pours out onto others. It is not
something we can or even wish to keep just for ourselves. A woman,
who became one of the great missionaries of the world, was being
carried in a sedan chair through the dirty, narrow, crowded streets
of a Chinese city after her first arrival early in the twentieth century,
as everything in her revolted at the strangeness and the dirt. "O
God," she cried, "how can I live among these people without love
in my heart?" Immediately her heart was flooded with the answer
– "divine love." From that moment on she forgot dirt, narrow streets
and strange surroundings; she saw only people for whom Christ
died. Instead of letting selfish love of herself draw her back, she
allowed God to draw her into an amazing creative service for those
beloved people.

When our soul is inwardly wed to Christ in complete surrender,
then there are responsibilities and tasks and opportunities given us,
for love can and will be creative.

Actually, living victoriously means there is a higher level of
all powers of the personality; our mind becomes sharper and more
creative, our emotions become broader and more sensitive, and
our will more active and decisive. Our entire life is reaching out to
others. Lives are changed, growth is started and creative impact is
made. Before giving our life to Christ we may pick and choose our
friends, but after being born again we take everybody in our heart.
Love is creative.

Prayer for today: O Father, thank You for the creative impact of
Your love in my heart. Make me creative each day. Amen.

April 8   Acts 2:37-39; Romans 7:18-20; 8:13

HOW DO I OBTAIN A VICTORIOUS LIFE?

The question as to how we obtain a life of victory deserves an honest, sincere answer. We must approach it with sincere prayer on our lips and in our heart. First of all, we are different now. When we first come to Christ, we come as a stranger and a repentant rebel knocking at Christ door for admission. Now we are a child in the Home looking for a deeper and more complete life in the spirit of that Home. We are seeking adjustment in that Home. We are asking Christ to take away everything in our life which will conflict with the spirit of this new Home of ours. We can now come to Christ with a sense of confidence and assurance, born out of contact with the Father. If any strongholds exists within us; Christ did not put them there – we did. Let's look at what we are not to do. Do not try to gain victory by fighting your individual sins. The way to victory is not accomplished in that way. Yet, that is the first thing many people think about – "I'll put up a good fight against my sins." Don't, you'll lose. For when you "<u>alone</u>" fight your individual sins, you are compelled to center your attention on those sins. It is a law of the mind, <u>whatever gets your attention—gets you</u>! Therefore, if you give your attention to fighting your sins, your sins will get you. Many people are astonished to find even while praying about their sins, and sincerely fighting those sins, they will yield to them. You may feel that God let you down when you were fighting so hard to overcome your sins, but later you will realize <u>you were fighting alone without God's power to help you</u>. We must find the right road and stay on it.

Prayer for today: O Father, take me by my hand and lead me, for without Your guidance I will stumble and lose my way. I must find the right way. I can no longer live without adjusting perfectly to You. Amen.

April 9   Romans 8:5-10; 2 Corinthians 10:5

THINGS TO AVOID IN SEEKING TO LIVE VICTORIOUSLY

Yesterday we said the first mistake to avoid in seeking to live a victorious life is not to try fighting your own individual sins. Let's pursue this a little further. Just suppose you are fighting sex sin. In fighting this sin you will have to concentrate on it. The result is your imagination is aroused. Then a battle ensues between your imagination and your will. Psychologist tells us whenever there is a battle between our imagination and our will, the imagination always wins. So if we go with the imagination, we fall into sin.

Our imagination must be called away from our sins and centered somewhere else. In other words our imagination must be centered on Christ. However, our imagination cannot and will not be centered on Christ until we have surrendered "ourselves" completely to Him. Remember, the imagination goes where its supreme treasure is. *"Where your treasure is there will your heart be also."* (Matthew 6:21). Your treasure must be in Christ – wholly and supremely. If so, your imagination will also be in Christ. So—shifting our imagination plus our supreme treasure equals the shifting of our very life. We must surrender our life to Christ completely. There can be no true love between persons unless there is a natural inward complete surrender. When one withholds their inmost self from the other, there is no real love. In the same way there can be no complete love between us and Christ until there is complete surrender to Him. When complete surrender takes place— true love blooms. It begins to burn within us. The imagination follows. Since love is centered here, the imagination is centered here. It now fights with the will and not against it. This is victory. The answer then is to shift that imagination. This can only be done by shifting the center of life itself from "self" to Christ.

Prayer for today: O Father, I want You at the center of my imagination. I completely surrender my life to You. Amen

April 10   Jeremiah 14:10; 23:17; Hebrews 12:1-2

THINGS TO AVOID (Continued)

We have seen the uselessness in trying to fight our individual sins alone, now look at another mistake to avoid. Do not try to <u>forget</u> your sins. Trying to forget will only bring them back to your mind. <u>To try to forget is to remember</u>. A scam-artist came to town with the county fair, he declared he could make gold. As the fair opened, a crowd soon gathered around him as he poured water into a large open container, and then pouring into the water a mixture of coloring he began to stir it with a large spoon and chant words claiming to have magical power. When their attention was diverted by his able assistant, he let some gold nuggets slip out of his long sleeved shirt into the water. He poured off the water and there was gold! The crowd was awestruck. A wealthy, naive young man offered him five thousand dollars for the formula. The scam-artist explained specifically how to make the gold, then added, "But you must remember this: do not think of a red-faced monkey as you stir, or the gold will not make." The young man promised to remember what he was supposed to forget. But try as hard as he could, the red-faced monkey was right there in his mind, the gold would not make! The only way to forget is to have your mind centered somewhere else. Self-surrender will produce new affection. Your sins will be completely forgotten, because Christ is completely remembered. One word of caution –you <u>can</u> succeed in getting your sins out of your mind by driving them into your subconscious mind, where there they play havoc in your life. So, whether you succeed in placing them there, thinking they are forgotten or call them vividly back to mind, either way it is defeat and disaster. Again, the bottom line: The only way to forget <u>anything</u> that needs to be forgotten is replace those thoughts with thoughts of Christ.

Prayer for today: O Father, as you lead help me to follow. Amen.

April 11   Matthew 7:17; Romans 3:21-22 & 27-28

FORCING OUR WILL TO AGREE WITH GOD'S WILL

There is one more thing we must look at that might cause us a problem – feeling that living victoriously will come to us if we only try a little harder. So we try to force our will to agree with God's will for our lives.

Much of our present-day Christianity is founded on the idea that we must try harder to do God's will by getting our will in line with His. It doesn't work that way. Why? When we say, "I'll try," that shows we still have "self" as our basis. It is self-effort. As long as there is conflicting desires within us, we cannot put forth any real effort. On the other hand, when we say, "I'll trust, or I'll have faith," then we shift our basis from self to Christ. Then we are no longer self-centered, but Christ-centered. Our religious moral fruits are not the result of our conscious effort to achieve them. Our will does not depend on our strength to force our will to be in agreement with God's but upon God's strength that enters our will.

Since our will is naturally self-centered it resists authority or control on impulse, the strength of our will is in direct relation to the strength of our "self".

But "self" can only be unified when it comes under the complete control of the power of Christ.

Prayer for today: O Father, we have tried to reach our goals by forcing our will toward Your will, but our wills are weak because we are weak. Unite and strengthen us at the center of our being. Then we will be able to reach our goals. Amen.

April 12   Luke 9:23-24; Ephesians 4:22-24

THE CENTRAL ISSUE

We have seen that we cannot merely try to fight our sins, or forget our sins, or force our will to agree with God's – we must go deeper, because our outer sins are rooted in something deeper. Just as our fingers are rooted to our hand, so our sins are rooted in our un-surrendered self. It is the thought of self-advantage in some form or another that lies at the root of our sins. **Why do we lie and steal**? We think the "self" will benefit. **Why do we argue with others**? Because "self" has been opposed. **Why are we envious**? Because we are afraid someone will get ahead of our "self." **Why do we yield to sex passion**? Because we think the "self" will find pleasure. The ego-urge is our central difficulty in life and is the very foundation for most of our unhappiness. **The central issue, then, in living victoriously is: self-surrender**. But, you ask, didn't I do that when I gave my life to Christ? Yes, you did to a point, but not completely. Now you see deeper depths that must be surrendered. The conscious mind was given to Christ at that time, now we see that the subconscious mind, the very center of our divisions and inner turmoil, must be given to Him as well. These basic instincts must come under Christ control and they must be cleansed. The self we now give to Him is a more complete self, both conscious and subconscious, for we want full salvation – complete salvation.

Now we allow Christ not only to treat our individual sins, (the systems of a deeper problem), but the very root, the self.

That self must be crucified in order to rise again.

Prayer for today: O Christ, You have touched the root of my disease. Help me not to be afraid, or ask for partial healing. Help me to surrender all. Amen.

April 13   Matthew 10:37-39; Acts 5:1-2

LETTING THAT LAST THING GO

The last thing we must let go is ourselves. It is the one and only thing we really own. And now it is with absolute necessity that Christ asks for that one last thing. It is here that the real war with self takes place. Everything else has been small battles. Jesus said with firm decisiveness, *"If anyone comes to me and does not hate his father and Mother, his wife and children, his brothers and sisters – yes, even his own life – he cannot be my disciple."* (Luke 14:26). I and my family must be placed on the altar. To "hate" means to "love less" according to the parallel scripture in (Matthew 10:37). *"Anyone who loves his father or mother more than me is not worthy of me; anyone who loves his son or daughter more than me is not worthy of me."* <u>These lesser loves are not to</u> be abandoned. <u>They are to be surrendered</u>. The interesting thing to note – in (Luke 14:26), the "life" or "self" was the last thing Jesus mentioned – (*"yes, even his own life"*). Why did He put that last? Because it is the last thing we ever give up. The missionary gives up their home and loved ones to go to another country, they give up everything except themselves. They find their inner self touchy over position, place and power. The minister sacrifices a great deal to go into the ministry – everything except the minister. They may find themselves preaching the gospel with a great deal of vanity and personal ambition mixed with their preaching. The layperson gives up much to follow Christ, but they find themselves easily offended even while following Christ. In each situation the "self" is still there controlling their life. It must be surrendered to Christ. <u>Christ must be the one we see in a person's life, not the person</u>.

Prayer for today: O Father, I come to You to help me with this "self" thing. I am reluctant to let go of this last thing, but I am willing to be made willing. Amen.

April 14   Matthew 19:21-22; James 3:11-12

COMPROMISES

We saw yesterday that we are up against Christ demand for self-surrender. This is the first step to Living Victoriously, and we must take this step. We do not give up "self" without a struggle. Our entire biological drive is against this. This demand reverses the process of our nature. Letting go of "self" is an invasion of our rights of self-affirmation. When we think too highly of ourselves, these driving forces will rise up within us like they did in the self-confident nature of Peter when he said to Jesus concerning the predicted denial of Him, *"Even if all fall away, I will not." "Even if I have to die with you, I will never disown you."* (Mark 14:29-31). But Jesus knew Peter was thinking like a human thinks. When we are about to take the step that makes us MORE for Christ, then the old carnal self will rise up within us and try to pull us back into self desires and urges and will plead for our existing state of life. Or "self" will suggest compromises. If our old self cannot conquer by denial, it will try to conquer by dividing. Compromise will result. A patriot making a speech, and glowing with patriotic pride, said, "For the sake of my country I am willing to sacrifice my own Mother – Yes, I am willing to sacrifice my own children, and, if necessary, I am willing to sacrifice myself." That person put themselves last! They were willing to let their Mother and children go first! We smile at the "patriot" but in them we see ourselves. The self presents compromises, maybe not quite so drastic, but it presents compromises to save itself. When Jacob was about to meet the angered Esau, he sent gifts before him, (Genesis 32:13-15) hoping this might save himself. There is much of Jacob in us. That nature within us that resist authority and control must be subdued and changed.

Prayer for today: O Father, help me not to blur this hour with compromises and by a patched-up truce between the old and the new self. I want to be entirely new. Amen.

April 15   2 Kings 5:18; Luke 9:57-62

COMPROMISES (Continued)

Last study we saw that "self" let go reluctantly and compromises arise. Remember that old Pharaoh, who had been ruling for ages, when asked to let the people go continued to change his mind, "yes –no, yes-no." But like Moses we must insist that, *"not a hoof is to be left behind."* (Exodus 10:26).

The "yes-no" attitude is sometimes covered up in a subtle manner. I gave away my tickets to the football game and felt so pleased with myself for doing so. Then I just happened to remember my friend who wanted to give away tickets that was five rows up from the fifty yard line, so I got those for myself. That satisfied two things within me – one the desire to not only be pleased with myself and have others pleased with me for giving my tickets away to less fortunate ones, but also the desire to have the better tickets.

Think about it – how many times do we offer the lesser of something and keep our essential self from being inconvenienced, or bothered. We offer our services and withhold our "self." We offer our talents on occasion to Christ and reserve for ourselves the praise that comes from those God-given talents. In this way religion becomes the window-dressing that hides our real motives. We are not necessarily hypocrites, for many of these motives we may not even be aware of – we are just half-way givers, selfish. This does not work with God. We surrender our lives completely to Him and then we cancel it by "amendments" always taking back part of what we just gave to Him. And then we wonder why we have no victory in life.

Prayer for today: O Father, search my heart to find any hidden secrets. I want absolutely everything about my life to be under Your control. I want my life to show You. Amen.

April 16   Matthew 6:24; Romans 13:14;
                                  2 Corinthians 6:15-18

COMPROMISES (Continued)

I do not want to tire you with the study of compromise. But this is so important we must stay with this even if it makes us uncomfortable, if that's the case then maybe we are getting somewhere. We have all seen or heard about the celebrity entertainers on a stage performing their worldly songs and dances. While an idolizing crowd throws themselves into a wild and uncanny, frenzy. The entertainers may treat the whole affair with just what it is – a self-gratifying, money-making project. After all what are they after if it isn't fortune, fame, and power? As the curtain closes the performer gathers up their treasures and heads for the next concert to do it all over again, for the same reason "self." The "all important self" may be so covered with all the hoopla that we hardly notice that "self" occupies the throne of that person's life. How many times do we see a display in our churches of similar proportion? Sounds the same, looks the same, and acts the same. Is it the same? Maybe yes, maybe no, but the compromise is there. Read again (2 Corinthians 6:15-17a), *"What harmony is there between Christ and Belial?* What does a believer have in common with an unbeliever? What agreement is there between the temple of God and idols? For we are the temple of the living God. *"As God has said: '…I will be their God, and they will be my people.'" "Therefore come out from them and be separate," says the Lord.*

When we decide to give up "self," the temptation to leave the "important self" untouched will be overwhelming, but to live a life of victory it must be done.

Prayer for today: O Christ, You see how we hesitate to give up "self" our most precious possession. But give us whatever it takes to do so. Amen.

April 17   Luke 7:36-50; 10:38-42

TWO WELCOMES

After having read the scriptures for today's study, perhaps we can see ourselves in one of these welcomes. Jesus was invited into the house at Bethany, and there Mary "sat at the Lord's feet listening to what He said." One of the Pharisees invited Jesus to his house for dinner. Jesus went into the Pharisee's house and sat down to eat. Then follows the story of the woman who anointed Jesus feet: The Pharisee said to himself, *"If this man were a prophet, he would know who was touching him and what kind of woman she is – that she is a sinner." (Luke 7:39).* Let's continue: Jesus says, *"Simon...I came into your house, you did not give me any water for my feet...you did not give me a kiss...you did not put oil on my head..."* (Luke 7:44-46). In other words Simon only allowed Jesus part-way into his house, Simon gave Jesus food, but not his heart, he gave a welcome – with reservations. Jesus was in, but not in. Jesus knew the woman had sinned in her flesh, and He forgave her, because in her heart she was ready to be forgiven. But Simon's heart was not ready; he would not let Jesus in. For Simon wanted to keep both his pride and Jesus. Simon wanted to have Jesus and yet not have him. He was divided – therefore self-doomed.

But Mary welcomed Jesus and gave Him food – and her heart. She sat at His feet. He was at home there. The welcome was complete.

Is your heart a Bethany to Christ, or a Pharisee's house?

Self-surrender will turn the proud, empty, critical, indifferent, self-righteous Pharisee's house into a Bethany.

Prayer for today: O Father, I open wide the door of my heart to You. You will be welcome there. Take the throne of my divided heart, for I give it to You. Amen.

April 18   John 16:12-13; 1 Corinthians 13:9-12

ALL I KNOW AND ALL I DON'T KNOW

You may have a lingering fear that you are still holding back from completely giving Christ your <u>ALL</u>. But if you are completely honest in giving all you know to give, then you can lump all the other unknown things and future contingencies in the words. "I give all I know and all I don't know." "All I don't know" has within it, the future as it unfolds. It means that in your giving there is an absoluteness and yet a relativity. <u>Absoluteness is a once for all time, and yet a relativity in that you will have to keep offering things to God as they come up day to day</u>. But do not be anxious about these things which will come up in the future – meet them as they show up. **If there is no inner voice telling you that you are holding something, then you have a right to believe that you have given your all to Christ, for when we hold something back, the Spirit will let us know.** The absoluteness and relativity in complete self-giving can be seen in married life. There is a once-and-for-all about giving all of yourself in real marriage, but there is relativity in that there are continuous adjustments and continuous developments where we must promise to continue to give of ourselves. Marriage is over in minutes and yet it takes a lifetime to be married. "<u>ALL</u>" <u>is a small word, but within it is an amazing capacity for development</u>. It holds within it pleasures and pain, struggle and sorrow, joy and peace, great relationships and difficult adjustments. It is best that we cannot see all that life holds for us. For we do not need to live life all at once – that would be exhausting. We can live it one day at a time. <u>What the future holds is not for me to ask</u>, but whatever it may be, <u>I know He</u> holds the future.

Prayer for today: O Father, I thank You that I do not have to worry about tomorrow. I know You have tomorrow, as well as today and You have me. Let that be enough for me. Amen.

April 19   Psalm 103:1; John 4:14; Colossians 2:6-7

ALL I DON'T KNOW (Continued)

We saw yesterday that "All I don't know" covers the developing future. It also covers something else: it covers the hidden depths of the subconscious mind. It reaches in length into our future, and in depth within us.

The subconscious mind is a well-established psychological fact. Long before psychology began its description of the subconscious mind sincere religious people had felt the fact within them. It has been described in various ways, such as: "something beyond my conscious working within me," "evil within," "inherited evil," "original sin," etc. All these point to a place within us which seems to be working against the conscious purpose of our life and over which we have little control. It is the subconscious – the place of inherited instincts, instincts polluted by the streams of ungodly tendencies which have poured into us for ages.

We do not know the subconscious mind except indirectly, also we can only control it indirectly. That control must come from God, who knows all things. We can surrender our subconscious mind to Him. When He takes control our subconscious mind becomes cleansed and Christianized to the depths. How do we know this? We do not know it except indirectly. But we look at the disciples after Pentecost. They seemed to be unified to the very depths of their being. Their new life came out from them like perfume from a flower – it was a natural expression of their unified lives.

The life that is controlled at the depths of the subconscious mind by the Holy Spirit seems to have no tension, no stress in regard to life itself. The conscious and subconscious are both now dedicated to the same purpose.

Prayer for today: O Father, Thank You for healing me at the center of my being; my conscious and subconscious mind now harmonious will sound out music much greater than before. You have control of both. Amen.

April 20   Mark 3:5; 9:22-23; 11:22; John 1:16

THE ACCEPTANCE

We are now at the place where we are prepared to take the step of complete deliverance. It is the step of faith. <u>Faith is an adventure in acceptance</u>. It counts on God being genuine. Faith believes that the character of God and His Word are behind His offer of complete deliverance. There is an element of quiet aggressiveness, on our part, when we reach out and take hold of this awesome God, we find inward peace, for we have given God our all, our everything, and now we have the moral right to accept all, all that God has for us. It is a step in mutual confidence.

But some of us having given Him <u>our all</u>, hesitate to receive <u>His all</u>. We stand at the revolving doors; waiting for it to revolve or open for us, but it will not open until we give it that aggressive push of <u>faith</u> and when we give it that aggressive push it will open.

You have given your all, now press forward, literally press against the promises God has held out to you and walk through them with peace and freedom. Walk into freedom with Jesus words found in (Mark 11:24), *"Therefore I tell you, whatever you ask for in prayer, believe that you have it, and it will be yours."* He awaits your acceptance. You cannot trust yourself, you cannot trust your own resources, but you can trust God. He will always be there for you.

Accept Christ in simplicity and with aggressive sincerity and He will never let you down. TRY IT!

Prayer for today: O Father, my Father, I know that I love You and I trust You for this gift of complete deliverance. Thank You! Amen.

April 21   Acts 1:8; 4:20

A PERSONAL WORD – from <u>M</u>ary <u>A</u>nn <u>D</u>otson-Moore

Perhaps a personal word might help as we talk about accepting Christ and giving Him our ALL.

As a child I was the only one of my parent's four children with a bad temper. I could get so mad it would literally make me sick. (Just an added note here – my initials spelled "MAD" and to be teased about it always made me MAD)!

Back to my story – I did not outgrow my temper as I grew into an adult. My temper grew right along with me.

My parents were dedicated Christians. God, Church, family, and all that each represented was the main thing in our life. So naturally I gave my life to Christ when I was an early teen. (I gave my life, not my temper). Actually, when I was young, I don't know if I heard any sermons on giving everything to Christ. At that time I relied on sermons I heard rather than studying God's Word for myself. That was a big mistake!

As time passed someone fell in love with me and married me in spite of my faults, (don't misunderstand, I was in love with him also). After several years of marriage and three children my husband was gloriously born again (saved). He was so happy. Why all the joy? I had been a Christian for years, but not with such joy and happiness that I was seeing in him.

One day not long after his conversion I got mad at him and let my temper flare. I do not remember what I was mad about – but one thing I do remember and I remember well – I remember the exact words he said to me, **"No one can live a Christian life and live with you."** He was not threatening to leave me and I knew that, but he was telling me the truth, and I knew that. That truth struck hard and deep.

Our pastor and his wife had several children and my husband and I had three. When I asked the pastor and his wife to pray with me about my temper, he asked the children to_kneel and pray as well, we were in their family room. I will never forget that

132

miraculous experience as we all prayed quietly together. I felt a burning sensation pass gently from the top of my head through every part of my body and out my feet. A divine cleansing wave that was over quickly and when it was finished I felt so clean and light with a sense of sacredness, awesomeness, and the most exquisite joy. A gift of the Holy Spirit!!

Very emotional? No, not at all. It was a wonderfully quiet and sacred experience. I knew then and I know now, that the very sources of my life were being cleansed. My will was just as much involved as my faith.

That experience happened many years ago when I was young. I have never had another **temper tantrum**. Have I been **upset** –**YES**, have I had a **temper fit** –**NO**. The fact is my whole life has been on a permanently higher level.

April 22   Romans 5:1-5; Corinthians 5:7;
                                            1 Peter 1:8-9

ALL EXPERIENCES ARE DIFFERENT

After reading my personal experience, you may need a word of caution: No one should feel that they must find exactly that experience or even one similar. This would be a terrible mistake. Two experiences do not happen exactly alike in emotional tone. We are all different individuals, so our experiences differ widely, and yet – there is the same sense of inner release, peace and joy, and thereby a higher power to live creatively. Never, never seek the experience of another, **seek Christ**, and let Him give you the special experience He has just for <u>you</u> and which will equip <u>you</u> for the purpose He has for your life.

Christ will give you His emotions and His emotions will be exactly right for <u>you</u>. Christ emotions are always healthy and always under the control of the purpose of His Kingdom.

You may wonder how such a profound experience such as I had could take place without extreme emotion. The wonderful feeling was a by-product of the facts that were taking place. We do not depend on emotions (feelings), we depend on Christ. He comes in to abide permanently among the flow and change of our feelings. But when Christ comes into our life – such a wonderful Guest, bearing such a precious gift, into such a heart – no wonder we have such good feelings, the wonder is that we can be so restrained. Life is untangled – we have found the way!

Prayer for today: O Father, my Father, Thank You that I have stepped out on the road to complete victory. If You are looking for a heart to refine and dwell in, You have mine, completely and forever. I do not depend on anything extraneous, but I do depend on You. Amen.

April 23   Isaiah 12:2-3; Joshua 1:5; James 1:17

ARE YOU AFRAID OF HAVING NO SPIRITUAL EMOTIONS?

Are you afraid of having <u>no</u> feelings of a spiritual nature? Spiritual feelings will come if we keep our eyes on the right place. If we look in, we will be discouraged, if we look around, we will be distracted, if we look at Christ, we will have peace. Emotions can be quiet, yet real. You may have to step out in obedience and faith. Keep positive in your heart, knowing that you have given yourself completely to Christ, and you <u>know</u> you accepted His gift of salvation, then relax. Talk faith to yourself and to God. Read God's answer to you, (Matthew 28:20b) – *"And surely I am with you always, to the very end of the age."* If Jesus said it, believe it! *"But thanks be to God! He gives us the victory through our Lord Jesus Christ."* (1 Corinthians 15:57). Victory is a gift. When we reach out and take the gift, the assurance that we have accepted His gift will come. Don't be discouraged if when you accept God's gift you aren't overwhelmed with emotion (remember what we said in yesterday's study, there is no two experiences the same). So if you feel emotion or if not, it does not alter your salvation. Your Father is there with you to stay. Trust Him!

A father, absent from home for a long time, the eager and excited family had expected him that evening. But he did not come and the family went to bed disappointed and discouraged. The next morning as they sat at the breakfast table silent and sad, the father walked in from upstairs. Since he was very late getting in he had gone to bed without disturbing them. However, he was just as much there the night before as when he was evident in the morning. So when you give yourself to Christ and accept His gift of salvation, even though the evidence of His presence, you may not feel, it doesn't mean He is not with you. <u>It will happen</u> that you feel His presence, and when it does it will be a great day.

Prayer for today: O Father, However I sail through this life, I sail with you in control. Amen.

April 24   Luke 4:37; Romans 1:8-10; 1 John 1:1-3

TALKING FAITH TO OTHERS

Yesterday we said that in taking this step to living victoriously we should talk faith to God and to ourselves. If talking faith to ourselves seems like something we suggest to ourselves, that's ok, for we all practice this power of suggestion in everything. It is a process of our thoughts. The question is, just <u>what</u> do we suggest to ourselves? If we are suggesting to ourselves to think positive and assume the best, then this is most necessary. You are suggesting to yourself what you honestly believe to be the truth as you know it, namely, that God's way demands that if we do our part, God will do His part. You are suggesting to yourself to step out on the path – that's faith. Also talk about your faith to others. It helps us grow spiritually to confess our faith. Tell others where you stand, where you are going and what your faith is doing for you. This turns our whole attitude of life toward faith and affirmation. It opens the channels through which new life flows through to us. It establishes new ways of thinking; it commits us to a higher level of spiritual life. The acceptance of God's free gift of salvation and all that He has for us drives us to the goal line. The confession of that faith to others takes us in for a touchdown. It gives our soul a punt or push in the right direction. That punt or push may be decisive. It may be the opening into conscious victory. It is reality. It is a confession of faith, not of accomplished fact. This faith will turn into fact, and the fact will turn into feeling. Our redemption is now an operating fact resulting from our faith.

Prayer for today: O God, my Father, I cannot confess to my being worthy, but I do confess to my faith in Your being trustworthy. You will see me through. Amen.

THE WITNESS OF THE SPIRIT

The witness of the Spirit
Is not a loud roaring sound
It is a meaningful experience
Very, excitingly profound.

The witness of the Spirit
Is not an explainable lot
But when you experience it
The explanation matters not.

The witness of the Spirit
Can thrill you to your toes
Often is just between us and God
And no one else knows.

The witness of the Spirit
May at times magnify and glow
In such an outpouring manner
Everyone is sure to know.

The witness of the Spirit
To our heart, we say
Is the definite way of knowing
That Christ dwells in us today.

Written December 27, 1976 by-MaryAnn Moore

April 25   John 13:10; Acts 20:32; 2 Corinthians 7:1;
                            Ephesians 5:25-27

WE ARE MADE "CLEAN" THROUGH GOD'S WORD

Jesus uttered these remarkable words, *"You are already clean because of the word I have spoken."* (John 15:3). What was the "word" that made them clean? Why did He use "word" instead of "words"?

The reason seems to be that Jesus "words" gathered themselves into such a living body of truth and insight, into such unity and oneness, that they were no longer words; they were "His Word", "The Word". *"In the beginning was the Word, and the Word was with God, and the Word was God." (John 1:1). "The Word became flesh and made His dwelling among us." (John 1:14).* In the naming of Christ we do not break the mystic spell of eternity – we interpret it, we are cleansed by it.

The cleansing Christ had been performing through His disciples for three years, was more than a personal cleansing. He was cleansing them and their world. It was a cluttered world they faced, and Jesus left them, as far as they were concerned, with a world of things and relationships, CLEANSED.

> The Word became flesh
> A way of life new and fresh
> He walked and taught
> Clean in every deed and thought
> He left us His Word –the B-I-B-L-E
> Written for you and me
> So we too can live as He lived
> Clean, victorious, and free.

Prayer for today: O Father, help us let Your Word be spoken in every part of our being and in our relationships, that both our relationships and ourselves may be cleansed. Amen.

April 26   Matthew 23:9; John 1:18; 14:9; 1 Timothy 2:5

THE CLEANSING OF THE DISCIPLES WORLD

Yesterday we said that the disciples came to Jesus with a much cluttered world. Superstitions, magic, wrong beliefs, and wrong practices filled their world. It is true that the prophets cleansed away many things by their forceful and penetrating words, and we can't realize just how much good they did because religion is still cluttered with magic, superstitions, wrong beliefs, and wrong practices and more.

First and foremost, Jesus cleansed our ideas about God. He cleansed away the gods and half gods, the national and local irresponsible kings, rulers, etc., and left us with God, our Father, who does not ask us to do anything He Himself will not do. "Anything" except one thing – repent for sins we committed.

Beyond that He shares everything with us. And yet, on the cross He even shared in the repenting of our sins, did He not?

If our eyes are on Jesus then our life-force is God the Father. We have looked into the face of the Son. And that one look makes us feel that, whatever the explanation, this is the explanation. This is what Jesus meant when He said, *"No one comes to the Father except through me."* (John 14:6). The emphasis is on "the Father", we cannot see the Father unless we look on the face of the Son. There we see God's likeness. And what a likeness!

He has forever cleansed our ideas of God through the Word which He has spoken to us.

Prayer for today: O Father, how can we ever cease to love such a God as You! Our hearts bend in deepest gratitude that such a God fills our world – and us. Amen.

April 27   Luke 17:20-21; Acts 1:3-8

THE CLEANSING OF THE KINGDOM

Christ did not only cleanse our ideas of God, He went farther. He cleansed our ideas of the Kingdom of God. The Kingdom of God was to the Jewish mind a setting up of a world State with God as ruler and the Jewish people as His deputies. Jesus took this idea and cleansed it from national elements and universalized it, and made the Kingdom to be ruled by a new dynasty of deputies – the Servant-Kings. God as the Chief Servant is the greatest of all, and power will now be distributed to us (deputies) according to service rendered. This is beyond all thought of origin, race, sex, class, or color, and will be given to each individual as we are cleansed.

In this kingdom all unclean rulers will ultimately break themselves, if you think about it you can surely name a few who have done just that, broken themselves and their countries.

But the Kingdom of God has been forever cleansed for us, and we cannot rest this side of it. The Kingdom of God is ultimately our life's world – and as Christ lives within us, it is truly a beautiful world.

God also cleansed the material. Jesus cleansed away many bad ideas and gave us a world of matter which God looked upon and saw it was "good". My body is not an enemy, but the handiwork of God and as such it is to be kept fit and well and used in the purpose of the Kingdom of God. This is my Father's world and should be enjoyed; it should be used to His glory and dedicated to His service. Since we have seen the Word become "flesh" we can no longer be afraid of "flesh" the material, for it has within it the possibility of expressing the Divine. We never really saw the material until we saw Christ. Then our world was new. And an amazing worth-while world is the scene of the coming Kingdom.

Prayer for today: O Father, we thank You that we live in a world of matter. Help us not to fear it, but to use it – in Your Kingdom. Amen.

April 28   Matthew 5:31-32; 43-45; James 1:27

CLEANSING (Continued)

<u>Christ cleansed the family</u>. The home was the only institution Christ defended. He not only defended it – He cleansed it. He cleansed it from polygamy on one side and homosexuality on the other, and founded it the life partnership of <u>one man</u> and <u>one woman</u> on the basis of total equality.

<u>Jesus cleansed love</u>. He cleansed away lust and left it as pure love. It is possible to love everyone of either sex – and without lust, because Jesus has cleansed love.

<u>He has cleansed prayer</u>. Christ saw prayer was being used as magic and mere petition; He cleansed prayer and left it as communion. Prayer was no longer getting something from God, but God getting something from us. It is connecting ourselves to God through higher contact with higher power that we might achieve God's higher purpose.

<u>Christ cleansed religion</u>. He made Himself the definition of religion. To be religious is to be Christ-like, and that definition forever cleanses our minds from unworthy and lesser concepts. We have looked into a Face, and we can no longer think of religion except in terms of His Life.

Finally, <u>Jesus cleanses His disciples</u> – cleanses us to the depths of our being through His Word. What a cleansing of ourselves and our world!

Prayer for today: O God, our Father, thank You for the depth of this cleansing! Help us to accept it completely. Amen.

April 29   Matthew 4:19; 28:18-20; Luke 22:31-32

JESUS DECLARATION OF FAITH

Last week we saw where Jesus cleansed His disciples and their world through the "word" spoken to them. It was a courageous thing for Jesus to speak to His disciples like this, because He was declaring a faith, rather than a fact. It was true that the disciples were cleansed from many things, but at this point in their lives they were not "completely clean." They were arguing over who would be first, proposing to call down fire from heaven, and asking other disciples to stop their work because they did not belong to their group. This is hardly being "clean" and yet Jesus knew their heart and He knew they wanted to be completely "clean." The power they needed to be perfectly clean was available. Jesus knew this was a fact, so He declared it already done. This statement was the expression of Jesus knowing that this was all provided for in His "word" and also the expression of Jesus faith in the disciples that they would connect with that "word" and accept the cleansing. It took about sixty days before it was actually accomplished. This cleansing was accomplished at Pentecost, so this statement – *"you are already clean because of the "word" I have spoken to you."* (John 15:3*),* is made with about "sixty days of grace" attached to it. But at the first moment they were **willing to surrender completely to Christ**, it was theirs for the taking. In other words, Jesus had given them a check and all they had to do was endorse it and take the cash. That is what the disciples did at Pentecost they endorsed it with all their hearts – the check that gave them cleansing.

Prayer for today: O Father, we thank You for the wonderful feeling within us of Your sufficiency and Your faith in us. Help us never to disappoint that faith. Amen.

SOMETHING EXTRA –

GIVE ALL – RECEIVE ALL

I was a Christian for many years. I had been there and done that, working, working, doing God's work! "I" was doing God's work. If you could get to heaven doing good works, I would have had a first class ticket. Was I satisfied deep within my soul? NO!!

There was always a nagging feeling deep down inside that there was something missing with my Christian experience. Did I study my Bible and spend quality time in prayer? No! I did just enough to feel my "Christian duty" was being met. But the longing, the emptiness within was always present. And I knew why, but I still went for years trying to fill that emptiness with God's work.

Try as hard as you want, but you will never be completely happy and content in Christ until you let go and let God. Until you surrender **completely**. He has a plan, it is His plan, not ours, and He has to be in control for that plan to come to fruition. Isn't that the reason "self" must be surrendered to Him? If we give our all to Christ – our very all – He will cleanse us and fill us with His all. Then the emptiness is filled with the joy, peace, and love of Christ. It satisfies, I know, I finally gave my all, (my everything), in turn He has filled me with His all, (His everything), my emptiness has been replaced with God's satisfying joy, peace, and love.

It is never too late, at my age I am proof of that.

MaryAnn

April 30   1 Corinthians 2:12; 1 John 4:4; 5:4-5;
                                   Revelation 21:7

OVERCOMING THE WORLD

Among the most penetrating and hope-filled words Jesus ever gave us were these, *"In this world you will have trouble, but take heart! I have overcome the world!"* (John 16:33).

Someone might say, "Yes, He did overcome the world over two thousand years ago – but what about the world today?" Two ideas belong together: Jesus was identified with the hunger, sickness and imprisonment of people – *"whatever you did for one of the least of these brothers of mine, you did it for me."* (Matthew 25:40). And the verse telling us that *"in me you may have peace...I have overcome the world."* (John 16:33). In other words, as Jesus is identified with us in our defeats and sickness and hunger, so we are also identified with Him in His victory – His overcoming the world, provided, of course, that we enter into and relate ourselves to a complete relationship with Him and make His life our very own.

This opens up amazing possibilities – we can make every one of Christ victories our own. We can so relate our life to His in complete adjustment that when He overcomes, we overcome. We actually live by the life and victories of Christ. His victory will be our victory.

Prayer for today: O Father, I thank You that as unworthy as I am, I share with You the most magnificent thing this world has ever seen – Your overcoming. Help me relate to it completely and make it mine. Amen.

May 1   Luke 16:10; Acts 6:1-6; 2 Timothy 2:15

OVERCOMING THE ORDINARY WORLD

Jesus overcame the world of the ordinary. To live in a village for thirty years in the middle of dull humanity and work at a carpenter's bench, to support a widowed Mother and the family, is not difficult if you see nothing beyond that. However, if you feel the call of the living God upon you, and know in your heart that you have the one thing this sad world needs, and then be compelled to stay in these cramped surroundings, and do ordinary work for ninety per cent of your life in order to live the remaining ten per cent in fulfilling your real life purpose – if you do all this happily, then that is victory. Do you know what makes humans the most suffering of all creatures? It is that we have one foot in the limited and the other in the unlimited, and we are torn between the two worlds. But Jesus had one foot in the hard ordinary facts of Nazareth and another in the center of the world's needs. Two terrible conflicting worlds – but was He torn between them and therefore unhappy? <u>No</u>, because He made these worlds one. He brought the unlimited into the limited and the limited into the unlimited. The bringing of these two worlds together would make it worthy of a world's Redeemer. It has been said, "<u>If we do a small thing as though it were a great thing, God will let us do the great thing as though it were a small thing</u>." So day by day in commonplace Nazareth Christ wove with unlimited patience the seamless robe which He would wear before the world. Before sewing machines, when the task of sewing required every small stitch to be made by hand, a woman was asked if she did not tire of the tedious job she was so patently doing? "Oh, No," she replied, "this is my wedding dress." These stitches were no longer ordinary – they were related to something special.

Prayer for today: O Father, You did overcome dull task and dull hours, for You did relate them to the unlimited. Help me to do the same. Amen.

May 2   Judges 6:15; John 1:46; Acts 4:13-14

OVERCOMING THE HANDICAP OF AN ORDINARY FAMILY

Jesus overcame two handicaps: He had no formal education and He did not belong to a prominent family. *"How did this man get such learning without having studied?"* (John 7:15). He suffered in the eyes of the educated and cultured because He had no "formal" education. But Christ overcame that, and made what He did have so real and worthwhile that the people who followed Him saw that He knew life and could give it. We can enter into that victory. Then, there was victory over being from an ordinary family. He came from a family of low social rank, from a despised place. And when you look at His family history as seen in the genealogy you see some rather evil blood in that family tradition. Many of us can identify with this, for we, too, do not come from "the best of families," but from very common stock. However, that very handicap can help us start a new tradition. Let us remind ourselves at this point that – Shakespeare was the son of a bankrupt butcher and a woman who could not write her name. Beethoven was the son of an alcoholic. Schuber, the Austrian composer, was the son of a peasant father and an uneducated mother. Michael Faraday, English physicist, was born in a stable, his father an invalid blacksmith, his mother a menial worker. When the people objected to a lady marrying Matthew Henry because of his lowly birth, she replied, "I don't care where he came from, I'm only interested in where he is going, and I want to go with him."

We too can enter into that victory which Jesus gained and made people forget or not care where we come from as they watch us going with Christ.

Prayer for today: O Father, we thank You that You did overcome these two things, help us that we may begin in You a new learning and a new heredity. Amen.

May 3   Matthew 6:1-6; John 7:2-8

OVERCOMING THE WORLD OF THE SPECTACULAR

Jesus was fiercely tempted at the place of being spectacular. Christ had the power, could it not be used to impress people if He yielded to Satan's temptation? Of course it would be to advance the Kingdom, so therefore would it be right? But Jesus turned down very decisively this temptation. He overcame the world of the spectacular. Christ would win by <u>worth</u> and <u>service</u> alone. Everything else was of the devil. Christ was right. Had He advertised Himself, we would have forgotten Him. His reticent style was more vocal than His self-display would have been. Because Christ refused to listen to Satan at the Pinnacle of the Temple (Matthew 4:5-6), we put Him on the throne of the universe. Jesus also refused a miracle before Herod and we forget the asking and remember the refusal. Today for us to Live Victoriously we must find victory away from trying to be spectacular, from promoting ourselves. Several years ago a television audience watched as a televangelist and his group appealed for money to build a large building to "advance the Kingdom of God." When the building was completed, it was dedicated to a <u>man</u> and a large picture of him hung prominently in the foyer for all to see. Would it not have been the appropriate and right thing to do to dedicate this building to the ONE it was supposedly built to honor and to have hung a huge picture of Christ in that space for all to see? Eventually, those people, their beautiful building and everything they were doing, folded – and rightly so. We shudder to see the light of Christ turned of, while the stream of light pours upon the pastor as he prays, the audience silently approving as it keeps it's eyes open to watch the <u>display</u>. Their music has been lost. Christ kept His music, for He refused to blow His own horn. And millions now sing His praises! We too can enter into this victory and make it our own.

Prayer for today: O Christ of the quiet heart, teach us Your humble ways, for we see they lead to humility. Amen.

May 4   Psalm 57:7; 112:7; Isaiah 30:15; John 11:6-7

OVERCOMING A HURRIED WORLD

The man who had most to do seemed never to be in a hurry. He was launching a Kingdom which would turn out to be the ultimate order for all people, and yet as He built this Kingdom He seemed to be in no feverish, fussy haste. Not that He was idle or wasting time, He was far from it. He never wasted a moment, and still He was never hurriedly busy, and always on time.

Jesus said to Martha, *"You are worried and upset about many things."* (Luke 1:41). Martha probably said under her breath, "Yes, but if I'm not careful and anxious, you'll go hungry." But Martha in all her rush and haste fell down at the very place in her life where she thought she was strongest. Note this passage: *"Early in the morning as He was on His way back to the city (Jerusalem from Bethany) He was hungry." (Matthew 21:18).* Why did she let Him go from Bethany without anything to eat? She fell where she thought she was strongest. This hurried state of our day has also fallen in its strongest place. We speed up our technology and civilization and then leave thousands behind unemployed, idle, unloved and hungry. We fail where we think we are strong.

We must regain victory at the place of the unhurried heart. We must make King of our heart, a calm and unhurried Christ. And His quiet will spread to every part of our being.

Prayer for today: O Father, we thank You for victory over restless haste. Give us Your victory of the Quiet, assured heart that knows in the end God's victory is certain. Amen.

May 5   Luke 9:46-56; 22:49-51

OVERCOMING IMPATIENCE WITH INADEQUATE TOOLS

The Kingdom which Jesus launched required delicate handling. Its virtues might very well turn into vices by the slightest twist. Its light might turn into darkness. If such should happen He could have tremendous temptation to be out of patience with the inadequate tools of His Kingdom. It is a wonder He didn't dismiss His disciples at a number of places along the way. When they twisted His teaching into something else, why didn't He let them go and try it with another group? He didn't, because He would eventually make this group victorious.

Often we face the same temptation – quit this job and try another; get rid of trouble (a wife or husband) and start all over again; dismiss these Christian workers and build the congregation with a fresh group; get rid of the pastor and try a better one; change churches; and so on – all this is really just running away from the problem – an escape mentality. It is not victory – it is an attempt at escape.

After all, the next group will probably have the same streaky human nature. The new seems clean for a few days – and then the dust! That second wife or husband will not be an angel! The fact is obvious that they are pretty poor "stuff" at best, if they are so quick to take another after having just ditched one.

Jesus overcame this impatience with inadequate tools and made those tools into changed men, who changed the world. That was victory.

We must learn to adapt to people around us – remembering that as we tolerate them Christ has to tolerate us. Even when we do our best we may fall short. But we are all <u>convertible</u>!

Prayer for today: O Father, we thank You for Your patience and for Your persistence with us. Help us to deal with others in the same patent, redemptive way. Amen.

May 6   Luke 23:34; Acts 7:59-6; Colossians 3:12-15

OVERCOMING RESENTMENT

A person of faith is usually a person with a sensitive, eager disposition. They see beyond the normal and want something different and work to achieve it. That person will almost immediately come across opposition, for people do not easily give up the "what-is" for "what-ought-to-be." The person with faith will be tempted to resent people who do not see what they see and how they see it. This person must have victory over resentment. It is interesting that Jesus linked faith in God and forgiveness to others. In (Mark 11:22-25), "*Have faith in God," Jesus answered*. *"I tell you the truth, if anyone says to this mountain, 'Go, throw yourself in the sea,' and does not doubt in his heart but believes that what he says will happen, it will be done for him. Therefore I tell you, whatever you asked for in prayer, believe that you have received it, and it will be yours. And when you stand praying, if you hold anything against anyone, forgive him, so that your Father in heaven may forgive you your sins."* Jesus put faith in God and forgiveness to people together, they belong together. Faith without forgiveness makes religion unpleasant and extreme. Forgiveness without faith makes religion soft, not progressive. But faith and forgiveness together makes religion Christ-like. Forgiveness puts love in faith, so now faith works by love. The person of faith forgives those who strike back because they do not agree with them in changing "what-is" to "what-ought-to-be." That person follows a man who saw His attempts at changing an old world into a new world end up on a cross, deserted by the multitudes whom He would save and by disciples who professed loyalty to Him, and seemingly by the Father who sent Him. And yet on that cross was a prayer of forgiveness upon His lips. This was VICTORY!! We too can have that victory. Resentment has no place within us.

Prayer for today: O Father, help us to have a heart that is not resentful. Make us full of faith toward you, and full of tenderness toward others who do not agree with us. Amen.

May 7   Matthew 15:15-20; 22:34-40; 23:23-24;
                                   Philippians 1:8-9

OVERCOMING THE UNIMPORTANT

If we are to live a victorious life, we must live <u>what is important</u> – <u>a life connected to Christ</u>. Many people do not – they live their life around unimportant issues, which occupies and absorbs most of their time. A true story: A terrible train wreck happened. Many were killed. And many injured were groaning under the wreckage. The few unhurt were trying desperately to help the wounded and give them needed attention. In the middle of all this, a woman sat beside her luggage which had been torn open and she kept repeating, "Oh, my expensive shoes!" She repeated this over and over; it mingled with the cries of the injured. A pair of shoes was the center of her attention with a wreck around her! This portrays vividly what we often do: **we become so absorbed with personal things that are so unimportant, that we miss the important issues of life**. Let's examine ourselves, go over everything that has a place in our lives and ask this question: Is this relevant to the really big issue? Does it keep me from the really important things? It may not be a bad thing, but is it relevant? If there is anything in our lives that cannot be considered important to our Christian life, then out it should go. The Christian must have a wastebasket, not only for the bad but for the unimportant.

Jesus was never once led into an inferior issue, never once missed the real point, never got side-tracked, and was always occupied with what was important. He overcame sin and also the unimportant. We must free our lives not only of what isn't good, but what isn't good enough. Jesus did that, and we can share His overcoming and enter a world of what is truly important.

Prayer for today: O Father, we thank You that You want to save us from both sin and the unimportant. We consent to let go the trivial and irrelevant. Help us. Amen.

May 8   Matthew 6:25-34

OVERCOMING ANXIETY

"Do not be anxious about anything, but in everything by prayer and petition, with thanksgiving, present you request to God." (Philippians 4:6). Do not be anxious! Was there ever a message so deeply needed as now? Anxieties fill the air – and they fill us. Jesus conquered the world of anxieties. Three basic things that we are anxious about – we spend our time worrying about: food, shelter, and future security. Not one of these was Jesus assured of. He had no food except what was given to Him day by day. He had no assured home. Often He slept under the stars, huddled beneath a tree. As for future security – He knew there was none, for His road would end on a cross. The three things that we may worry about most were absolutely missing from Jesus life. He shared our disabilities – but not our worries. How did He do it? His prescription was simple: OBEY GOD, TRUST GOD. Those four words were the cornerstones of His life. And when the storm of His life came, the foundation stood. Note how He puts them together. You cannot really trust God unless you obey Him. If you do not obey God then you cannot trust Him to do what He says He will do. A woman told of the loss of her faith: "The Bible says, *'Ask whatever you wish, and it will be given you,'* and I prayed for my father's recovery, but he died. So my faith is gone." But she did not quote the complete scripture: *"If you remain in me and my words remain in you, ask whatever you wish, and it will be given you."* (John 15-7). Obey God, trust God! (And read the complete scripture). This is a practical working faith: first, **it is our business to do the will of God**; second, **God takes special care of us as we do His will**, third, **we should not be afraid of anything.**

Prayer for today: O Father, there is no deterioration of Your heart. Give me a heart like Yours. Help me to always be obedient to Your will and therefore free from worry. Amen.

May 9   Matthew 16:21-23; Luke 13:32; Acts 21:11-14

OVERCOMING THE SPIRIT OF WITHDRAWAL

There is a real tendency to try to win victory by withdrawal. We surround ourselves with the hard shell of refusal to face certain issues, withdraw within ourselves, and hope for victory. We try to maintain peace by dodging the battle. Sometimes we try to maintain a high spiritual level by never coming to terms with any issue, never taking sides, never crossing anyone – we make for ourselves a deserted island and call it victory. You may see someone who looks peaceful and like they have it altogether. However, if they have no cares, it is because they don't care, if they have no burdens it is because they take none, that is not having it altogether – that is refusing to face life or withdrawing from it. Jesus overcame the tendency of withdrawal and found victory. He found victory not by getting out but by getting in. One of <u>the most important verses</u> in the history of Jesus is this: "*Jesus <u>resolutely</u> set out for Jerusalem.*" (Luke 9:51). This meant that He would face issues, would bring on the crises at hand and see the whole thing through to the bitter glorious end. But in setting Himself in such a determined direction, He showed us the way and we can do no less for Him. We can never be true to Him <u>now</u> unless we are true to Him at this point. All withdrawing from real issues is withdrawal from Jesus. Think about it – it is true.

One of <u>the saddest verses</u> in the Bible is this: "<u>*Wanting to satisfy the crowd*</u>, *Pilate...handed Jesus over to be crucified.*" (Mark 15:15). And for us one of the saddest days of our life is the day we allow the fear of the crowd to conquer our better judgments and instincts of our soul. Sometimes we are "content" with the crowd when we should "contend" with them. Jesus was taking a baptism of responsibility for everyone. Pilate was crawling out – withdrawing. Jesus was marching in – going for victory!

Prayer for today: O Father, Give me the determined nature and the power to come to terms with issues as they arise. Amen.

May 10   Matthew 7:14; Luke 13:32; John 16:32;
                     2 Timothy 4:16-18

OVERCOMING THE UNWILLINGNESS TO BE IN A MINORITY

Sometime truth is found in a minority. (Mark 9:26-27) A stricken boy lay on the ground in front of Jesus. The story says, "...*The boy looked so much like a corpse that <u>many</u> said, 'He's dead.'*" At that time had a majority vote been taken, they would have decided the boy was dead and needed to be buried. But the truth was in the minority of <u>one</u>. Jesus called the boy back from collapse to restored health.

The majority decides again and again in its elections that any new law, which will replace the present law with its injustices and wrongs, is dead. But again the majority is wrong. For the idea of a just social society, in which every person will have an equal opportunity, is God's idea, and will not be put down.

We cannot gain spiritual victory unless we <u>are willing</u> to be in the minority, if necessary.

If you look at the scene in Gethsemane, you will see the size of the crowds: Jesus <u>alone</u>, then <u>three</u>, then <u>eight</u>, and then <u>the majority of Jerusalem</u>. <u>If it is your desire to be in the majority you will probably find yourself in the crowd farthest from Jesus</u>.

Living Life Victoriously means you are released from the desire to be on the popular side – you become willing to stand alone if necessary. But alone, "<u>if in the right</u>," He will be with you.

Prayer for today: O Father, I had rather be alone with You, than in a crowd without You. I want to be with You wherever You are, with many or with a few. Amen.

May 11   Romans 6:1-7; 6:18-2

OVERCOMING SIN

One of the things most necessary in Living Victoriously is to realize that when we are fighting evil we are fighting a <u>conquered</u> enemy. Jesus met every sin and conquered it. If we do not realize or remember that we are fighting an already conquered evil then we may develop an inferiority complex before our enemy. In which case we would allow evil to bully us, and make us feel that it is a permanent part of life and cannot be eradicated. Hence, we are defeated in our mind before the battle begins. We must understand that sin has been conquered – every sin has been conquered, both within us and in the world. We need only to accept the gift of complete victory and then proceed to make it a reality in us and in the world around us. So when sin starts to bully you, calmly and joyfully tell it to bend its head and let you see the footprints of the Son of God on its neck. (Joshua 10:24-25) –and your inferiority complex will be gone. You will not meet one single sin today that has not been defeated. We walk the earth among conquered enemies. There is an old story told about a warrior in the ancient days. While leading a battle his head was cut off, but he was so intent on fighting that he fought on even with his head gone. This headless warrior killed many. But he collapsed only when a woman saw him and cried out, "But your head is gone – you're dead!" So he fell down and died! You get the idea – when evil seems so strong and invincible and is about to do you in, stop and say, "But your head is gone! Did not my Master conquer you? Did He not sever the head of evil by the sword of the cross? Your head is gone, you are dead!" Evil fights on. But it is brainless. It depends on prejudices, old habits, and unreasoning emotions. Reason is on the side of good. We fight a fierce but brainless enemy.

Prayer for today: O Father, I thank You that You did not give-in to a single temptation. Show me how to accept and enter into this completed victory. Amen.

May 12   John 15:1-11; 2 Corinthians 2:14; Galatians 3:27

THE SECRET OF OVERCOMING

In the past few days we have been thinking together on the amazing statement, *"Take heart! I have overcome the world."* (John 16:33). You say, "well and good, wonderful, but how do I grasp this and make it mine?"

The entire verse reads this way, *"I have told you these things, so that in me you may have peace. In this world you will have trouble, but take heart! I have overcome the world."* The disciples were distressed when Jesus informed them that He would soon be leaving. Jesus understood their feelings, but He needed them to understand that in Him they would have peace. In the world they would have trouble: *"but take heart! I have overcome the world."* "In the world" – trouble. "In me" – peace. What does this "in me" mean?

It means being identified with Christ, merged into Him, so united with Him that His victories become our victories, hence – His peace becomes our peace. Surrender of ourselves means identifying completely with Christ. Life flows into life, mind into mind, and we share a common life.

In (Isaiah 63:11-12) it says, *"...where is he who set his Holy Spirit among them, who sent his glorious arm of power to be at Moses right hand...?"* God's power and Moses' efforts coincided. When Moses raised his right hand, God's right hand was there beside it. God's arm didn't do everything, for that would have kept Moses from growing spiritually. Moses' arm had to put forth the effort, but when he tried, God was victorious.

Say this to yourself today: "I am in Christ, and so His power is identified with every single thing in my life. Today His glorious arm will be at my right hand. As I do my work today there will be an unusual strength within me. As I face uncertainties there will be unexpected solutions. As I face relationships with others there will be a love beyond my own, making those relations sweet and beautiful, nothing will meet me today that Christ will not be in, and together we will go through it. He will cause His glorious arm to go at my right hand."

"Around my incompleteness flows His completeness,
Around my restlessness flows His rest."

Prayer for today: O Father, thank You that I am "in" You and You are "in" me. Help me to grasp the full meaning of this and live by it today and forever. Amen.

May 13   Romans 6:13: 1 Corinthians 15:9-10;
                           2 Corinthians 5:16-17

PURIFYING THE OLD SELF INSTINCTS

Last study we ended with the idea of being "in Christ," and we saw that meant identifying with His purpose so that His victories become our victories. Let's now look at some of the results of being "in Christ." Paul says, *"If anyone is in Christ, he is a new creation, the old has gone, the new has come."* (2 Corinthians 5:17). Actually the (old things) have just become (new).

There was a feeling that old things (instincts) had completely left us, and yet there was a feeling in which they had been completely transformed and made new. This "new creature" is entirely different from the "old creature," and yet he is fundamentally the same, "only new." Ancient Persia used the peach to get poison to put on the tip of arrows. Can you believe our beautiful, delicious peach once poison? Today's peach is a new and different creature, old things are gone and they have become new. It is new – the poison has been eliminated, but the fundamental life of the tree remains; only now, instead of being used to bring forth poison, it brings forth luscious, health-giving fruit. That is purification.

Paul saw that the poison of his old self-instincts had been purified and made new. Before they had been used in purposes that ended in death, they were now being used for purposes that ended in life. He found that he was the same Paul with his fundamental Jewish human nature instincts intact, and yet he was so fundamentally changed that he had to change his name to express a new fact. The past was discontinued, but the future continued. Paul's conversion (2 Corinthians 9) meant his spirit was under new control, directed toward a new end – purification had taken place.

Prayer for today: O Father, I thank You that You do take this raw material of human life and cleanse and refashion it, and make it serve other purposes-Your purposes. I give it all for Your disposal. Make me what You want me to be. Amen.

May 14   2 Corinthians 5:14-15; 6:3-10

PURIFYING THE OLD SELF-INSTINCTS (Continued)

The instincts are our driving life-forces. Life's energy flowing through us breaks into three instinctive channels: Self, Sex and Group. Minor instincts that we have usually turn out to be phases of the above dominant instincts. Concerning these instincts there are these possibilities: biological expression, suppression or self-control, and purification. The difference between repression and suppression seems to be that in repression the instinct is pushed down into the subconscious and the top closed. There it works havoc. Someone has said, "Repressed instincts are like bad boys who, when suspended from school, begin to throw rocks at the windows." But in suppression the instincts are kept within the conscious mind and are suppressed at certain places in order to be purified at others. In other words, keep the bad boys in school under observation and direction, and teach them to direct their energies to constructive ends. But suppression without purification may end in repression and is therefore dangerous to handle.

Christianity believes in biological expression, but always under the control of its standard of excellence. That means expression at certain levels and suppression at others. However, the suppressed can always be purified – the turning of the instinctive forces to higher expressions. That opens the door upward.

Prayer for today: O Father, we thank You that You have made it possible that we can be wholly dedicated to Your purpose and that human nature is not to be eliminated, but redeemed. Redeem me, I pray. Amen.

May 15   Acts 14:19-23; 26:29; 2 Corinthians 11:23-29

SOME OLD THINGS MADE NEW

Paul said, *"Therefore, if anyone is in Christ, he is a new creation; the old is gone, the new has come!"* (2 Corinthians 5:17). We are now discovering just how old, old is. The instincts are very old. They go back to untold ages, race tendencies have gone into them. They have become indented and set in certain directions. And yet they can be abruptly changed and redeemed.

Take a phase of self-instinct, the belligerent instinct in Paul. Before his conversion he was very hostile, he breathed out slaughter against the Christians - then the change. After his conversion he was still hostile. But now this hostility was directed against evil. Sometimes it came close to being directed at his associates. But mainly his hostile instinct was bridled and harnessed to the chariot of God's purposes, and Paul drove it toward Kingdom's end. The hostile instinct was purified and made constructive.

Do you have a hostile spirit? Don't try to get rid of it. Let Christ cleanse from it that selfish, aggressive hostility that stands for its own ways, and then let Him harness it to the task of fighting evil of every kind. Then you can say, "My old self-instinct of hostility has gone; and the new has come."

Prayer for today: O Father, take this hostility of mine. I lay it upon Your altar. I ask You to purify it and use it to Your glory. Amen.

May 16   John 15:16; 18:20-23; 1 Corinthians 11:1;
                            Philippians 4:9

PURIFYING THE SELF-INSTINCT

The ego instinct is probably the most haughtily domineering of all instincts. It is the reason for most of our actions. We must face that fact. When we think of a person being "a selfless person," we are simply thinking of that person as not having a lot of concern for themselves. Christ was not selfless, neither was Paul, and as a Christian we should not be selfless.

It makes for hypocrisy to say the self is less or not there. Self is there and should be there. But the question is: what kind of self is it?

The self was purified in Jesus, the meekest of men and the most self-assertive. He renounced power, refusing to be made a king, and yet the self was satisfied by gaining the most amazing power ever exercised. Paul became the servant of the churches – their troubles, his troubles, their weaknesses, his weaknesses. As you look at Paul you say, "The man has lost his ego." No, not at all. That ego instinct was purified, and therefore satisfied by having an authority over people by the very fact of his renouncing himself. He did not renounce himself for that purpose; had he done so, it would have spoiled it all, but the power over others was a by-product of the losing of himself. The self was not lost – it was turned loose.

Your old ego must die, be crucified. Then it will come back and you can say, "The old ego has gone; and look, it has become new."

Prayer for today: O Father, take this ego of mine and cleanse it from all egoism, and use it for Your purpose, so that I may be able to live with it, and perhaps rejoice in it. Amen.

May 17   Matthew 2:11-12; 23:37-39; Galatians 4:18-19

PURIFYING SEX

Life is heavily loaded when it comes to "sex," much too heavily loaded, in today's society. But whether it is overemphasized or rightly emphasized in our individual self it is an integral part of us, and as such must be dealt with frankly and with good sense.

To confess sex-desire to oneself is no more shameful than to confess desire for food. Both are essential parts of us. Where it is functioning biologically for the purpose of procreation, the problem is normally solved. Even there it must remain under the restraint of the high standards of our life. For if one part of our nature demands satisfaction at the expense and sacrifice of the rest of yourself, then the result is not satisfaction but inner division and therefore unhappiness. But the problem becomes more acute when the sex instinct is denied biological expression. In that case it may be suppressed, which is dangerous, setting up complications. Or the sex instinct can be purified.

The sex instinct was purified in Jesus. He was creative in both mind and spirit. He was bringing into being a new culture, a higher type of humanity. He was parenting the family of God. "*O Jerusalem...how I have longed to gather your children together, as a hen gathers her chicks under her wings!*" (Matthew 23:37). That is purification. Paul, denied a family life, was not unhappy, because he was purifying his sex-life, by being procreative in the higher reaches of life, the mind and spirit. Wherever he went he saw new birth take place. He was a spiritual father.

If a man be in Christ he is a new creature, the old sex instinct that could have been used for self-satisfaction, has now become new – purified to be used as God intended.

Prayer for today: O Father, I thank You for release of inner bondages. Loose my soul in creative activity. Amen.

May 18   Philippians 1:9-11; 1 Thessalonians 2:19-20

PURIFYING THE INSTINCTS OF CURIOSITY AND PRIDE

The instinct of curiosity is shown early in the child as it ask questions concerning everything. In adults it may show itself in ugly ways by prying into other people's affairs and meddling in their private life. On the other hand the curiosity instinct can be a great factor in deciding to help the spiritual life grow. The Christian should purify it from lower ways to higher ways.

The Christian belongs to a Kingdom where there is no limit of knowledge. The Christian, therefore, is under the influence of a high standard of excellence always reaching for a swiftly moving goal. Accordingly the Christian has the possibility of great curiosity. As a Christian our mind and spirit should grow as we stretch forth that curiosity to learn. The curiosity instinct is purified from useless, pointless prying, to the purpose of unlimited growth.

The pride instinct can also be converted, can be purified. There is a foolish pride, which thinks in terms of a showy, gaudy manner in order to attract attention to it self. That pride needs to die. BUT pride can be attached to our Christianity. In (1 Thessalonians 2:19) Paul says, *"For what is our hope, our joy, or the crown in which we glory in the presence of our Lord Jesus when he comes. Is it not you? Indeed, you are our glory and joy."* Here was the old Pharisaical pride turned redemptive. Paul was not rejoicing in his ancestry and his learning, but rejoicing in this new creation taking place before him – proud of his new humanity. The instinct of pride was turned from being petty and was rejoicing in the worth-while work of his own hands.

As a Christian we should be able to say, "The old curiosity and pride have gone; and now they have become new."

Prayer for today: O Father, kill within me foolish pride and then raise up within me a more noble pride that will tolerate nothing less than the highest. Amen.

May 19   Isaiah 32:20; Matthew 13:1-9; Romans 8:29

PURIFYING THE MATERIALISTIC AND THE SOCIAL INSTINCT

The materialistic instinct is the driving force in many lives. It is the basis of many of our difficulties. It drives us to worship – "things" – "stuff." This instinct needs converting, can it be done?

Jesus knows it can, because He said, "*Do not store up for yourselves treasures on earth...But store up for yourselves treasures in heaven.*" (Matthew 6:19-20). The materialistic instinct is still operative, <u>but now toward higher values</u>. In other words, we now <u>invest in people instead of things</u>. We are eager for these new changed people and this changed society. The old materialistic instinct has gone; and it has become new. The social instinct can be used for narrow-minded, selfish, individualistic means. It can assert itself against its neighbors, friends, and others, pushing their world into turmoil. In Christianity it must be purified. The social instinct is now connected to the ultimate plan in human relationships, namely, the Kingdom of God on earth. Then one can say, "*Who is my mother, my brother, and my sister.*" (Matthew 12:48). "*Those who do the will of God, those are my mother, my brothers and my sisters.*" (Matthew 12:50). The social instinct is not done away with, it is enlarged, enlightened, enlivened. It now has a real place to dwell. It now takes its meaning from the highest loyalty – the loyalty of the Beloved Community, the Kingdom of God. <u>Every power of our life is to be purified and presented as instruments of our new life</u>. Paul says in (Romans 6:19) "*I put this in human terms, because you are weak in your natural selves. Just as you used to offer your body in slavery to impurity and to ever-increasing wickedness, so now offer them in slavery to righteousness leading to holiness.*" Paul taught purification long before it was named.

Prayer for today: O Father, I thank You that my instincts are all at Your service not at the surface but at the depths. Amen.

May 20   Matthew 15:19-20; 18:3; John 3:3

LIVING VICTORIOUSLY AND THE SOCIAL ENVIRONMENT

So far in our search for Living Victoriously we have concentrated on the causes of evil within us. It is where we should begin, for we are like a person with fever, tossing in bed to find a cool spot, when actually the fever is within. Finding a cool spot on clean sheets will not cure the fever as long as the germs causing the fever are within. In our modern age we must not lose sight of this fact while we are so intent on social change as the cure-all for human ills. We have a way of brushing past our 'inner" problems and concentrating on "outer" difficulties.

In this day and age it is not so much that we have lost our sense of sin as that we have developed a technique by which we are able to connect it to those we dislike and to those of whom we disapprove. For example, large company CEO's, corrupt leaders, wicked government officials, etc. This transference of guilt to others is dishonest. Christian religion is a force of belief cleansing us within, therefore the primary religious virtue is sincerity, a penetrating sincerity.

That sincerity must begin with us. Beginning any other place is insincerity. It is an escape mentality. No one is in a prepared state of mind to face the problems of the world unless they are ready to face honestly their own life **and make it right**.

We have, and rightly so, started with ourselves. But we cannot stop there.

Prayer for today: O Father, we thank You that You have put Your hand upon our own heart first of all, now help us to follow You as far as You go. Amen.

May 21   Matthew 11:20-24; Acts 19:23-27;
                          1 Corinthians 15:33

ADAPTING TO BOTH PERSONAL AND SOCIAL
ENVIRONMENT

Yesterday we said that the first emphasis in our search for Living Victoriously should be on ourselves. However, while it may be the first, it must not be the last. To go to our social surroundings and pass over the personal, is an escape mentality, but to stay at the personal and refuse to go to our social environment is also an escape mentality. Many hindrances to Living Victoriously are within us, many or <u>NOT</u> within us. They are in our social environment. It will not do to counter this by saying that the social environment is made up of individuals, because it is and it isn't. Our social environment is not entirely made up of individuals <u>now living</u>. It is a product of accumulated attitudes and customs passed on from generation to generation and may be only modified slightly by existing individuals. Therefore it can be very impersonal. The question is: Does our social environment help or hinder our new life? Life depends on two factors: <u>Adaptive individual</u> (us – our new life) <u>and a suitable</u> <u>environment</u> (Christian surroundings). As an individual we may be very adaptable, but if there is no suitable environment (Christian environment), we will die spiritually. On the other hand, if the Christian environment is there and the individual is not strong enough to adapt, they still die spiritually. If our Christian life depends upon response to our environment, the question is: do my present surroundings provide an environment to which, as a Christian, I can respond? **Does it feed me, or poison me**? If our present environment feeds us, preserve it at all cost. But if it is poisoning us and we cannot purify it from poison to spiritual food, then we must replace our present surroundings with a new environment that will feed us.

Prayer for today: O Father, as we look at the surroundings about us take from our heart the blinding prejudices that keep us from seeing things as they are. Open our eyes and our heart. Amen.

IS A "PRIVATE" ENVIRONMENT SUFFICIENT?

We saw yesterday that life depends on a suitable environment. No matter how healthy the palm tree may be, if transferred to a cold climate, it will die. "But," you say, "The analogy doesn't hold, for the Christian has their private favorable environment – the Kingdom of God." As the diver down in the sea has a life line leading to the air supply, so the Christian has their personal contact with a higher power. However, the diver cannot stay down forever and is restricted at every point by the hostility of the environment. As Christians we can exist in this world society of ours, but we are restricted at every point. It is not our native air, so unless we periodically rise to the atmosphere of a co-operative society, (our Church, Christian groups, Christian friends, Christian family members, etc.) and take off our helmets and breathe freely, we shall probably suffocate. And what about those who are compelled to live in this world-society without any contacts with the Kingdom? How shall they live who have to breathe one atmosphere and one alone – the poisoned atmosphere of the modern social society?

As Christians, God's servants, we must create an environment that will minister spiritual life, to those around us, an environment in which we can live freely and fully. We must live a Christian life in spite of our environment.

Besides, did Jesus intend for us to have a private favorable environment here on earth? He did ask us to pray that the Kingdom might come on earth as it is in heaven. (Matthew 6:10). If there, why not here!

Prayer for today: O Father, we pray again, "Our Father, may Your Kingdom come and may Your will be done on earth as it is in heaven." Help us to put that into our plans as well as into our prayers. Amen.

May 23   Mark 13:9; John 18:25; Acts 12:20-22

ALL CAUSES OF SIN

In (Matthew 13:41) there is this remarkable statement: *"The Son of Man...will weed out of His Kingdom <u>everything that causes sin</u> and <u>all who do evil</u>."* Note the two emphases: "<u>Everything that causes sin</u> and <u>all who do evil.</u>" The last emphasis refers to <u>personal, individual sins</u>; the first emphasis refers to the <u>impersonal causes of sin</u>. One kind of sin was in the individual will and the other in modern society. We have been dealing throughout our quest with sin in the individual will; we must now look at the cause of sin in society. Our modern society may cause sin and it may cause good. It may cause people to do evil, because they cannot live in this modern society without doing evil. <u>Sometimes it is not easy for us to see the causes of evil in the society to which we belong</u>, especially if we are in a favored position in that society. We think emotionally; our reasoning tries to make rational emotional attachments. This fact of emotional thinking will put us on guard about the validity of our social attitudes. A man who owned most of the liquor stores in a particular city was given a prestigious title by that city's government because of his "cleverness in the detection of crime." However, he never thought of his own liquor stores as the cause of much of the crime! He prided himself on his righteous endeavor against crime, for his reasoning went around one of the most prolific causes of crime – his own system. He was probably not a conscious hypocrite – he didn't see it, for he thought emotionally. We all do. We therefore need open-eyed wisdom as we look at the causes of sin in our society.

Prayer for today: O Father, You do pierce beneath to the real and exposed hearts of us all and You put Your finger on our sore spots in our Temple system. Give us Your clear-eyed vision and courage. Amen.

May 24   Mark 14:11; John 2:14; Acts 24:26;
                                    1 Timothy 6:10

SOME CAUSES OF SIN

In searching for causes of sin in modern society we are compelled to brush aside the lesser causes and go straight to the central one – **selfish competition**. The competitive greedy spirit in modern society is probably the most prolific cause of sin. It sets the stage for evil. It becomes easier under a competitive situation to be hard and ruthless than to be loving and generous. It stacks the cards against goodness. When this is said, probably a real objection comes to mind: If competition is taken out of life, will we not lose individual initiative? This is a real fear to many. But note that we were referring to "selfish" competition. There is a higher competition which is not selfish. In a co-operative situation there would still be competition, we would still compete as to who could give most to the good of all. But this friendly competition would be constructive and not destructive. As the individual self-instinct must be redeemed and turned toward constructive ends, so the collective ego-instinct must be redeemed and made to serve the public good. In either case you cannot eradicate the ego; you must control it to the making of a better situation. It must be purified. Competition there will always be – now Christianized and controlled for God's purpose. However, this "selfish" competition which holds the center of our life is a very different thing. It has been softened and civilized, but underneath that softness and civilization is ruthlessness. If you don't believe it, ask the thousand who have recently lost jobs because of ruthless competition, to show you their wounds of soul and body. They know. We all know. For civilization is bleeding from a thousand wounds – bled white by competitive struggle. The selfish competitive, greedy spirit of society is one major cause of sin.

Prayer for today: O Father, we ask You to help us face this matter calmly and courageously and make it right. In Your name we pray. Amen.

May 25   Proverbs 20:14, 21: 6; James 5:2-4

SELFISH COMPETITION –THE MAJOR CAUSE

Yesterday we said that selfish competition was the major cause of sin. We must pursue it. Here are two boys brought up in a refined and loving home. The basis of life in that home is co-operation – it is in any good home. But suppose when meal time came the older stronger boy would snatch as much food as he could from the younger and weaker boy and stack it on his plate, would not the family be outraged and bad manners severely dealt with? Good families are simply not built that way. Each meal is not a scramble to get all we can get, and keep all we can keep. Each gets his proper share of whatever there is, and the older and stronger ones look after the younger and weaker. (At least that is the way it should work). The entire family attitude and mind-set makes it easier for the children to be co-operative and helpful. A good family life is built on co-operation. So also is our best education built on co-operation? But the moment one of those boys steps out of that home or out of college to go into the business world most of his values are reversed. In order to be a good family member he had to develop in sympathy and mutual helpfulness, respect, and service. Now, in order to be successful in a competitive world, that training must be reversed. He must drive hard bargains, without paying too much attention to the ruination of others. Side blinders have to be put on the eyes so that he looks straight ahead at what he wants. He would be shocked to find that around this table of business he is grabbing all he can from the weaker members and stacking it up around his own plate regardless of whether he can eat it or not. And yet that is exactly what he is doing. The family spirit is dying in him. The competitive world is a cause of sin to him. **But—doesn't he have knowledge and ability to choose how he handles the system?**

Prayer for today: O Father, You who did come to make us one family, forgive us that we have not put that family spirit into our total life. Help us yet to get it right. Amen.

May 26   Matthew 20:10-14; 1 John 4:19-21

LOVING YOUR NEIGHBOR IN A COMPETITIVE SITUATION

When that young man, the one we talked about yesterday, is slowly becoming hardened and is losing his ideals, picks up his briefcase and goes back home for a visit, he looks at his father in a puzzled way and says: "Dad, the business world is different than I expected. I am unlearning everything I was taught at home, why such a difference?" His father, remembering with a sigh the reversal of his own ideals, helplessly replies, "Son, business is business." They are both caught in a system which can be a cause of sin to them. <u>Human society is the legalized struggle of humans to "out-do,"</u> <u>exceed</u>, and <u>surpass one another</u>.

Question: Isn't the very center of Jesus' teaching that we are to love our neighbor as we love ourselves, and if we did that, wouldn't we have a different world? In a small city, where there were already <u>many</u> drug stores a new pharmacy chain opened, with big fanfare, cut prices and enticed the community to support it. Now a much loved and faithful family owned pharmacy, who served the community for many, many years, was forced to close their doors and go out of business, because of ruthless competition.

The only way out of the world's difficulties is to love your neighbor as you love yourself. Can we apply that in the struggle we are entering? It isn't impossible, but it is highly improbable. The deck is stacked against us. On one side we are to, "love our neighbor as we love ourselves." And on the other, "Get all the business we can, no matter if your neighbor gets hurt in the process." Which side will be our history? We will probably try to compromise. The competitive situation could become a cause of sin to us. Hopefully not!

Prayer for today: O Father, help us to make a world in which the light within us will not be blown out. You are calling us to make society better, help us to step up. Amen.

May 27   Leviticus 5:1-10

HANDS-OUT OR HANDS-IN

We have been dealing with selfish competition as a cause of sin. Let's look at it again until it burns itself into our souls. America is a poor-rich country, rich and poor side by side. The poor will say, "My salary is not enough to feed my family." When your salary is not enough to feed your family, other necessities are not even in the realm of possibility. In the midst of this a devoted, hard working, well-meaning person says, "What we need is more help for the poor, the government needs to do more. Though the statement is made with sincerity and thoughtfulness, do you feel like you've been slapped in the face? Here is a loving, gentle, well-meaning person talking about the "necessity" of handing out more to people, "many" of whom would prefer to help themselves if given the opportunity. Of course there are always those who think the world owes them a living and everything else, while they sit and do nothing and these could be the ones benefiting most from the "free hand-out programs." But given a chance most people had rather earn their way through life. In today's selfish society this kind of thinking is wrong. We do not need more hand-outs, we need more hands-in the work places. When our hands are busy working we don't have time to get into trouble (and our world certainly needs less trouble). We cannot tolerate a society that causes kind, gentle people to say we need more handouts from the government – no, we need a society who cares about our neighbor, a society who represents genuine love and respect for everyone. A people who will help restore society to a working society, so all have an equal opportunity to make something of themselves. "Sounds good," you say, "but it will never happen." It could happen – it could begin with us. After all it must start with "me."

Prayer for today: Father, we ask You to forgive us that we have tolerated and still tolerate a society where more and more hurt seems to be the suggested remedy. Amen.

May 28   Amos 5:11; 8:4-8

EMPLOYER AND EMPLOYEE

A phase of this competitive system works out in relations between employer and employee. Does it become a cause of sin – on both sides? It can.

Here is an employer who is gentle, kind and desires to be Christian. Their Christianity tells them that they should do to others as they would like for others to do to them, if they were the employee, instead of the employer. If they were the employee, they would like to be paid at least minimum wage. But they must compete with others, so they hire at the lowest possible wage and still get workers. The competitiveness loads the situation against their being Christian – causing them to sin.

Some of these employees may be young people, and because of the insufficiency of their salaries they are tempted, yes, influenced to sell drugs, sell their bodies, steal, cheat, etc., especially those from poor families who are trying to help a single parent who is also making low wages. The employer's forcing down income becomes a cause of sin. Or the employee may not go that far, but may simply take it out in resentment. To harbor resentment according to the Bible is sin. The system causes that sin too. **However, we always have a choice**!

It could be the employee's resentment is shown in doing poor work, loafing on the job. Skimpy work is not honest, stealing time from your employer is not honest – it is sin. Again the system may be the cause, **but it is our choice**. **We choose to do right or we choose to do wrong, regardless of the system.**

Prayer for today: O Father, Help us to work our way out of seemingly impossible situations. And let us not produce situations that torment our very souls. Amen.

May 29   Matthew 26:52; Psalm 68:30; Isaiah 2:4

ANOTHER CAUSE OF SIN – WAR

Another phase of selfish competition is war. Selfish competition works out into international relationships and then – war!

Let's not be completely hopeless about eliminating war. Look how far we've come! The Old Testament says, "*In the spring, at the time that kings go off to war...David remained at Jerusalem.*" (2 Samuel 11:1 & 1 Chronicles 20:1) Kings went to battle when springtime came exactly as a farmer went to his spring planting – and as regularly. It was news when David remained at home. We have come a long way since then. Some countries are beginning to be more conscientious of each other and when their country is attacked instead of turning their heads and looking the other way, the government and people are profoundly stirred. A conscientious country banished slavery and it can banish war.

We are not more war-like than we used to be, we are far less. But science has thrown us together as a world by its rapid communications, and it has at the same time put into some of our countries hands terrible weapons of destruction. The result is FEAR! That fear has driven us to war either as nations or individuals, not because we enjoy war.

If the very center of life could be changed from competition to co-operation, then war against nations as well as war against individuals could be greatly reduced. But war is almost inevitable in a world and/or society based on competition. Let's pray for a co-operative world as a whole.

Prayer for today: O Father, we stand before this appalling fact of war. If we ever needed Your help, we need it here. And if we ever needed to follow You, it is here at this place. Help us to do it now! Amen.

May 30   1 Thessalonians 5:12-15; Hebrews 12:14

ANOTHER CAUSE OF SIN – CONFLICT

Yet another phase of selfish competition is conflict among families, friends, church members, co-workers, etc. Again selfish competition works its way into our relationships and then – conflict.

These situations are not without hope. They are acts of the sinful nature and that sinful nature is contrary to the Holy Spirit. (Galatians 5:17): *"For the sinful nature desires what is contrary to the Spirit, and the Spirit what is contrary to the sinful nature. They are in conflict with each other, so that you do not do what you want."* We can't always do just what we want. Selfishness is wrong. Instead of shrugging our shoulders when we see trouble about to explode, form a conscience. A good, moral conscience can banish a world of trouble before it leads to sin.

If the very center of lives could be changed from competition to co-operation, then conflict would drop off like leaves drop from trees in the fall. In our individual world based on competition conflict is inevitable.

Selfish competition makes people sin the major of collective sins – conflict with one another. Therefore we need and want a co-operative individual world.

Prayer for today: O Father, we stand before this ugly fact of conflict. We need Your help here, and we need it now. Help us to follow You. Amen.

May 31   Proverbs 6:12-14; 16-19

DEVELOP AN ATTITUDE AGAINST CONFLICT

Doesn't it seem the right thing to do to protect the defenseless? Most, if not all of us have a built-in defense system.

The difference between offensive and defensive conflicts is hard to distinguish. Conflict causes people to sin in the following ways:

(1) It poisons the air with <u>lies</u>. The first casualty of conflict is <u>TRUTH</u>. You cannot stir up conflict unless you make the enemy a devil. Lying propaganda sees to that.

(2) Conflict poisons the air with <u>hate</u>. So – the second casualty is <u>LOVE</u>. Bitter, burning hate settles into the hearts and minds of those we influence and steps into our war against <u>whomever</u>. The very air around us becomes noxious with hate. You cannot breathe without breathing it, hellish hate.

(3) It causes people to <u>sin</u> against people. It cost many good and godly reputations to be destroyed directly or indirectly. What a waste of God's creation.

Prayer for today: O Father, we pray for an end to this madness. Amen.

June 1   Matthew 5:21-24; James 4:1-12

DEVELOPING AN ATTITUDE AGAINST CONFLICT
– (Continued)

Continuing from yesterday – reason conflict causes sin –

1. Conflict kills the <u>conscience</u>. When you are out to destroy another person's reputation, for whatever reason, it hardens you. It takes away from <u>your</u> good conscience and kills it. Conflict does that to people.

2. It takes a person's finest <u>attributes</u> and uses them for no good. It takes on conceit, haughtiness, hatefulness and many other unchristian-like traits and turns them to destruction.

3. It <u>produces helplessness</u>. Many parents, spouses, children, family and friends weep helplessly over the ruined reputation of a loved one, whose reputation should not have been ruined at all. Is it right? No, it isn't right, it is evil. **But until the rights are no longer wronged, and the wrongs are righted, it is our job to pray.**

Prayer for today: O Father, Help us to show Your peace to everyone. And in doing so let that peace spread throughout our world. Amen.

June 2   Matthew 5:43-45; Romans 12:16-21

GOD'S PRESCRIPTION FOR CONFLICT

Over the course of our time here on this earth, we will have countless opportunities to be involved with others through relational, theological, philosophical and methodological differences. On occasions those differences may lead to conflict, and our opponent may appear to be our enemy. At such times, we as Christians, must remember the words of Jesus in (Matthew 5:43-45) – "*You have heard that it was said, 'Love your neighbor and hate your enemy.' But I tell you: Love your enemies and pray for those who persecute you, that you may be sons of your father in heaven. He causes his sun to rise on the evil and the good, and sends rain on the righteous and unrighteous.*"

God's prescription for conflict — <u>LOVE YOUR ENEMIES!</u> Pure and Simple.

Prayer for today: O Father, help us pursue a lifestyle that expresses Your love and grace as we relate to others. Amen.

June 3 — Amos 9:7; Luke 22:29; Acts 10:34-35; Colossians 3:11

ANOTHER CAUSE OF SIN – PREJUDICE

We have looked at two causes of sin in our social system – selfish competition and conflict. Now, let's look at a third – prejudice. It justifies and holds together a base for the idea of others being of little or no value, morally low – hence: cruelty, dislike, distrust, detested. What an error in our world!

Prejudice of <u>any kind</u> is self-starvation among many other things. A woman said, "Oh, can't I have an American doctor instead of this "foreign" doctor?" Why? This doctor had more than the average medical training, was a specialist in his medical field, an artist of very rare ability and a musician of high achievement, and a Christian gentleman. But this woman would close herself off from all that culture and skill because of one thing – <u>prejudice</u>. She was practicing self-starvation through prejudice. Prejudice caused her to sin against herself and the doctor.

When we open the door of our heart to people of all <u>races and class</u> as Christ did it will be a most enriching experience. What love, what friendships, what wisdom, what Christ-likeness, what nobility will come to us through that open door! Close your door of superiority and your life will be richer for it.

Prayer for today: O Father, open my heart wide to the people of every race and class and perhaps You too will come through that open door. Amen.

June 4   Ephesians 2:14-18; Revelation 5:9-10

PREJUDICE AND SNOBBERY

Yesterday we talked about opening our heart to the people of another race and class. But if you open the door, you must go through it, people will know whether it is sincerely open and if you have sincerely gone through it.

Some new missionaries on board a flight to a new country were studying the native language. A person who had visited this country before listened to them as they tried to get the proper pronunciation. Finally she spoke to them saying, "Of course I believe in speaking the language correctly, but I don't believe in pronouncing it like the "foreigner." Is she still wondering why the "foreigner" is so hard to understand? She would leave this country starved, having denied herself many enriching friendships, because she felt a <u>superior</u> attitude and demonstrated snobbery.

An upper-class youth rescued a boy, known to have AIDS, from drowning and his parents were angry with him, saying he should have let the boy drown rather than touch an AIDS victim. But if that youth had let the boy die, something would have died in him. He chose to let servant-hood find brother-hood.

Peter came close to keeping his superior-hood, *"Surely not, Lord! Nothing impure or unclean has ever entered my mouth."* (Acts 11:8). But he threw it all away, went to the Gentiles and found brother-hood. Had he refused to open his heart, he would have shriveled and died. You and I will shrivel and inwardly die if we refuse to open our hearts to every person, of every race, of every class. **It will be worth it all!** Do not let race and class prejudice shut you out from that!!

Prayer for today: O Father, I pray for victory at this place – the place of my prejudices. If I do not gain victory here I will be poorer for it. Amen.

June 5   Matthew 19:16-26; James 2:1-4

ECONOMIC INEQUALITY – CAN CAUSE SIN

In tracing back various causes of sin we come across the fact that unequal wealth can be a cause of a great deal of sin. First, it can work harm to the individual who has more than they know what to do with. It often produces in that person the feeling that they must in some way deserve all this and that God must be pleased with them, when the fact is they may have inherited it all from hard-working parents, grandparents or such. Inequalities can produce <u>superiority complexes</u>. We often think because we have more we are worth more, which isn't necessarily so. It might make us decidedly worthless. Without it we might give a <u>great</u> contribution to life, with it we may only give contributions. It also sets the stage for lack of ambition, selfish devotion to pleasure and self-gratification, and wasted time in general.

Again, it can create a mentality which tries to justify this condition of inequality. Rationalization sets in and with it an unconscious hypocrisy. Furthermore, it keeps us from fellowship. How can you have fellowship across these chasms? One of the most severe charges that can be drawn up against those with much wealth and those with not so much is that it sends division through life and separates person from person. And one very deep need in our world is fellowship. The Christian must question everything that makes fellowship more difficult.

Let's not allow inequality to put up barriers!

Prayer for today: O Father, You did come to break down barriers, forgive us that we have set up barriers between ourselves and others for whatever reason. Amen.

June 6   Leviticus 19:13-15; Job 32:13-22

INEQUALITY – CAN CAUSE SIN (Continued)

Unequal wealth can cause hurt to those who have more, but it can also cause hurt to those who have less. It tends to create in one a superiority complex and in the other an inferiority complex. In a society where we tend to seek to acquire more and more, people are judged as to their financial worth, so – not having wealth brands one as inferior. This is a positive sin against personality.

Furthermore, from a Christian standpoint it stacks the cards against inward peace and harmonious relationships. Irritation and bitterness are produced. It is not enough to preach that such bitterness is unchristian. We must uproot the cause that produces that bitterness.

To preach contentment and good cheer to the underprivileged, while leaving untouched the cause of their gloom and lack of contentment, is to add insult to injury. "An optimist is hopeful about other people's troubles." We have no message for that gloom and misery unless we are willing to work at uprooting that misery. And what is the root? The society we live in is financially controlled to intercept the gains of economic progress, by means of higher prices to consumers and financial gain to insiders. Note the phrase: "To intercept the gains." When we realize that this produces bitterness will that bitterness not continue until the cause is removed?

Prayer for today: O Father, we pray that You will help us to hold steady here, and not excuse or explain away, but in Your name be straightforward and courageous. Amen.

June 7   John 18:25; Acts 10:28;
                                    Philippians 2:14-16

NATIONALISM – ANOTHER CAUSE OF SIN

The greatest danger to the peace of the world is nationalism. It has taken that lovely sentiment called patriotism and turned it into a deadly enemy. It causes people to sin where they otherwise would not. The people of one nation usually have no reason to hate the people of another nation. But nationalism takes hold of people, subjects them to propaganda, instills fears, inspires hate, puts weapons into their hating, frightened hands and explodes them against the people of another country. Why? Who knows? The smiling devil that inspires this madness is nationalism.

Nationalism becomes preposterous beyond words, reaches in and puts its dominating, determined hand on the one thing that is sacred between us and God, our conscience, and says that it is sovereign in there. God is secondary, nationalism is primary.

This nationalism, sees that Christianity is a brother-hood stretching across all barriers and since Christianity is determined on brother-hood of all people everywhere, hence: nationalism looks on Christianity as its most deadly foe. So it produces a new paganism that would oust Christianity, or it proceeds to render Christianity as weak and harmless to their cause, which amounts to the same thing.

The Church must continue to preach the gospel of "The Savior and Redeemer of all nations and races" this gospel bridges over all worldly and human changes.

The gospel "bridges" these canyons but nationalism rules at both ends of the bridge. And Christianity rules over what? The canyons – emptiness!

Prayer for today: O Father, we are asked to follow another god, nationalism. How can we? We love our native land, but we love You more and we love You supremely. Amen.

June 8   Exodus 1:14; Jeremiah 34:8-17

CONTROL – ANOTHER CAUSE OF SIN

Another cause of sin – the control of one group of people by another group or control of one person over another.

We know that government control in general has been the cause of an amazing amount of advancement to minorities as well as others. Nevertheless, one groups rule and authority over another group of people for a long period of time, no matter how well intended, causes resentment on both sides and resentment leads to sin. This is not limited to groups, such as governments, religious institutions, etc., it happens in our individual homes and the result is the same: life is weakened, loses initiative, is driven down, loses self esteem, loses freedom, becomes untruthful, not dependable, and resentful, that is certainly the tendency of people controlled by another.

It also causes inner deterioration in the person or persons doing the controlling. Because they believe in freedom for themselves, but feeling compelled to deny it to another, an inner contradiction takes place. A defense mechanism builds up which fights against their personal ideals. Deterioration is bound to become a fact under these circumstances.

When control is out of control everybody loses.

Prayer for today: O God, our Father, help us to share our freedoms with everyone, everywhere, for we know if we do not share them, we cannot keep them. Amen.

June 9   Jeremiah 22:13-16

ANOTHER THING THAT CAN CAUSE SIN – INADEQUATE
HOUSING

Our weakest and most unfortunate members of society have
been crowded into dwellings called low income housing – "proj-
ects" for short. Here many families are compelled to live in a small
overcrowded space. In these cramped conditions they eat, sleep, and
live. At every moment of their lives in that place called home where
their human personality is invaded. There is no privacy. Now, preach
to that group of human beings that modesty is a virtue, and purity
is a necessity and quarreling is bad, and your words sound hollow.
Why? Because their entire situation is loaded against modesty,
against purity, and against a good temper. Resentment may follow.

The picture haunts our imagination: Drive-by shootings, killing
of innocent people, drugs, rapes, and much, much more. Young
people growing up in such surroundings may be hindered in their
battle for success. The very physical basis of their life works against
our message. But it is our Christian duty to make sure they know
there is something better, much better to life. When the potential
for better is present in a life let's be there to help them along to a
brighter future, a future that includes the One who *"will meet all our
needs according to his glorious riches in Christ Jesus."* (Philippians
4:19). And even more importantly, know the LOVE OF CHRIST,
*"and to know this love surpasses knowledge – that you may be filled
to the measure of the fullness of God."* (Ephesians 3:19).

Prayer for today: O Father, we bring to You those who are crowded
in inadequate housing as well as the homeless. Forgive us that we
have not done more to change these situations in our civilization.
Help us to do more. Amen

June 10   Matthew 20:7; Deuteronomy 14:15

LOW WAGES AND UNEMPLOYMENT CAN CAUSE SIN

Low wages can set the stage for sin. The temptation to be dishonest is very great when your income is small and inadequate. The story is told of a little girl from a poor family, who went to visit a wealthier family where there were many beautiful dolls, and she had none. She felt she had a right to one, so she stole one, and for many years suffered untold misery from her sensitive conscience. Her poverty made it easier for her to take that doll and suffer those years of misery. Stealing may happen more often when money is scarce. However, that fact doesn't make it right or even excusable.

But if low wages can cause sin, unemployment is worse still. It causes deterioration. To be unwanted and unneeded in human society is enough to take the light out of our eyes and make our head droop. But in some an amazing thing is – often the light still shines in the eyes and the head is still held high after months of fruitless searching. This has to be admired as a faith-like attitude.

It is all so unnecessary and inevitable, but in a co-operative system it would not be. Let us therefore stand for a co-operative system, and give what strength and influence we have to bring it to fruition. We probably all know someone who is unemployed, don't stand around and watch day after day as they deteriorate.

Unemployment not only can cause sin in the victim, but also in those who allow it to continue, because they selfishly refuse to co-operate in ending it. Are we all guilty?

Prayer for today: O Father, Our Father, forgive us that we have tolerated so long this inhumanity, and give us, we pray, the strength and wisdom and courage to help end it. Amen.

June 11   Acts 10:19-20; Philemon 1:8-17

THE EXISTENCE OF CLASS

Another cause of sin in society is the existence of class. As long as society is based on class, causes of sin will be in the social structure.

The consciousness of class produces the consciousness of those who are not of that class. That produces division. In that division, misunderstanding arises.

Some wealthy people may seem to have inflated egos and exploit the poor. It isn't always so. There are many wealthy people who are the salt of the earth.

Class divisions cause us to feel class-pain and class-disabilities, but not human pain and human disabilities. It causes us to sin the sin of indifference, of being insensitive, to people of another class. It tends to dry up our sympathy for them. Therefore these class distinctions turn the situation in an unchristian direction and make it easy for people to sin against those of another class.

We must not think these class divisions are rooted either in nature or in the will of God. They are rooted in the will of humanity. They are nothing less than artificial barriers placed by the wrong organizations of human society between person and person.

This idea of class on both sides can cause sin, and its roots must be cut if we are to live victoriously in the fullest sense!

Prayer for today: O Father, whose heart went across these barriers and gathered people of all classes into a new living fellowship where there was no class, give us, that same spirit. Amen.

June 12   Matthew 19:3-10; Galatians 3:28

CERTAIN ATTITUDES TOWARD WOMEN CAN CAUSE SIN

With all the progress women have made in our modern society, our economic and political system is still largely the result of man's organizing. And in the organizing, woman has been fitted into it largely on the basis of a sex-being, and she is supposed to be treated and act as such. Even though women's organizations have tried to change the image for today's woman, women, in general has accepted the false mentality and has given herself the petty business of being attractive to men. This has been the cause of much sin in human society.

The position of women is rapidly changing throughout most of the world. There have been and will continue to be many casualties in the transition from woman as a sex-being to woman as a person with equal rights and duties. Women, in driving this new force called freedom, is making a wreck of many refined feminine styles and many strong distinguishing characteristics. But we cannot stop until woman arrives at the place where Jesus placed her as a human personality and NOT a mere sex-object. She must be given an equal place and an equal opportunity in the reconstruction of the world. Women need to step in the system with a spirit of peace, not a take-over spirit.

Prayer for today: O Father, help women to be treated as equal persons and help them to set up a Christ of peace on every dividing line in human life. Amen.

June 13   Ezekiel 3:5-6; 12:18-20; Isaiah 33:15-16;
                           Philippians 4:19

FINANCIAL INSECURITY

This cause of sin is mentioned last, for in many ways it is the most prolific cause of sin in human society. Under the principle of unrestricted competition, financial security can decline quickly for both the employer and the employee. For both of them financial security can reach a vanishing point. Under unrestricted competition many business ventures fail. How can a business person be sure they do not belong to a failing business venture? How can that person be sure they belong to the successful few? And if they are sure they do belong to that successful few, can they be sure of their moral position, because in a competitive society, has their success caused the failure of others? When we have more business than we really need, someone will have less than they need. However, we never feel that we have more business than we need, no matter what business we are in. So it is hard to be morally uncomfortable in business, or is it? The very fear of insecurity drives us to acquire much more than we actually need in hopes of meeting that insecurity. This creates an enlightening greed that is appalling. And now to the wage earner: Their financial destiny is not in their own hands, nor in the hands of their co-workers, but in the hands of those who own the capital. They therefore live in constant dread of joining the growing ranks of the unemployed. That haunting fear is one of the most desperate things in human life. It may make people feel inferior and destroy them and their usefulness to society. In this way financial insecurity causes fear – the employer is afraid if a higher salary is paid, then their competitor will undercut them and they will go under financially; the worker is afraid of losing their job. What a mess!

Prayer for today: O Father, help us to produce a system in which fear will have no place. We could do it if we knew how to love. Help us to love, we pray! Amen.

June 14 Matthew 14:15-16; Luke 3:15; 1 John 3:17

WHAT CAN WE DO ABOUT IT?

We have seen that certain things in our society set the stage for sin, can cause sin: selfish competition, the wage system under competition, controversy, prejudice, economic equality, the existence of classes, unemployment, control of one person or group by another person or group, nationalism, wrong attitudes toward women, and financial insecurity. These things, and many others, deeply rooted in the structure of our society block living victoriously. They do not make living victoriously impossible, but certainly make it very difficult, and often under the pressure of these things, living a victorious life in the individual is suppressed completely. If Christian religion has no message at this point, if it undertakes to live victoriously without facing these issues, then the method used is evasion, and this violates two fundamental principles of living victoriously, namely, honesty and courage to face facts. To attempt to win by strategic retreat is to run into the pitfall of mental insincerity and without mental sincerity living a victorious life is impossible. The process of evasion is therefore self-defeating. Obviously, the first thing to do is look at these things as causes of sin and therefore an evil in society – something to be eradicated and not tolerated. Many think these things in our society's structure cannot be done away with. They accept them as fatalistic. This defeatist attitude is a big problem. It must be broken. Just as an individual in order to have personal victory over personal sins must have faith that it can be done, so we must have faith that these social ills are disease, and as such are no normal part of human living and can be eradicated. The health of our society demands it.

Prayer for today: O Father, we need to be reborn spiritually and mentally at this place, we need to come into a faith that believes anything is possible with You. Give us this faith for our society. Amen.

June 15   Matthew 27:39-42; Acts 24:5-6

FACING SOME HALF-TRUTHS

Yesterday we said that one of the first things to be done is have faith that these social evils can be overcome. In order to have this faith we must clear our minds of half-truths, for if we get caught in these half-truths, we will never be able to acquire full faith.

1. Half-truth – Individuals can rise above any combination of social circumstances.
2. Half-truth – Since individuals control institutions and systems, it is enough to change individuals.
3. Half-truth – You can change society without changed individuals.
4. Half –truth – Society is relatively immoral and man is relatively moral.

Half-truths can become more dangerous than whole lies. For there is nothing in a whole lie to hold good people to its loyalty, but a half-truth often gains the loyalty of good people, and with their eyes fastened on the half-truth they are oblivious of the lurking evil it can cause. Jesus was crucified on half-truths. Religious people, seeing those half-truths, were blind to the other side and allowed themselves to commit the worst deed in human history. They did it clinging to half-truths as justification of what they were doing. (He did say that He was king. He did say if they destroyed this temple, He would rebuild it). He said almost everything they accused Him of – minus their half-truth twist.

Today Christ and His Kingdom are being crucified on half-truths. Wrong ideas cause as much damage as wrong wills. The wrong ideas are usually half-right ideas. Again it is the fatal <u>twist</u> that sends the whole thing in a wrong direction.

Prayer for today: O Father, You suffered and are still suffering from half-truths, open our eyes that we might see if we hold any half-truth that keeps us from seeing things as they truly are. Amen.

June 16   1 Kings 17:1-24; 2 Kings 17:6-11;
                           Proverbs 22:6

INDIVIDUALS AND THEIR CIRCUMSTANCES

The first half-truth that we must notice is – individuals can rise above any combination of social circumstances.

The possibility of using one's adverse circumstances and sufferings to further their spiritual life must be understood. This is all right for the spiritually mature, for the exceptional person, but for the ordinary Christian it is hard to understand. And if it is difficult for ordinary Christians, what about the people who have no Christian faith? Can they use pain and sorrow? Some Christians like to believe that to USE suffering is the privilege of the ordinary Christian. We cannot close our eyes to the fact that **the majority of people do not change their circumstances, but are changed by them**. Someone has said that if a letter were sent to that most "influential person" called "Circumstance," most of us could end it by saying, "I am, Sir, your most obedient servant." For <u>most of us are</u> the obedient servants of our circumstances. We must think in terms of the weaker members and produce a society in which it will be easier for them to grow. **All of us are weak the first of life, and it is at that weakest period of life that we are most conditioned by our surroundings and influenced by it. For the sake of each succeeding generation we must produce a society that will <u>work</u> <u>with</u> and <u>not</u> <u>against</u> the total growth of Youth. When we are young most of us are not self-contained, but environment-conditioned.**

Prayer for today: O Father, forgive us for producing a society which cause little ones to stumble, and help us to make it right, for their best interest as well as for ours. Amen.

June 17   Luke 11:42; 24:52-53; Acts 17:5-7

WILL CHANGED PEOPLE CHANGE SOCIETY?

We know society is made up of individuals so – if a sufficient number of individuals change, society will also change. Changed people <u>have</u> changed society. But – these are only half-truths. It is not completely true that individuals make up society. Society is made up of individuals, but it is also made up of inherited customs and attitudes which have become a part of the social structure and which exist apart from the will of the individual. To change the individual "will" may leave entirely intact this inherited social structure. Let's look back in history for example: Changed individual slave owners did not get rid of the slave system. That could only be accomplished by what someone called a "wide-scale frontal attack." Both in England and America slavery was ousted by the frontal attack of legislation. It is true that other factors played a part in abolishing slavery, but it was only after adequate people at the government level attacked it was it completely abolished. An attack on a personal level alone would have left the slavery system to this day. Government coercion supplied personal change to those slave owners who did not want to change. Change can start where the individual will is directed toward the change of a system, however, that change will not take place, in the social system, unless you have this wide-scale, concerted, frontal attack. But, suppose, instead of our changed will being directed toward social change, it stops at the half-way mark of "contentment" then this is even worse, this often happens. Our Christianity instead of becoming the life of social change often takes the place of social change. It sometimes makes our attention glance either toward ourselves or toward heaven, and leaves the essential problems of life untouched. Half-change may become whole perversions. Change must be complete.

Prayer for today: O Father, Put the content of social change into my individual change. Amen.

June 18   Proverbs 4:23, Isaiah 1:16-17;
                                                Jeremiah 1:6-10, Matthew 12:33

CAN SOCIETY BE CHANGED WITHOUT CHANGED INDIVIDUALS?

Another half-truth is you can change society without changed individuals. The individually-minded say that the greatest necessity is for changed individuals, and the society-minded say the greatest necessity is for a changed society. Each contains a half-truth, but only a half-truth. It is only a half-truth to say that you can change society and neglect individual change.

A changed society needs changed individuals to sustain it. The whole outer structure of life rests on that delicate thing called character. If character breaks, confidence breaks, and if confidence breaks, society breaks. Take communism for instance: it is not as strong as it once was, it seems to be declining – hopefully with this decline the dynamics of communism and the confidence people once had in it's destructive ways will weaken until a new generation of individuals will not embrace it but will secure and support the structure of a better and different society placed on them. The best plans of a changed society need changed individuals to make it work.

As an individual member of society if you see a smaller immediate advantage compared to a larger long-term advantage, have enough character to resist the immediate in behalf of the future. A changed society needs changed people to keep it changed.

Prayer for today: O Father, it is here that we need your power. For how can we go into a new day with old life? Cleanse our heart, that we may do our part in cleansing society to its greatest limits. Amen.

June 19   Deuteronomy 16:18-20;
                                 Isaiah 59:14; Habakkuk 1:4

A CORRECTION

Yesterday we insisted that you cannot change society without
changed individuals to sustain those changes. But a correction to
restore a balance needs to be made at this point – a changed society
WOULD tend to change individuals. That is a point which Christian
leaders have largely missed. We should welcome these wide-scale
basic changes in the structure of society in the very interests of individual change.

We know now the power of our environment in the making of
us as individuals. Many things which we think to be inborn in us are
actually socially influenced into our life at an early age, so early that
we mistake them for being innate.

We know this to be true – take a child out of an undesirable environment at birth, let the child be subjected to a new social heredity
in which it would know nothing of its so-called inferior birth, and
let the child be given the privileges, education and culture of other
children in that better environment, and in almost every child a new
personality will emerge, whereas had that child stayed in the lesser
environment most of the time the child would have taken on the likeness of its surroundings and would have caught the average outlook
and conformed to it.

A competitive system works against individual change at every
point; a co-operative system would work toward change at every
point. You can make a co-operative system by the very things so
deeply rooted in spiritually changed character, namely, a change
from Ego-centered to Christ-centered, from Self to God and others.
In living a changed life in such a system you would be working, not
against the grain of the social system, but with it.

Prayer for today: O Father, we pray that we will have a changed
society, that we may more easily have changed individuals. For we
know You want to see people changed for Your glory. Amen.

June 20   Exodus 23:1-8; Leviticus 19:13-15

THE HALF-TRUTH OF MORAL PEOPLE
AND IMORAL SOCIETY

To insist that a person as an individual is comparatively more moral than society is partly true. A person as an individual is not prepared to do many things which as a member of society is expected to do: for instance, ruthlessly compete to ruin others.

If the system were reversed – and we were not in a competitive society but in a co-operative society – society would be comparatively moral and individual comparatively immoral. There are organizations and their basis is sharing fellowship –**according to each need and from each according to their ability.** This collective system in its organization is fair and loyal, but now and again individuals break this fairness and loyalty by individual wrong moral acts. Those individuals are not as moral as their collective fellowship organization. It would be the same on a wider-scale when society comes to a co-operative system – it would be moral society and immoral individuals.

It has been said that because society is immoral this is all rooted in our nature, and must be dealt with as such, again this is only half-truth. What seems rooted in our nature may be rooted in wrong social environment, namely, a competitive system. Change that system to a co-operative one and many things which now appear rooted in our nature will be seen to be rooted in a wrong social environment and are not born within us, but collectively imposed upon us. Much that seems to be our nature actually comes from the way we were raised under a system which produces wrong attitudes. This gives us a basis for hope rather than a basis for pessimism, for WE CAN CHANGE what we have made, namely, a wrong social environment.

Prayer for today: O Father, we come to You for strength and courage and clear-sighted love that we may not sink back into the pessimism of our natural self, but that we may rise to the optimism of Your redemptive grace and power. Amen.

June 21   Matthew 11:23; 24:42-51; 25:1 & 13

THE HALF-TRUTH OF THE COMING OF THE KINGDOM AS ONLY GRADUAL

Modern liberalism has insisted that the coming of the Kingdom will be by gradual changes. It has drawn its inspiration from two sources: from modern democracy and from certain teachings of the New Testament which teach a gradualism. Modern democracy has committed itself to a faith in democratic processes of change according to constitutions. This means by vote instead of by sudden, catastrophic revolution. Liberalism has felt that the processes of the Kingdom would be the same. In this they have been supported by passages in the New Testament – (Matthew 13:33) *"...yeast...mixed into flour until it worked all through the dough."*(Mark 4:28) *"... first the stalk, then the head, then the full kernel in the head."* These passages seemed to fit in with the spirit of democratic, evolutionary change. But with the decay of faith in the democratic government much of this faith in gradualism has decayed with it. Dictatorships, veiled and overt, have risen. Now liberalism is partaking of that changed outlook. It is saying in some places that change can only come suddenly and in a catastrophic manner. This change of policy shows how liberalism is dependent on modern culture; in fact, liberalism is modern culture. It is most unstable. It should hold to its principle of gradualism. For that lets the responsibility rest where it should rest, namely, on Christians, to bring in that Kingdom by individual and collective endeavor co-operating with the redemptive God. This outlook keeps us from flying off at tangents of various short cuts and keeps us with our souls at work. For gradualism in the New Testament is a living part of the gospel. It is ineradicable. But it is only half-truth – we should remember that. There is another side.

Prayer for today: O Father, keep us from evading responsibility by throwing it on You, as well as future circumstances, and help us to fulfill our purpose to Your glory. Amen.

June 22   Matthew 13:31-33; Mark 4:26-28;
                                 Luke 17:20-21

THE HALF-TRUTH OF THE COMING OF THE KINGDOM AS
ONLY SUDDEN

Modern fundamentalism in many cases has rejected the principle of gradualism and has said in the Second Coming of Christ the
Kingdom will in fact be set up. This coming will be sudden and catastrophic. In this they have been supported by scripture in the New
Testament which teach His coming as a thief in the night, by the
nobleman who went into a far country to receive a Kingdom and to
return to set it up, and so on. That the New Testament does teach this
sudden and catastrophic phase of the coming of the Kingdom there
is no doubt whatever. BUT it is a fact that holding onto this phase
alone has produced a mentality that has withdrawn interest from
social change by gradual process, has made those who hold onto it
discount great changes, and has made them look for things to get
worse in order for a final, sudden triumph at the coming of Christ.
This has been and is a moral and social drain. Christian thought has
moved back and forth from one to the other again and again – thesis
producing antithesis. It is now time to combine the two – come to
the synthesis. And the synthesis is this: There is in the pages of the
New Testament both the teaching of gradualism and the teaching of
the apocalyptic. Both are there and are integral parts of the account.
They cannot be explained away, for we need both phases. Each is a
half-truth that needs the other to complete it. We need to understand
that the task is ours and must be assumed as such, and we must also
see that it is God's and that He will complete it, perhaps even when
we least expect it.

Prayer for today: O Father, we thank You that You have taught us
that the task is ours and the communication is Yours, and the task is
Yours and the communication ours. We shall work it out together,
and together we will triumph. Amen.

June 23   Matthew 24:14-30; 25:1-13

THE SYNTHESIS
(A complex whole formed by combining)

From many angles we have been working toward a synthesis. The Christian world is working through these half-truths to a synthesis, a larger truth, a combined whole. That larger truth is that the New Testament teaches both.

Modern minds have hesitated to take the apocalyptic at its face value. They have thought it was something read into the account, but the extracting of it has been impossible. IT IS an integral part. (Matthew 24:36) – Jesus says, "*No one knows about that day or hour, not even the angels in heaven, not the Son, but only the Father.*" Should we not look on every hour as the possible hour?

To accept this synthesis of gradualism and apocalyptic would leave us just where we should be as Christians – within the stream of human history and yet above it, within the process of the world to suffer and bleed and in that way remake it for God's glory. As Christians should we be above this process of the world as its judges through Him who is to be its final Judge?

Prayer for today: O Father, You are leading us into the larger truth of the Kingdom. We accept it, for the Kingdom is our one and only hope. Amen.

June 24   Matthew 23:4; John 12:31-32;
                          Romans 14:10-11; James 2:12-13;
                          Revelation 2:23

IS THE CHURCH TO TAKE THE ROLL OF JUDGE?

Let's look at one more partial emphasis. There are those who would tell us that the function of the Church is to stand back from all these movements of social reconstruction, to commit to none of them, but to be the constant judge of all. This would be an escape-mentality.

Isn't this escaping from the problem by assuming the role of judge, instead of being in it as a participant, suffering along with it, and in that way saving it from within? If we assume the role of judge in the struggle ahead of us, would we not turn out to be a Pharisee, instead of a Christian? Did not Jesus reject all the methods of trying to save the world by standing outside the process? Did He not accept the way of standing within it, making its sorrows, its problems, its sins His very own, the cross consequently becoming inevitable?

We as Christians must reveal the Christian attitude: *"For God did not send his Son into the world to condemn the world, but to save the world through him."* (John 3:17). Jesus rejects the role of judge. But a strange thing happens. Through this very identification He becomes Judge. The Christian Church today can only become the judge of actions of social reconstruction to the degree that she is in the actions and suffers vicariously. The Church gains a moral authority which makes her a judge, not otherwise. To take the attitude of an indifferent judge is to assume and unchristian attitude.

Prayer for today: O Father, You judged us from a cross. Help us to gain our moral authority over the world from the same place – the place of our own suffering for others. Amen.

June 25   Luke 1:78; 7:16; Philippians 2:5-8;
                           Hebrews 2:9-18

VISITED AND REDEEMED

We saw yesterday that the only way of redemption is for the Christian to get into these actions and make a difference from the inside. It will not do to assume the role of judge and leave it at that. As this is essential to the whole Christian attitude we must look at it firmly. Zacharias said a penetrating thing in (Luke 1:68 KJV), *"Blessed be the Lord God of Israel; for he hath visited and redeemed his people."* Note the phrase, "<u>visited and redeemed</u>." Zacharias probably had little idea just how amazing in its sweep redemption was, and how deep the visitation.

For in the redeeming of the world God might have issued orders from heaven or He might have been incarnate as a Teacher, an Example, or He might have done just what He did, namely, become One with us, and let everything that falls on us fall on Him – plus. This was visitation.

At this point the Church must follow in His steps. The Church must not merely issue condemnations of the social system from its sheltered sanctuaries; it must not be a detached spectator of world struggles; it must not merely take the role of teacher – it MUST visit, and that visitation must mean what it meant in Christ visit – <u>a visitation that means identification</u>.

Can the Church become specific enough to save itself? Jesus' visitation was specific – ours must be too. It must be sufficiently specific to gain a specific cross. Dealing in pious generalities is usually evading the issues. We must find the places where the real issues are being debated and take sides.

If we refuse the visitation, we shall renounce the redemption. We cannot have one without the other.

Prayer for today: O Father, we pray that You will save us from the spirit that would save ourselves while others perish. Give us courage to be specific. Amen.

June 26   Matthew 18:6, 10, 14; 21; Hebrews 11:40

THE BLENDING OF TWO EMPHASES

We have now arrived at the place in our study where we can see the necessity of blending the individual and social into a living whole. Jesus did just that. Of Him it was said: *A bruised reed he will not break, And a smoldering wick he will not snuff out, Till he leads justice to victory. In his name the nations will put their hope.*" (Matthew 12:20).

Here we find this blend – tenderness toward individuals, a refusal to break the bruised reed or quench a smoldering wick and a demand for social justice. For "judgment" was not a deciding of legal points, but a giving of a fair, equal opportunity to all – the words "social justice" express it. First, there was tenderness toward individuals – the bruised reeds which have been bruised by storms of nature, or by the trampling of life. The gospel comes as an infinite tenderness to those who are hurt by the awful powers of unconscious nature, or by the conscious inhumanities of person to person, or bruised by their own follies and sins. Also to those who are a smoldering wick, those in whom life and hope are very dim, in whom the fires are about to go out, the gospel comes as an inspiration, hope, life. We must never fail the stricken individual by withholding this message of tender healing and life-healing hope, in the badly wounded world. However, even though we are interested in individuals we must not neglect to give our attention to and act on any opportunity that would end social injustices through which many lives are being bruised, and many being made to burn dimly. Just because we are passion-ately interested in individuals we must be passionately interested in social justice. You are really not interested in either in the fullest sense unless you are interested in both. Neither can be fully effective without the other.

Prayer for today: O Father, to You these two worlds of individual and social were one, help us to cease our divisions at this point and make them one. Amen.

June 27   Psalm 82:2-4; Proverbs 22:27;
                                   Isaiah 1:17; 59:14-15; Luke 11:42

THE MEANING OF JUSTICE

The blending we saw yesterday was that of <u>tenderness toward the individual and a stern demand for a social justice</u> – the bruised reed was not to be broken, and justice was to be sent forth to victory. <u>These two are integral parts of the work of Christ, so the scripture says</u>. If so, then we must look more closely at the meaning of "justice." It does have a history. It came down through Hebrew tradition, where the individual and the social emphases were one. The Jewish people in their corporate life were to express the will of God. **The idea of religion being a private affair between the soul and God is unthinkable to the Old Testament prophets. The nation as a nation was the chosen people of God, and as such were to express the mind of God in their total life. So the word "justice" came to express equality, fairness, divine law and divine love operating from the center of the whole life.**

Jesus took this same attitude. He expected the nation to exemplify the Kingdom. When they refused, He said, *"The Kingdom of God shall be taken from you, and given to a **nation** bringing forth the fruits thereof."* (Matthew 21:43 KJV). Note it was to a **nation**. His final appeal was to Jerusalem, representing the **nation**, *"O Jerusalem, Jerusalem...how often I have longed <u>to gather your children together</u>,"...* (To embody this Divine will), *"<u>but you were not willing</u>."* (Matthew 23:37). He also demanded of the cities of Capernaum and Bethsaida <u>a corporate</u> <u>repentance</u> because He had expected a <u>corporate obedience</u>. <u>(Matthew 11:20-24)</u>. We forget that particular scripture in the gospel and because we forget it, the world is corporately adrift, without guidance. We have allowed this scripture of the corporate expression of the will of God to largely drop out of Christianity. We must rediscover it – or allow humanity to perish through internal discord.

Prayer for today: O Father, You came to bring justice unto victory, help us to learn anew Your word and fearlessly apply it to our total living. If we do not, we perish. Amen.

June 28   Psalm 72:2; Isaiah 1:27; Amos 5:24

THE WISDOM OF THE RIGHTEOUS

We see that a very deep need is to put social justice, into human affairs. This passage concerning John the Baptist emphasizes the same: *"He will...turn the hearts of the fathers to their children, and the disobedient to the wisdom of the righteous – to make ready a people prepared for the Lord."* (Luke 1:17 KJV). Note: *"a people prepared,"* a nation was to stand ready to do the will of God. And how were they to be prepared? Two things – *by turning the hearts of the fathers to the children*; in other words, by making the generation now in power to cease from its own selfishness and to think in terms of making the rising generation better; this to be done by demonstrating – *"the wisdom of the righteous."* Note that phrase *"the wisdom of the righteous."*

It is true that what the poor and the homeless need is not charity but justice, and it needs to be said again and again. We have seen no wisdom in injustice – (unrighteousness). We have built a society in which those in control have intercepted the gains brought by science and technology and have kept a big part of those gains from passing on to the people, the result – economic disaster to too many. Each nation wants all the advantages, wealth, weapons, power, etc.; for itself regardless of what happens to others. The result? International anarchy, fear – and war! Talk about the Kingdom of God not being practical and workable? Let those who have not made a mess of things by injustice bring that criticism! This generation is disqualified.

A basic, complete justice for everybody would be social wisdom. If we will not listen to this word from the Bible, then we must listen to it spoken by fiery tongues of a world in flames. For God speaks! And the wisdom of the righteous is His message.

Prayer for today: O Father, we pray that You will save us from our own foolishness, and help us to be lovingly righteous in all of our relationships. And help us to begin now. Amen.

June 29   Habakkuk 2:4-14; Matthew 15:13;
                            Luke 10:18; Colossians 2:15

JUDGMENT UNTO VICTORY

Yesterday we saw that God speaks, and His word is that we should learn the wisdom of the righteous. But we are afraid for two reasons: it will cause loss to us, and it won't work.

We can't say that it will cost nothing to be righteous. You will have to have the selfish self removed before you can become fundamentally righteous and willing to give everybody an equal opportunity. It will mean a real renunciation – a fellowship of sharing. When the master in the parable said to the grumblers concerning his equality, where the last hired got as much as the first hired, "*Friend, I am not being unfair to you.*" (Matthew 20:13), he spoke to a common fear. We are afraid that an equal justice will do us wrong. And an equal justice <u>will</u> do us wrong if we benefit from our unsocial self. But a new, righteous, brotherly or sisterly self can be born, and to that person it can be said, "Friend, I am doing you no wrong; in fact, I do you supreme good." But we are afraid it won't work. Remember - the verse concerning Jesus says, "*Till He leads justice to victory.*" (Matthew 12:20). Will He, Can He do it? He is doing it! Today He is breaking down the unjust and decaying the social system. Injustices are breaking down. It is the hour of judgment – judgment in the sense of <u>condemnation</u>, in order that the hour of judgment in the sense of social justice might come. The condemnation falls on us that the construction might begin through us. He is leading justice to victory! The eternal God will not fail in His redemptive purpose and His redemptive purpose includes the total life.

Prayer for today: O Father, we thank You that this whole redemptive process is until Victory. I do not want to fail You. In the end there will be one word upon our lips "VICTORY!" Help us to take up that word now and make it our own. Amen.

June 30   Isaiah 50:5-10; 54:2-4, 10, 14, 17; John 6:68

OUR ONE HOPE

We need a renewing of hope. Attitudes of distrust and despair have bitten deep into our souls. And this is serious; <u>despair closes the doors against the redemptive purposes of God</u>. So – where shall we find a renewal of our hope?

The scriptures we have been studying say, *"In His name the nations will put their hope."* (Matthew 12:21). The hope lies with Him who will not break the bruised reed, and will lead justice to victory. In other words, our hope lies in the <u>ONE who blends in His message to humankind a tender redemptive-ness to the individual</u> **and** <u>a stern demand for social justice</u>. **These two together will equal victory.**

However, one without the other will not equal victory. Our hope does not lie in changed individuals alone. It may leave the social problems untouched.

Our conversion to Christ often has us going through a process of personal readjustment which leaves us confused by preconceived ideas about many things, not the least of those the knowledge of an unjust society. The content of social justice must be put into our new life with Christ. Social reconstruction without individual conversion will not lead to victory. Even a change of climate will leave untouched many of our inward maladjustments which would continue in any climate.

No, <u>our hope lies in neither social justice nor social reconstruction, but in</u> **CHRIST**, <u>**in Him is our hope**</u>.

Prayer for today: O Father, whether we take the road of personal need or the road of social reconstruction, they both lead us to Your feet. We are there, because You are the one hope for our troubled world – and for us. Amen.

**This information may be helpful for several pages following -

Definition of—

Idealism – the cherishing or pursuit of high principles, purposes, or goals that are thought to be in reality out of reach.

Idealist – a person who represents things as they might or should be rather than the way they are.

Realism – a person who tends to view or represent things as they really are.

Karl Marx – 1818-1883, German economist, philosopher and socialist.

Marxism – the system of thought developed by Karl Marx and Friedrich Engels, especially the doctrines that class struggle has been the main agency of historical change and that capitalism will inevitably be superseded by a socialist and classless society.

Socialism – a system of social organization in which the means of production and distribution of goods are owned and controlled collectively or by the government.

Capitalism – an economic system in which investment in and ownership of the means of production, distribution, and exchange of wealth is made and maintained chiefly by private individuals or corporations.

July 1   Ephesians 4:16; Colossians 1:17; 2:10; 3:14

THE HALF-WAY POINT

We have completed half our journey in our quest for Living Victoriously. One theme running through the pages, which will continue in the pages to come, is this – if we are to Live Victoriously, there must be NO paralyzing divisions, there must be UNITY. This is psychologically and spiritually sound. But we have only begun to see how wide this demand for unity will be. It must take in everything. We saw that there must be no conflicting division between the conscious and the subconscious mind. The process in which mental harmony is produced is by making the subconscious conscious. In other words there should be no hidden disagreement between the conscious and the subconscious minds. We also saw that there must be no conflicting division in the conscious mind itself. When we try to give ourselves to a mutually competing end, we find defeat. There are some things that cannot exist together without causing paralysis. If we are going to have victory we must decide between them. Again, there must be nothing between us and God. Every barrier between His will and our will must be removed. And now we can see the necessity for a greater unity – the unity between the individual and society. If we allow a division to grow between these two through lack of emphasis on either, there will be spiritual defeat. The social without the personal is a body without a soul, and the personal without the social is a soul without a body – one is a corpse and the other a ghost. But together they make a living person. This division between the individual and the social has been the root cause of the major defeats of religion in modern life. The hope of the world is in healing this division. In order to get victory are you prepared to heal that division **as far as you are concerned**?

Prayer for today: O Father, You are leading us to unity. Help us to hold back at no point, but to go forward to complete unity. Amen.

July 2   Matthew 7:15-27; 23:2-3

UNITY OF THE IDEAL AND REAL

Yesterday we begin to see how wide the demand for unity will be. This demand for unity will confront us at the place of the ideal and the real, of theory and practice.

Are you an idealist or a realist? If you say you are an idealist and pity those who say they are realist, have you ever thought that you just might be wrong and they might be right?

Would we be prejudice of a truth if it came from Karl Marx? (Karl Marx – 1818-1883, German economist, philosopher, and socialist). Well, we will have to get over those prejudices if we are going to discover reality and through it victory. Marx proposed the idea of the unity of theory and practice. This means that you have only one theory and you put it into practice, at least in its beginning. The only thing we really believe in is the thing we believe in enough to put it into practice – at lest in the beginning. This unity of theory and practice searches us deeply and should prove a cleansing effect to Christianity.

Someone says that the next giant step forward for Christianity is to get rid of idealism. Just what does this mean? The belief is that we have built up high ideals as mental compensation for our not so high ideal practice. **The very fact that we hold these high ideals gives us comfort that we are a person of superior character, at least, in our own imagination. This compensates for our lower behavior and excuses us, or lets us down easy.** Our mental world becomes a world of fantasy while something else holds us in reality, because reality holds us at the place of action (practice).

Must idealism go and realism replace it or can they be united?

Prayer for today: O Father, we need Your guidance at this place. Help us to be willing to let go of our ideals if they interfere with reality, for we must be real. Amen.

July 3   1 Corinthians 6:20; 2 Corinthians 3:13;
                                Philippians 3:4-7

LOSING OUR IDEALS TO FIND THEM AGAIN

Yesterday we said that one of the first steps toward unity of life is to break down separation between idealism and realism. To have unity one or the other must go, or they must come together. To totally reject idealism, would be to reject that on which much of society turns. Idealism is profoundly irreligious, because it distorts Christian religion into something unreal. The ideal of false-Christianity consists in the separation of desire and love, through which love becomes an ideal, and desire is left to control and determine action. Love becomes a feeling that accompanies the contemplation of an idea.

If we lose idealism, does it mean that we should have no ideas? On the contrary, if we should lose idealism as something built up above and apart from life, if we should plant it into the soil of the real, our ideals would spring up again and bloom into renewed beauty. We should lose them and find them again. It is like this – now we do not have them, for they stand apart from life; then we would have them, because they would be deeply rooted in life itself. Our ideals were air castles – now they are houses to be lived in here and now.

In suggesting this we find ourselves very, very close to God in our thought and spirit. Christ had no idealism apart from realism. He says, "*The words that I say to you are not just my own. Rather, it is the Father, living in me, who is doing His work.*" (John 14:10). Here "words" and "works" were used synonymously – His words were works. They were one.

They must become one in your life and mine. But how?

Prayer for today: Dear Father, You are searching us with Your realism. You are calling us to overhaul and throw away useless thinking that we do not intend to put into practice. Help us to not ask for compromises. Help us to be true. Amen

July 4   Luke 4:16-24: 2 Corinthians 4:2

HOW DO WE APPLY THIS PRINCIPLE?

Yesterday we ended by asking the question – how can we make our idealism and our realism one? Here we will have to walk softly, pray for understanding, and be transparently honest. First of all, let's take an inventory of our ideals which we are now using in our lives as mental compensation – (things we hold to comfort us mentally), but do not guide us morally. Example: A little three year old girl not wanting to go to bed was hiding from her Mother. She said to someone sitting near, "If my Mother asks where I am, tell her I'm not here, but don't tell a lie." That last phrase was idealism used as mental compensation for what she was doing. We find many such things in our lives. At the close of a Christian Seminar where there was a session for questions, a member of the audience quietly complained to another as they were leaving, "It is our business to ask those scholars questions and it is their business to answer, even though none of us expect to do anything about it." This showed that the person believed religion was idealism not realism. We must close this gap. As we examine our lives in the quietness before God and come across such ideals, we must renounce this idealism in the name of Christianity. It will hurt us to the core to renounce our idealism, for it will mean that it will appear to us that we are not quite as good as we had led ourselves to believe. But at the very least we will have gained mental honesty. And that is the beginning of a fresh, new approach. So—

"Down with every barrier,
Off with every mask,
Out with every sin, and,
Away with every fruitless ideal."

Prayer for today: O Father, of the kindly searching eye, we open our lives to Your gaze, and we open our will to Your full obedience.

Help us to be completely honest and completely responsive. Then we can go forward. Amen.

July 5   James 1:22-27; 1 John 3:16-19

APPLYING THIS PRINCIPLE TO SOCIAL SOCIETY

When we began to apply this principle of unity and try to put it into practice in social society, we will find ourselves in a difficult situation, and for here the realization of our ideals does not depend entirely on us. Other people are involved and <u>social change must wait on their co-operation. What, then, can we do as individuals?</u>

We can ask ourselves two questions: First, in what direction is my face turned? Is my attitude right in regard to doing away with a competitive society in favor of a co-operative one? Am I really inwardly set against ghastly inequalities between people? Am I inwardly committed to wiping out distinctions based on class and color? Have I inwardly renounced controversy? Am I inwardly free from the dominance of narrow nationalism? Am I inwardly set against all exploitation of people? Do I want to see all people free? Do I really want fellowship with everyone?

Second, what steps am I taking to make real these <u>inner attitudes</u> in <u>outer life</u>? **<u>As far as</u> it depends on me and on the circumstances which I control,** am I here and now, taking steps to end the things that are wrong? Am I going as far as I can in realizing the things that are right? I may not have reached the goal, but am I on the right path, with the consent of my whole being, — NOW?

This "NOW" is important! For without it, even good intentions to do it <u>some time</u> become a mental compensation and therefore inaction. Every reality has a "NOW" in it.

Am I prepared to put a "NOW" in all these intentions?

Prayer for today: O Father, the Christ of the beginnings – help me here and "NOW" to have the right attitudes and take the first steps. Being used to living in two worlds it will not be easy to begin to live in one. But help me do it. Amen.

July 6   Luke 16:9-12; Acts 6:1-3; 1 Corinthians 10:31

UNITY OF SECULAR AND SACRED

One of the most disastrous divisions that ever took place in Christianity was the division of the sacred and the secular. In early Christianity they were one. When the disciples wanted someone to look after the food arrangements, (Acts 6:1-7 KJV), they said they must choose men *"of honest report, full of the Holy Spirit and wisdom,"* to look after this matter. Wisdom and the Holy Spirit were to make it a sacred act. All life was to be saved.

Now we have divided life into the sacred and secular, sacred callings and secular callings, sacred days and secular days, sacred books and secular books, sacred music and secular music, etc, etc. I'm sure you get the picture. The secular has become materialized, and the sacred etherealized, with emphasis on the "ether." It has been Satan's very strategy to divide and rule. And were there is division Satan does rule. We can never live victoriously as long as we try to live a compartmentalized life. They must be brought together. They need each other.

As Christians we want to live victoriously in our workplaces. However, when our jobs are dull and uninteresting and not to our liking, we may make ourselves feel better about the whole thing with the lofty thought, "if I do this job someone else will be spared the misery of it." Very sweet of us. And yet in the back of our mind did we not feel that the job was less than spiritually done by us? Instead could we have looked at it as a part of our spiritual life – our spiritual life can and should be evident in and through our job? The word of God must become flesh or die as a word.

Prayer for today: O Father in whom everything became one, and in whom the workplace was no longer the commonplace, but glowing with meaning and purpose, help us to make them one. Amen.

July 7   Exodus 31:1-6; Romans 12:1;
                                            1 Corinthians 6:19-20

SACRED AND SECULAR – (continued)

We cannot leave this division between the sacred and the secular, for if we still keep them divided, then we are defeated and defeated where it counts most.

You may or may not have heard about the man who said he sold cars for a living while he served God. But should he not have thought of serving God through the selling of cars. Can not our job itself show evidence of our spiritual life? Is not the thing that attracts us to others the fact that they show the presence of God in and through their jobs?

The business person must be able to handle their accounting (books) with the same sense of sacredness and mission as the minister handles the sacred BOOK in the preaching and teaching of God's word. Of course that would mean the break-up of many companies, both large and small, because you cannot manage crookedness with sacredness. It would be far better to lose the business than to lose one's soul. But legitimate business can be made a sacred act. "The extension of the incarnation" should mean this: today I stand in this business, workplace, classroom, or wherever, to become the embodiment of the spirit of Christ in this "situation." I will work out His mind and spirit in my relationship with things and persons. As Peter offered his boat to Jesus to teach the multitudes from, so I offer to Him my "boat," my job, my life from which He may teach through my "situation" the meaning of the Kingdom. I am an extension of the incarnation.

Prayer for today: O Father, we thank You that You can make life shine with meaning when we bring You into it. Help me to do that very thing today. I will need Your power, but I know I can count on You for that power. Amen.

July 8   Romans 6:13; 12:1; 1Timothy 4:8;
                          Hebrews 10:5-7

THE UNITY OF BODY AND SOUL

We have been taking up one by one the places where there have been divisions, trying to see the possibilities of bringing unity, hence – power into the total life. We now come to the division between the body and the soul.

The body has been looked upon as the enemy of the soul. To have freedom in our bodies we sometimes think they must be suppressed; some parts we would like to get rid of or trade. Are you ashamed of your body? Religion as well as society has intensified this war between soul and body.

But not so in Jesus. Jesus accepted His body as He accepted His soul – gifts from God. "*A body prepared for me.*" (Hebrews 10:5). His body and His soul were in one accord. He did not neglect His body, nor pamper it, or suppress it – He offered it as the instrument of God's will and purpose. And He kept it fit for God. There is no mention of Him ever being sick. Tired – Yes, but never sick.

Christ, not weak Christians, must be our pattern for the way we are to act toward our bodies. Just enough food to keep us fit, anymore than that might keep us fat. Why carry excess baggage anyway?

We may sometimes become ill, but why be more ill than we should be. Many of our ills are self-induced. Just enough sleep to make us lively and fresh, anymore than that might make us dull and lazy. Just enough exercise to keep up healthy, with an eye on the fact that too much attention to ourselves may drain us of higher interest.

If we keep our bodies fit like a well-tuned violin, then the music of God will come from every fiber of our being.

Prayer for today: O Father, we thank You that Your body and Your soul were well tuned, so let the ages bend low that we may catch the rhythm of that harmony. Help us to be like You. Amen.

July 9   1Corinthians 6:13 & 9:27; Romans 12:1;
                                    1Timothy 5:22

THIS IS MY BODY

One of the most astonishing things Jesus ever said was this: *"Take and eat; this is my body."* (Matthew 26:26). He offered His body for humanity to feed upon. It is an astonishing offer.

Never let dim the idea of the atonement in these words. That idea is there and we are grateful. But is this idea not there also: that He made His bodily appetites instrumental in promoting the purpose of the Kingdom, the way He purified His sex impulses, and the way He kept pure in act and in thought – in other words, does He not offer to us His whole bodily victory? Feed upon that fact, He says. And we do.

If we can say the same thing to others, then we really know victory. Are we able to feed others at the place of our victories which we have in and through our bodies? Can we say to others who are tempted and harassed, "Take and eat of this victory I am gaining with my bodily appetites?" If so, we are in line with His spirit. We are an extension of the incarnation.

So when tempted to indulge our passions in thought or in action, stop and say: No I cannot do this. Because if I do, when others come to feed on my victory I will have nothing to give them. I cannot offer others the possibility of feeding upon my soul, unless I can offer them the possibility of feeding upon my bodily victories. They both go together. I will keep myself pure today, by feeding upon His victory that others may feed upon mine.

Prayer for today: O Christ, of the pure body, make me like that. May no impure thought or deed incapacitate me from offering to other tempted souls my victories. Please, keep me pure. Amen.

July 10   Leviticus 17:14; Matthew 26:27-29;
                                               John 6:53-56

THIS IS MY BLOOD

Jesus said another astounding thing: *"Drink all of it; for this is my blood..."* (Matthew 26:27-28 KJV). Again we repeat that the idea and the fact of the atonement are in these words. But is not this idea also heredity of a higher race, and now we can have the source of our blood heredity, not in tainted, contaminated past of which we are inheritors, but in a new, pure, untainted source of inherited life.

My ancestry may be a poor, contaminated, streaky human blood-line – whose isn't? So what? Now I step into a new blood line from a new Ancestor. I am no longer a victim of the past – I begin a new life – in Christ! Christ is my very blood. He becomes Life of my life, Blood of my blood when my life conforms to His in obedience and trust.

This also has another side to it. We must be able to say the same thing to others: "This is my blood – drink it. You will find coursing through my blood a new victory and a new purity – drink of that victory and of that newness." If this is true, then we must let no impurity, no disease get into our blood stream – it must be kept pure and healthy so the present and future generations may inherit from us a new heredity. So when we are tempted we must say, No, to do wrong would make me unfit to say to anyone, drink of my life and of my new blood line. No, for the sake of others I sanctify myself – yes, my very blood, that I may be able to feed, <u>not poison</u>, this and future generations.

If Christ is your very blood, then rejoice and give it!

Prayer for today: O Father, I thank You that You can offer to me Your blood and that I belong to a new heredity. Help me to be worthy of such a blood line. And help me to hold within me the dignity of the life to which I belong. Amen.

July 11   Matthew 10:8; Mark 7:34;
                                 Luke 13:16; John 11:33

UNHEALTHY BODY – AND OUR ATTITUDE

Our victory in life should extend to our bodies. Our bodies should be as fit as possible. We say "as possible," because there are those with a handicap. Even so, it can be made better.

First of all, never let your mind entertain the idea that your unhealthy body is God sent. It isn't. God is fighting against disease. Christ never said sickness was the will of God – He cured it. God's Kingdom is displeased with <u>everything</u> that cripples life, including disease. If you believe it is God's will for you to be anything but well and healthy, that your sickness is God-sent, then obviously, no matter how much your spiritual life may develop, its power will not reach your physical body: you have put it out of reach. <u>A British Medical Journal</u> says that "there is not a tissue of the human body wholly removed from the influence of spirit." If that is so then we must let the power of our spiritual lives pour into our physical lives. *"And if the Spirit of him who raised Jesus from the dead is living in you, he who raised Christ from the dead will also give life to your mortal bodies through his Spirit, who lives in you."* (Romans 8:11). All things being equal, the Christian should be healthier than the one who is not a Christian, for the Christian has tapped a source of power for the body.

The greatest source of power for physical health is the absence of inward conflict and strife in the spirit. <u>Many people would be well physically if they were well spiritually.</u>

Remember, then, these two things – your sickness is not the will of God, and it may depend on the state of your soul, <u>of course it certainly MAY NOT</u>. But if it does, the first step to physical health is to get rid of all <u>inward</u> conflict and complications.

Prayer for today: O Christ of the healthy soul and body, make us like that. Help us not to pass on to our body's weariness of our soul. May we be as healthy as we know you want us to be. Amen.

July 12   Job 10:1; Isaiah 5:27; 40:31; Matthew 11:28

ARE YOU TIRED?

Many of us are tired because we pass our mental state on to our body.

In the early part of the twentieth century, a then famous physician, who had cured thousands in her hospital, said nature balances out its assigned duties about every twenty-four hours. That is, if you are tired and will give nature twenty-four hours of rest, it will throw off the fatigue toxins within that time. She said that you do not store up fatigue toxins for weeks and months, that if you did you would not be a tired person, but you would be a dead one. Beyond the twenty-four hours the tiredness is in the mind, unless there is a physical basis for the fatigue, if not – then it is mental and spiritual. She therefore scorned the idea of laying up for weeks and months for bodily rest. Twenty-four hours will do the trick, provided there is no physical problem and the soul is spiritually and harmoniously adjusted. It is amazing what the body can stand if the soul is spiritually unified. Most people do not wear out from overwork, but from under-existing.

There are two ways to keep your spiritual motor running. One is to stop and fill your tank. The other is the American way – try and keep your tank filled without stopping. Stop and fill your tank with the fuel of power and victory Christ is waiting to pour into you. Say to yourself, not just as you fall asleep at night, but again and again throughout the day, "*I can do everything through him who gives me strength.*" (Philippians 4:13). Its balm will soothe your nerves and will quicken every fiber of your being.

Prayer for today: O Father, Who went through the strain of the day without strain, give us that inward sense of Your quiet healing upon our spirits, that we may be ready for anything. Amen.

July 13   Exodus 23:25; Proverbs 17:22;
                           Matthew 8:7; 9:12

HOW DOES GOD HEAL?

The healing of God does not come through only one way. He heals in many ways. He heals by physicians, by surgeons, by climate, by mental suggestion, by the direct touch of the Spirit upon our bodies, and by common sense.

By "common sense" we mean that, while God gives grace to undertake greater tasks than we are normally made for, nevertheless He may be saying through this sickness: "Lighten up. You are carrying too heavy a load." You cannot do everything, and, it may be that by doing less, you can do the most important things better. There is a positive side to sometimes refusing to do good. If we find that we have "too much on our plate," then we must take less – take only as much as we can digest. We must go the limit of our strength, but then we must watch our margins, and not go beyond them.

Common sense tells us to exercise. We may have to do it early in the morning, during our lunch break, or before we go to bed at night, but we will find that it not only gives us needed exercise but it distributes the blood through our system, and helps our mind relax. Common sense tells us many other things about the physical bodies we live in, and we must obey that common sense. It is one of God's methods of healing. It may not be a spectacular method, but often God comes to us from some very lowly, dusty roads. Listen up – do not despise any way He comes to us because from the beginning He came to us from a lowly dusty road.

Prayer for today: O Christ, You called Your disciples aside to rest from many things and the many people; help us to rest by Your side, and perhaps to let go of the many things we strive to do so that we may do one thing well. Amen.

July 14   Matthew 4:23; 12:9-13; Acts 4:14;
                                       James 5:14-15

HOW DOES GOD HEAL? (Continued)

Christian people have at times discredited Christian healing by choosing only one method, healing by prayer and treating lightly or completely rejecting other methods. This is a mistake! And doctors should not completely reject the method of prayer, but use it.

God does sometimes touch and heal the body directly through prayer. We have all heard, seen or been a part of Christ direct healing, And why should we be doubtful or surprised, He healed the sick, blind, lame, etc., in His time on earth and (Hebrews 12:8) tells us, *"Jesus Christ is the same yesterday today and forever."* So – where is our faith? Hopefully, - not misplaced.

Science could and should say much in favor of divine healing. And Christians in turn should look favorably on the ways of healing through science as God's ways – and use them. For God's will is for health.

Prayer for today: O Christ, help us to touch Your robe in faith and rise into health. Amen.

July 15   Philippians 4:6; 1 Peter 5:7; Psalm 37:8

LIVING RELAXED

In our search for Living Victoriously one of the most important things to learn is to live <u>inwardly</u> relaxed. This day and time
seems against it. Its entire demand is high tension, high pressure,
high maintenance. So we do not die of the diseases our forefathers
died of – we go at high pressure until the heater cracks.. Nervous
disorders, heart failure, high blood pressure, depression, etc., <u>often</u>,
but not always, are outcomes of inner tensions. And all this not only
destroys the body but the mind and soul as well. For freedom and
efficiency depend upon relaxation.

A bee was beating itself against the windowpane in a frantic
endeavor to get out to freedom. I tried to rescue it, but the more I
tried, the more it beat its head against the windowpane. Finally it
fell to the windowsill exhausted. As the window was raised a bit,
it crawled out and immediately flew away to freedom. Some of us
are all inwardly tight, screwed up and frantically beating ourselves
against the window panes of our circumstances and tasks, and vainly
trying to find freedom and power. We will never find it until we let
go. So the phrase, "let go, and let God," is more than a catch-phrase,
it has profound meaning in it. We so much want to be both good and
effective but the more we earnestly try, the more we get nowhere.
We need to relax and trust – which of course, means a self-surrender
– and then goodness and effectiveness will be ours. We will be a
relaxed soul.

Relaxation means we have ceased to worry. We are trusting, and
trusting means drawing on the inexhaustible resources of God.

Prayer for today: O Christ, we thank You that surrounded by the
stress of things You had a relaxed spirit. Give that to us, that we too
may fully live. Amen.

July 16   Psalm 112:7; Isaiah 26:3; 30:15;
                           Mark 4:38; Romans 15:13;
                           Philippians 4:7

LIVING RELAXED - (Continued)

Have you ever watched the pathetic performance of someone trying <u>too</u> hard to do a good job, but is failing miserably because they are so tense and tied up on the inside that it is showing through to the outside? How often has that someone been you? (Been there, done that?)

Have you watched a young lady trying hard not to blush, or a speaker without experience trying to address an audience, a beginner trying to hit a golf ball, a patient trying to go to sleep, or a person trying to remember a name – the secret of mastering these situations is not in aggressively trying to apply your will to them, but in each case relaxation would bring the desired results.

Jesus said, *"Who of you by worrying can add a single hour to his life?"* (Matthew 6:27). He was talking to us adults about the foolishness of worry. He's saying, "LIVE RELAXED."

A good music teacher will insist the student relax every muscle so that their very soul can come into their fingertips. Then they will master their musical instrument. Some of us live spiritually that way. We let the very power of Christ into every portion of our being – and it is all done so easily. And. Oh, how effective!

Jesus was so relaxed that the power of God had an unhindered channel within Him. Spiritual relaxation meant spiritual release. The mechanism of life can be so lubricated by the peace of God that it will run without friction.

Prayer for today: O Christ, I come to You for strength, for courage, and for power in every portion of my being. And for this I thank You. Amen.

July 17   2 Samuel 23:5; Psalm 3:3-6; 16:1, 8,
                                     11; 18:32; 2 Timothy 1:12

RELAXED IN OUR CHRISTIAN WORK

Have you ever had the privilege to address an audience, small group or even an individual with your personal testimony for Christ? If so, were you relaxed as you spoke for Him or were you so frightened you could hardly speak at all? Did you remember (Matthew 10:18-20)? *"On my account you will be brought before governors and kings as witnesses to them and to the Gentiles. But when they arrest you, do not worry about what to say or how to say it. At that time you will be given what to say, for it will not be you speaking, but the Spirit of your Father speaking through you."* When we relax in Christ He will do the same for us. Whether it is governors, kings, enemies, friends, or family it is the same, Christ <u>will</u> use us to speak through. Ask yourself this question: If Christ can't use me, then who?

Try doing Christ work on your own power and you become mentally and physically exhausted. However, if His power is doing the work through us then He will give us calm confidence, unruffled assurance and peace. <u>Only His power can give that.</u> Then through the rough-and-tumble of things, by His grace we will have inward relaxation, in other words, <u>faith</u>.

Prayer for today: O Christ, give me more and more this day this assurance that will take away all worry, all stress, all conflict and make me at Your best. Amen.

July 18   Micah 7:7; 2 Corinthians 4:8, 9, 16, 17;
                                 Philippians 1:19-21; Revelation 1:8, 17

RELAXED WHEN SURROUNDED BY OPPOSITION

It is comparatively easy to be relaxed in our work, at school or wherever, but when surrounded by opposition, sometimes unfair opposition, then it is not so easy. We may often be defeated here, but if we can only remain relaxed in Christ, and retain our cool, it will work amazingly.

If we have someone picking to pieces everything we say and do, we must tolerate it, because if we are God's child they may pick us to pieces but it won't kill us. Depend on your faith, have faith in your faith! Then you won't have to fret and worry. Most often the person with the hostile attitude comes out the broken one. They cannot keep hidden forever, that ugly and unfair heart, eventually they will be exposed.

You cannot be relaxed surrounded by opposition if your agenda is your own, you can be sure of that. But when we are proclaiming Christ message, however poor and partial our interpretation may be, we know that at the very core of this message is something eternal, something standing within Time, yet above Time, something that does not need to be defended, but to be proclaimed and lived, something that has been proven in our lives. Therefore we can be relaxed even when surrounded by opposition.

Prayer for today: O Christ, You who stood surrounded by the crowd of opposition, the only calm one in that howling crowd, give me today a touch of that calm assurance. Amen.

July 19   Matthew 6: 25-34; Colossians 1:29

STRETCHING POINT

Are we afraid living relaxed might cause us to stop stretching to reach "perfection?" Aren't stretching points growing points? Therefore, if we stop stretching will we not cease to grow and become weak? Doesn't our vigorous effort and inward relaxation balance the scales?

It is correct to say that we must keep up a vigorous effort in our <u>moral</u> life. This vigorous effort keeps out weeds and any other obstacles that would hinder our <u>spiritual</u> growth. Jesus emphasized this very thing when He said, *"See how the lilies of the field grow."* (Matthew 6:28a). The emphasis was on the method of growth – *"see how they grow."* They do not grow by working themselves up into a mental agitated state, by anxiety, or by worry - <u>they grow by obeying the laws of their own nature and by absorbing from</u> <u>without</u>. Do the same says Jesus; obey the laws of the Kingdom now within you, draw nourishment – and calm. The fact is we cannot draw nourishment unless there is relaxation and trust. The agitated soul is a starved soul.

Remember it is the calm and relaxed people who are the vigorous - strenuous people, strenuous, but not strained. It is like the <u>center</u> of a twisting tornado, a place of absolute calm. The center is the place in the tornado where the resident forces reside. Out of that calm comes the power of the tornado. Out of the relaxed, coordinated spirit comes the power that reshapes the world.

Jesus was never more powerful, never more confident with His call, never more gripping as He stood before Pilate calm and silent. That calm, that silence is not weakness – it is dynamic. Out of it come the resident forces that reshape the world.

Prayer for today: O Christ, I know that the days, in which I am fussy in my efforts, I will not reshape the world around me. Give me <u>Your calm</u> – <u>Your dynamics</u>, I will be weak with only one, I must have both. Amen.

July 20   Psalm 55:22; Matthew 11:28-30;
                                 Revelation 2:3

RELAXING UNDER OUR DIFFICULTIES

If you should go to bed and lie there with all your muscles tight and strained because you are afraid the bed will break down under you, you would not rest and in the morning you would get up exhausted. Of course there are many reasons we may go to bed at night and our muscles are tight and strained because we are worried or afraid of one thing or the other, the least of which is our bed breaking beneath us. However, the point is <u>we must trust to rest</u>. Some of us are still holding ourselves <u>inwardly tight</u>, afraid if we let go, the grace of God will not sustain us. So we live exhausted lives, worn out from within.

An <u>old, old story</u> is told of an elderly woman who trudged along the rough road carrying a heavy pack on her back, when a man in a wagon came by and offered her a ride. Grateful beyond words she climbed in, but sat there continuing to hold her pack on her back. When the man suggested that she put it in the back of the wagon, she replied, "Oh, but it is so kind of you to carry me, I don't want to make you carry my burden too. I'll carry that." We may smile at the old lady, and yet how many of us do just as she did! We believe that the grace of God can save our souls, but we do not trust that same grace to carry our daily burdens, our daily cares and anxieties, the worries of business and our family – these we still continue to keep on our backs. Exhausted souls! Do you remember the Bible verse in (1 Peter 5:7) – *"Cast all your anxiety on him because he cares for you."* Believe it, trust in God's word and He will carry us through to Living Victoriously.

Prayer for today: O Christ, You do offer to carry us and our troubles. Help us to surrender our difficulties as well as ourselves. For You will carry both. We thank You. Amen.

July 21   Psalm 86:11; Matthew 12:30;
                            Acts 4:32; Ephesians 4:3, 13, 14

DISTRESSED AND SCATTERED

We have been saying that there is no possibility of Living Victoriously unless we are inwardly unified, no longer inwardly stressed but relaxed. In this verse Jesus diagnoses our condition and suggests the remedy: (from the KJV) – *"But when he saw the multitudes, he was moved with compassion for them, because they were <u>distressed and scattered</u>, as sheep not having a shepherd."* (Matthew 9:36-37). "<u>Distressed</u>"- inward strain, no inward unity. "<u>Scattered</u>" – literally, "drawn in different directions" – no outer unity. Two things lacking in humankind: inner and outer unity, at peace with oneself and at peace with others. And the reason for this was then and is now: "No shepherd," the lack of a CENTER around which our life can find inner and outer unity. Until we can absolutely center in on Christ, the perfect Life, we will lack unity. The CENTER can only be CHRIST. Even our Western religious world is distressed and scattered because it is often missing the Center. Religious people often jump from issue to issue, emphasis to emphasis, from doctrine to doctrine, and the whole thing lacks <u>togetherness</u>, unity. If we would take our stand with Christ and work out these issues, emphases and doctrines through Him, then there would be unity, because Christ would be the Center. Life needs a personal, enduring Friendship to keep it centered and immovable. Christ offers Himself as that Friend. When our love is completely and unconditionally connected to Christ, we are no longer lonely, no longer drawn in different directions, no longer at war with ourselves. We have found a Center – a Center of unity. And there is no center for the outer unity in the world except that we find it around the Son of God.

Prayer for today: O Christ, You are our Center as Your power alone can hold the forces of our souls from breaking our unity. Father, hold us, and then we know that we are held. Amen.

231

July 22   Proverbs 1:33; Isaiah 8:11-13; 1 John 4:18

FEAR – THE DESTROYER OF INNER UNITY

Of all the things that destroy our inner unity <u>fear</u> is possibly the most devastating and the most prevalent. Our biological fear tends to keep us moving, but there are other fears which paralyze us. The victory over fear is an essential part of our victory in Living Victoriously. Without this victory over fear there can be no Living Victoriously, because fear divides and paralyzes us.

A doctor told one of his patients, whom he had operated on, that he was ready to be discharged from the hospital, he was completely well. But before the man left the hospital he was visited by his astrologer, the astrologer told him the crisis of his illness <u>had not</u> passed and would come the following week, that he should remain in the hospital. The next week the man died – died from <u>no other apparent reason</u> except fear. Fear had taken his will to live and killed him.

There is no doubt that fear is the most paralyzing thing in human life. *"I was afraid, and I went out and hid your talent."* (Matthew 25:25). Fear not only paralyzes us but paralyzes our efforts as well.

We must find victory over all our fears – can it be done? Yes, thank God – yes it can be done!

Prayer for today: O Christ, I thank You that I do not need to be the victim of any fear. But teach me the clear road to that victory and I will walk in it. Amen.

July 23   Psalm 34:4; Ecclesiastes 12:1-5;
                               (KJV) 2 Timothy 1:7; Hebrews 2:15

FEARS FROM EARLY CHILDHOOD

Some of our fears come from early childhood. The mind, always trying to forget the unpleasant, drops the incident that caused the violent disturbance of our emotions down into the subconscious mind and closes the door on it. There it works silent havoc, causing nervousness, depression and distress.

The story is told of an officer who during World War I, would stand on the side of the trench rather than get down into the dugout. Some thought it bravery, but it was really fear- fear of a small close place. He found the reason: when he was a child he met an angry dog in a narrow alley and the dog attacked him. That attack in a narrow space left him with a fear of small close places.

Now, what do you do with a fear like that? Repress it? Try to forget it? No – it must be brought to the surface and dealt with. The incident must be gently and quietly looked at. Confronting it and looking at it will draw the wound to the surface where it can be dealt with. It will then be seen for what it truly is, a childhood incident, with no rightful basis of a lifelong fear.

If you have a fear that has troubled you forever, try to remember why you have that fear, confront it, talk about it, pray about it and see if it doesn't disappear.

Remember – 2 Timothy 1:7 – *"For God hath not given us the spirit of fear; but of power, and of love, and of a sound mind."* (KJV)

Prayer for today: O Christ, I come to You to take all basis of fear from my inner consciousness, for I know if You are my Redeemer, and You are, then I have no right to be afraid of anything. Amen.

July 24   Nehemiah 6:10-14; Matthew 14:5;
                                Luke 22:6; 23:23-24; John 9:22;
                                Acts 26:17

FEAR OF OUR PEERS

The fear of our peers suppresses the Christian and makes us conform to being an average individual, and the average individual is always below Christ's plan for our lives. We take on "protective resemblance" to our surroundings and fit in; we become mediocre, and are slowly but surely de-Christianized. We are afraid of being different. And yet it is just that difference that may be necessary to save us and our peers. Often the group survives only when some member becomes different and shows a higher method of survival.

Nevertheless, our peers demand conformity, and they will persecute those who depart from their standards. Fall below their standards and they will punish you, rise above their standards and they will persecute you, or they may ridicule you. And sometimes that can be even worse. We have all been laughed at, at one embarrassing moment or another at some time in our life. How did you react to the ridicule? Did you become upset and show an ugly attitude or did you laugh with the group? If you laughed along with the others you saved yourself from more embarrassment and showed a godly attitude.

So the suggested remedy – when ridiculed or laughed at, simply laugh with them, knowing in the end you will laugh longest and perhaps loudest, a great basis for laughter. Still, to get rid of the fear of our peers we must surrender them; we must acknowledge in our deepest spirit <u>no dominance except that of Jesus Christ</u>.

Prayer for today: O Father, deliver me from the fear of what my peers might say, and give me a deeper realization of what You say. I know I must be delivered from all fear. Amen.

July 25   Isaiah 40:29; Matthew 25:25;
                                     Luke 21:26; Hebrews 12:3

THE FEAR OF FAILURE

Like the man who received <u>one</u> talent, many do not attempt to do anything with their talents because they are afraid if they did they would fail. So, like this man, who went out and "dug a hole in the ground," they too end in emptiness and futility – a hole in the ground. Fear produces the very failure that we fear. Many do not give their lives to Christ because they are afraid they would fail if they did. So they never do. Fear feeds on failure and failure feeds on fear.

To know how to live victoriously we must conquer this fear of failure. But how? First of all by looking at fear at its worst. Suppose we do fail at "whatever," would we be any worse for it than we are now? Hardly! Because in this world by doing nothing **IS** failure. By doing nothing we are living in a constant state of failure. Again, suppose we failed in obeying what we felt was the call of God, did we really fail? No, because our very obedience is success. It is not our business whether we succeed or fail – it is our business to be true to the call of God as we know it. The results are in His hands. Anyway, God has a way of turning even failure into ultimate victory. <u>The cross is the world's supreme failure</u>. When Christ dropped His head on His pulse-less bosom and died, everything crashed, or did it? Ask your heart! If it is like mine, it clings to the failure as the one hope. So God has a way of turning the cross of your failure into supreme success. The seed sown fails and dies, but in its failure a new life springs up.

Therefore away with fear and forward with Christ! Where? Anywhere - provided it is forward!

Prayer for today: O Christ, who saw Your Kingdom crash about You on the cross and still held Your heart above the crash of things, give us the power this day to be unafraid of fear. Amen.

July 26   Matthew 6:24-33; Philippians 4:19; Isaiah 46:4

FEAR OF BEING DESTITUTE IN OUR SENIOR YEARS

Fear of growing old and not being able to take care of ourselves financially is real. Most of this fear should be satisfied by godly living. In a world of plenty we should not be haunted by the fear of being financially insecure in our senior years.

So – what do we do? Do we spend our entire life working to prevent this fear, and miss living our life as God planned? Would it be worth it in the end? Jesus said it wouldn't. In His own words from (Mark 8:36) *"What good is it for a man to gain the whole world, yet forfeit his soul?"* Jesus also said, *"Seek "first" his kingdom and his righteousness, and all these things will be given to you as well."* (Matthew 6:33). What were "these things"? "These things" were food and clothing. He guarantees us those two things – if we put His Kingdom first.

And if our "needs" exceeds food and clothing – read again the verse in Philippians that began our study for today: *"And my God will meet "all" your "needs" according to his glorious riches in Christ Jesus."* This promise was given to a church who had sacrificially given to meet Paul's need. This is a true measure of God's blessing to us when we, "seek first His Kingdom and His righteousness."

Prayer for today: O Christ, I thank You that I can live, as You lived, a happy, trustful child of the Father, without fear. Help me to maintain that trust into my senior years. Amen.

July 27   Psalm 71:9-18; Romans 15:1;
                                     1 Corinthians 12:20-27

FEAR OF BEING DEPENDENT ON OTHERS

There are those who are afraid that their actions in obeying God will bring suffering and difficulties to their loved ones. To decide your life's course on this basis is a tragic mistake. Our obedience to Christ may cause suffering to those we love as well as ourselves because we are all bound up in a bundle of life together, but we cannot wait to obey God's plan for our life until we know the consequences. If we wait, we will never act. Jesus' acting on the will of God involved His whole family in a cross – and also in a resurrection! It works both ways. A part of this fear of hurting our family members is the fact that we may be dependent on them later in life. Some of this of course comes from false pride. We don't want to be dependent on others. However, think about it – we are all dependent, every moment of our lives, both on God and others. To act as if we aren't is silly, superficial pride. If we help others during our productive years, shouldn't others help us if we should need it when we are older? You've heard the expression "what goes around, comes around" - we took care of the younger generation when they were helpless, why shouldn't the younger generation take care of the older if need be? It might help them to be more responsible; might even save them from selfish isolation. So the crucifixion of selfish pride by the older ones may turn out for the younger ones redemption. Also, if as an older person we accept the situation joyously and sweetly, you may be the kind of person anyone would delight in taking care of – and would miss you if they didn't have the opportunity. So turn your fear over to God – be dependent on Him, He will see us through.

Prayer for today: O Christ, we thank You for showing us the way. Even though You broke the heart of Your Mother – You made it well again. Help us to obey You, no matter the cost – to whom. Amen.

July 28   Ecclesiastes 12:5; Isaiah 51:12-13;
                            Matthew 5:15; 1 Peter 3:13-16

NEGATIVISM

Another form of fear is negativism. People who have inner conflicts find it difficult to be positive in their attitudes and decisions, so they retreat into being negative. When a suggestion or opportunity is presented to them, their first thought is to reject it. Almost everything seems difficult to them. Consequently they live in an almost chronic state of "NO." Their very nature has become negative.

Such negative natures cannot lead others. It takes the positive, hopeful, affirmative type to become leaders. Being negative is to be unchristian. The Christian is positive, hopeful, and affirmative. Sometimes as Christians we may say "No," but only to say a greater "Yes" or a huge "Divine Yes." To be in Christ, then is to take a positive attitude toward life.

(John 18:3-4) says, *"So Judas came to the grove, guiding a detachment of soldiers and some officials from the chief priests and the Pharisees. They were carrying torches, lanterns and weapons. Jesus knowing all that was going to happen to him,"* (– **did what**?) Prepared to compromise? Prepared to escape? Prepared to soften the blow? <u>NO</u>, He "<u>went out</u>" to meet them! At the moment of the great "NO," the betrayal, He was positive. Be positive even in the face of impending misfortune. Squeeze victory out of it. Keep affirming to yourself, *"I can do everything through Christ who gives me strength."* (Philippians 4:13). Then your negative fears will disappear and there to take its place will be a new, abundant, affirmative life. For as Christians we belong to the great affirmation.

Prayer for today: O Christ, I thank You that in Your presence my negative fears are dissolved and I feel that anything – anything is possible. Help me to maintain this spirit from You. Amen.

July 29   2 Corinthians 3:17-18; 4:1-2;
                                      1 Timothy 1:5; Psalm 119:45

THE BASIS OF THESE FEARS

The fears we have been looking at are rooted in one thing – inward division. If our inward spirit is united we have no fears. So— what is the basic solution?

Two modern answers which are extremely similar: 1. Know what your desires truly are, don't expect too much and when they don't happen you won't be too disappointed. 2. Have in mind your expectations and hopes, then when life doesn't go as you expected and hoped your fears will be to a smaller degree. The solution: PULL IN. Or inwardly have no hope or real desire to see any good come from your life, the solution for this fear is PULL AWAY.

Christ solution – is this: *"There is no fear in love. But perfect love drives out fear,... The one who fears is not made perfect in love."* (1 John 4:18). Perfect love drives away fear! The answer then is not PULL INWARD or PULL AWAY, but PULL OUT all the Stops! Expand through perfect love. That expansion drives out all fear. Christ solution is in line with our Christian nature – it is positive, affirmative, and expansive. But first it pulls together. It narrows its love down to one Person – that Person, God, through Christ. We become single-minded, with one consuming passion that eats up the smaller passions in our life. This love of Christ fuses the divisions of our soul into a burning unity. There is no room for inner fear, for there is no room for inner division. Division confuses, love fuses. Fear cannot live in the burning fire of love – this love that wants nothing – except Christ, is therefore afraid of nothing. Bowing before Him, we now bow before nothing else.

Prayer for today: O Christ, You have conquered our inmost being, we thank You that no fear can make us afraid. For nothing can separate us from the love of Christ – absolutely nothing. Amen.

July 30   Matthew 6:22; Luke 9:28-36; James 1:6-8

FEARS AND DIVIDED LOYALTY

There is no deliverance from fears unless there is undivided loyalty to Christ. <u>Perfect</u> <u>love literally does cast out fear</u>, and, <u>fear cast out perfect love</u>. This is vividly brought home to us in the Transfiguration scene. The Jewish heart of Peter was divided in its loyalty, wanting to keep Moses, representing the law, Elijah, representing the Prophets; and Jesus, representing the new Revelation, all on the same level – *"Let us build three tabernacles."* (Luke 9:33). This was serious, for the entire future was tied up in that question – was Jesus final and should supreme loyalty be given to Him?

The moment that "division cloud" enveloped them, *"they were afraid as they entered the cloud."* (Luke 9:34). That inner division brought clouds and fears. Then God speaks out of the cloud.

Where there is division there will be clouds and fears. Take our world situation today, we have entered the war clouds and we fear as we entered those clouds. Why the clouds and why the fear? DIVISION! Each country is thinking of itself and not the unity of the world at large. Selfish nationalism emerges and controls, hence world division. The result – clouds come over us and we fear as we enter those clouds. And rightly so – but out of those clouds comes a Voice. God speaks! And because we would not listen to the Voice of God as it spoke through intelligent reason, now we must listen to His voice as He speaks through gun fire and the crash of civilizations. It says, *"This is my Son, whom I have chosen; LISTEN TO HIM."* (Luke 9:35). **Those clouds will never lift and those fears will never leave us until we do listen to Christ.**

Prayer for today: O God, You are speaking out of the clouds today. We tremble at Your voice of Judgment. Help us to not only tremble but to obey. Save us from our divisions. Amen.

July 31   Psalm 23; 1 John 1:1-7

IS THERE A CLOUD HANGING OVER YOUR LIFE?

Does a cloud hang over your life – unemployment, unhappy home situation, financial stress, sickness, depression, etc, etc? Brooding fears underneath that cloud are terrifying. Listen as God speaks out of that dark cloud. Is it conceivable, that God could be at once a God of wrath and a God of love? Does He have two hands, one of cold steel and the other warm and human? Is it conceivable that He would alternately seek us with the one hand and strike us with the other? If we could believe this, we might hear Him saying to us in tones of mingled sorrow and anger, <u>we can and we must have deeper fellowship with Him</u>. (1 John 1:1-4), John's letter includes an invitation to all of us to enjoy *"fellowship" with the Father and his son, Jesus Christ*. The word fellowship identifies with the word partnership. This refers to people who have something in common. God wants us to enter into a partnership with Him. '*Take either of my hands and I will lead you, I am your shepherd and I will lead you to springs of living water and I will wipe away every tear from your eyes – and every cloud from your horizon.*' (**Paraphrased** Revelation 7:17).

If we will hear and obey His Word, He will make our life an instrument for common good and a bond of fellowship between us and others. God is speaking out of our clouds of depression: *"This is my Son, whom I have chosen; listen to Him."* (Luke 9:35). And unless we do, that cloud will never lift and our fears will never disappear.

Prayer for today: O God, why do we not listen to Your still small voice? Help us to listen before we have to listen to Your wrath as it speaks through our catastrophes. Forgive us. Amen.

August 1   Romans 12:2; Colossians 2:8-21;
                                       1 John 2:15-17

THE CLOUD OVER OUR CHURCHES

No one has to argue, that as a whole, there is a cloud over the Christian Church. Our vague uneasiness has grown into a fear that all is not well. And why is that? Again the answer is divided loyalty, inner division.

The divided loyalty is this: In each nation, instead of keeping the gospel of Christ in a framework of universal reference, we have more and more identified it with national cultures. The conquest of the gospel of Christ by local national cultures is going on at a rapid pace, and this process means the slow de-Christianization of our churches. On the original Holy Grail, the figure of Christ is seen sitting above the Roman eagle. That was the position Christ occupied in those early centuries – Christ was first and the nation was second. Today the nation uses the national culture for its own ends, and because the Church has become so domesticated, so identified with the national culture the Church is also being used for its nationalistic ends. "A process which began with a culture molded by religious faith has ended with a religious faith molded by a national culture." Protestants are mistaking dynamic cultured forms for the content of their faith. And the triumph of culture forms over the religious content is deadly. We are divided between Christ and national culture. Which do you say is supreme?

The clouds come over us and again the Voice speaks: *"This is my Son; listen to Him."* And until we do the clouds will not lift and our fear will not disappear. Christ must be first!

Prayer for today: O God, Whatever wrong comes before us, clothed in national culture, and demands our supreme loyalty, help us not to bow to it. Amen.

August 2   1 Corinthians 1:9-13; 12:13; Romans
                                        15:5-6; Ephesians 4:3

THE CLOUD OVER CHURCHES (continued)

However, the division within the Christian world is not merely between loyalty to our national culture and the loyalty to Christ, there is division between the Churches. And as a result of our Church family divisions a cloud has come over us, and under that cloud we are fearful, as we should be, **for a divided Church has little moral authority in a divided world**. We must adjust our differences or relinquish our moral leadership. There was a man who owned a beautiful piece of property and built such expensive walls around it that he went bankrupt building those walls and had to sell his property. "BANKRUPT BUILDING WALLS!" Is that not dangerously near the history of the Christian Churches today? We have so exhausted our resources in putting up doctrinal walls between ourselves and others that we have little left to use in helping redeem the world. If the time, intelligence and action which we have spent in trying to prove that we are right and our brother is wrong, had been spent in united action against the problems that now confront our world, those problems would not be so far from solution. And we would be leading the procession of events instead of being led by them. These divisions have brought a cloud over our religious life – dark, rainless clouds, clouds that predict storms of revolt, clouds that produce fear. God is speaking out of those clouds and His voice is as of old: *"This is my Son, whom I have chosen; listen to Him."* (Luke 9:35). And what does the Son say: *"that all of them may be one, Father..."* (John 17:21a). When we become one, the clouds will lift, but not until then.

Prayer for today: O God, our Father, forgive us that we Your children have built walls against one another. Help us to feel and act upon the unity of Your family. Amen.

August 3   Acts 4:34-37; 5:3, Philippians 3:7-8;
                            2 Samuel 24:24

CLOUDS OVER OUR PERSONAL LIFE

Collectively we have looked at life where clouds of division hang; now let's look within ourselves and see if there are any cloud-producing divisions.

Have you ever started out to pay the full price to Living Victoriously and then pulled back? That hesitation would mean division within your spirit, and that division would mean a cloud, and that cloud would mean fear. Did you sit down in the middle of your victorious walk and began to count how much it was costing you? After the price God paid for His gift to us, do you think He may have been disappointed in you? We know God didn't move away from us, but did we move away from Him, even if just a little. And though we know He did not desert us because He said He wouldn't, (Hebrews 13:5, Deuteronomy 31:6, and Joshua 1:5), do we still feel estranged from Him? Does a cloud of uselessness, hesitation and ruin hang over our spiritual life?

You may have prayed very hard for that cloud to lift, but it hasn't and it won't, until we listen to the Voice speaking from that cloud: *"This is my Son,... listen to Him."* And if we stop hesitating, if we will decide to not only give, but to give up and give in and listen to that Voice, we will lift up our eyes and see Jesus and Jesus only. He will then have our complete loyalty, and the clouds and fears will have disappeared.

Prayer for today: O Christ, we know You will only fill our personal world when You fill our hearts. Help me to let You fill my heart completely. Amen.

August 4   Galatians 2:20; 5:16, 17, 24; 1 Peter 4:1;
                             Jeremiah 31:33-34

THE PURE IN HEART WILL SEE GOD

"Blessed are the pure in heart, for they will see God." (Matthew
5:8). When the disciples listened to the voice of God, their hearts
became united, and then their uplifted eyes saw Jesus and Jesus only.
But many of us refuse to listen to that Voice, so the clouds linger and
the fears cling to us. The reason we don't listen is because we are
listening to something else – something closer to our heart.

Is the sound of something else rattling in your ears? Something
closer to your heart, perhaps some personal loss or hurt, some bitterness, some resentment, some bad habit, some foolish ambition, some
infatuation, some love of money – these fill our ears and God's voice
is drowned out. And that Voice was calling to us something big and
important.

A beautiful island harbor accommodated small sailing ships,
but in order to accommodate large ocean liners they would have to
spend a large amount of money. Lesser voices of fear and hesitation
prevailed, they refused to pay the price and the city is now a dead
city. Had they listened to the voice of faith and courage, they would
be a growing city, but lesser voices filled their ears and won out.

Prayer for today: O God, save me from lesser things that incapacitate me from hearing Your voice, and help me to pay the full price,
that I may have full deliverance from fear, and full vision of You.
Amen.

August 5 Psalm 37:8; Proverbs 16:32; 22:24-25;
Matthew 5:22; Ephesians 4:31

CONQUERING ANGER

Two major causes of sin might be <u>anger</u> and <u>fear</u>. From the psychologist point of view they seem to agree that <u>anger and fear form the basis of most of our unhappiness</u>. Anger and fear are impossible to integrate into a healthy personality. We have looked at fear now let's look at anger and how to conquer it. First of all, note that there is a form of anger which is biologically helpful. Anger can be a protection against evil. Our soul will rise up within us and resist evil with righteous anger. If we were incapable of anger, we might become too comfortable in our passiveness. In (Ephesians 4:26) Paul writes to the Church in Ephesus concerning conflict management – *"In your anger do not sin..."* Jesus was angry: (Mark 3:5) *"He looked around them in anger and, deeply distressed at their stubborn hearts..."* Note that in His anger was grief – He was "grieved." That determines the legitimate from the illegitimate type of anger. Where there is a sense of moral hurt, of moral grief, and not just personal resentment in the anger, then it is right, worthy and helpful. Note again that Jesus anger was anger at something done against another. His strong displeasure came from the fact that the Pharisee crowd had no sympathy for the afflicted man. That too is a test of whether it is justified anger. BE SUSPICIOUS OF ALL ANGERS THAT FORM FROM HURTS TO <u>US</u>. They probably have in them more personal resentment than moral justification. Again Paul says, *"In your anger do not sin."* But if we are to be angry and not sin, then we must be angry only **AT** sin. Even this kind of anger Paul suggest should not be held overnight, *"Do not let the sun go down while you are still angry, and do not give the devil a foothold."* (Ephesians 4:26-27).

If held overnight, it might give the devil a foothold.

Prayer for today: O Father, give us an inward hurt over wrongs done to others, but save us from personal resentments, for they destroy us. Amen.

August 6   Colossians 3:8; Hebrews 12:14-17; James 4:1-3

THE ROOT OF ANGER

Yesterday we saw that anger could be Christian when it is controlled by moral grief, and only when it was anger because of hurts to others. But we usually dress up our personal resentments in the clothes of moral justification and try to make them respectable and Christian. This process of rationalization allows many Christians to tolerate unchristian anger. A pastor thought he was fighting for principle, but when he honestly looked at himself, he saw the fight was more personal pride than principle.

Those words "personal pride" point us to the root of anger. It is in self. Self has its pride, and when that pride is wounded, it boils with anger.

Therefore, does it do any good to say, "I'll try not to be angry?" We will almost certainly fail by this sort of trying. Why? We cannot kill anger in ourselves, but we can consent for Christ to do it. And how will He do it? He will do it by striking at the root – the self. You remember when Jesus withered the fig tree, (Matthew 21:19), the disciples saw it "withered away from the roots." That is the way Christ withers things - "from the roots." And how will He wither anger from the roots? By asking our consent to crucify "self," in other words – surrender our self to Him. By that surrender of our "self" we undergo a supreme death to our old nature at the roots. After that death we still survive. There is a resurrection – of a new person, a new "self." And that person is too great and too happy to be angered by petty annoyances.

Prayer for today: O Christ, make me too happy and too great to be angered by petty things. Amen.

August 7   Ephesians 4:31-32; James 1:19-21, 3:6

IF ANGER REMAINS

Often anger remains to trouble us after we surrender "self.." Why? Because of two things: Either the surrender was only partial or the growth of our spiritual life after our surrender has been neglected. Ninety percent of germs that fall on healthy skin die quickly. Health kills them. The way to kill sin germs is strengthen the organism upon which they feed. To neglect growth is to let our spirit grow weak; and when that happens, our resistance is also weakened, and the disease gets a strong hold on us, and causes havoc. After our complete surrender to Christ there must be growth or there will be collapse.

Sometimes our surrender is only partial, we don't surrender completely, and we hold things back. That partial surrender sets up division in our nature, and that division turns into a fight within our spirit. There is a struggle for command of our spirit. Anger results from that struggle. We are touchy among other undesirable attitudes.

Sometimes our temper comes back to us worse than ever, because we made a compromised effort to get rid of it. We try to please both God and our "self." We may put self out a little distance, but we have not decisively dealt with it. And the temper based in "self" just keeps coming back.

Prayer for today: O Christ, we pray that You will help us to let "self" remain dead within us and our new surrendered life blossom with no anger. Amen.

August 8   Isaiah 29:21; Matthew 7:1-5;
                                           1 Corinthians 13:4-6

ENCOUNTERING FAIR CRITICISM

Encountering criticism conforms to our thought of overcoming anger. Sometimes criticism may be fair, but more often it is not. Unfounded criticism is often based on partial knowledge, not on fact or reality.

What are we to do when faced with criticism? First, ask yourself if it is true? And if it is fair and true criticism, acknowledge that fact and learn from it and use it. One of the greatest helps to the spiritual life is healthy criticism. Hopefully you have friends who can do this for you and you for them.

Example: A speaker was giving instructions to a group at a retreat, a new convert said to him, "Whenever we put difficult questions to you, you make us forget the question by changing the subject and talking about something else that is very interesting. You dodge our questions. It isn't honest." Everyone laughed, but the speaker learned a lesson he would never forget. The student was right. Now when the speaker doesn't know the answer he says so, instead of trying, perhaps unconsciously, to save face by going off to something else. Sometimes our critics can become the very hammers of God to beat us into shape, for we are only Christians in the making.

Prayer for today: O God, Our Father, help me not to resent criticism, but to take it as from Your shaping hand – Your efforts to shape me and mold me. Amen.

August 9   Matthew 5:44-46; 6:14-15; Romans 14:4, 13

ENCOUNTERING UNFAIR CRITICISM

Some of our criticisms are unjust and unfair. They may come from partial knowledge of something or they may come from something that has been misrepresented. So what do we do about unfair criticism?

First and foremost quickly breathe a prayer for your critics and yourself. It is harder to hate a person after you have prayed for them. Prayer pulls at the strings of resentment. Our attitude toward them becomes redemptive instead of resentful. You want to help them get rid of their ignorance and/or spitefulness. Keep your thoughts bathed in prayer as you think of them. **A prayerless thought will become a resentful thought – a prayerful thought will become a redemptive thought**.

Second, keep saying to yourself, "My soul is too great to let anyone be my enemy." Keep an inner spiritual dignity that will keep you from descending to their level.

Third, begin to think of ways to do good to them. They will have their armor up waiting for your return blow. Strike them where they are unguarded – at the heart. Overcome evil with good. If someone foolishly does you wrong, return godly love to them. The more evil comes from them, the more good will come from me. The poison of the slanderer's words returns to them, the perfume of our good deeds returns to us. In loving our enemy, in turning the other cheek, as Jesus commanded and illustrated, we rise above our enemy, and we may win them to Christ. But if not, we have won our own soul, either way we win.

Prayer for today: O Christ of the smitten cheek and still loving heart, help us to follow You at this point in our life. Criticisms make us writhe in pain, but let that pain drive us closer to You. If we are attacked by criticism may we take it straight to You. For You are the ultimate painkiller. Amen.

August 10   Matthew 27:12-14;
                                              Romans 12:14, 17, 19-21

ANSWERING OUR CRITICS

Sometimes we will have to answer those who wrong us. We owe it to ourselves and to them to clear things up with an explanation. But whether this is verbal or by writing do it on your knees, as you will certainly need God's presence with you. Don't give them a piece of your mind – you will lose your own piece of mind if you do! And don't be so misguided by your hurt or anger that you think by acting like the devil – you can influence the devil out of someone else. Satan can't cast out Satan, nor does he want to. Speak to your critic as you would like to be spoken to. Or if you are writing a letter, after you have written it, don't mail it that day, sleep on it, your subconscious mind might enlighten you. It will if the spirit of Christ is in your subconscious mind.

Or perhaps you shouldn't answer at all. Let Jesus answer for you. In (Luke 5:30) it says, *"But the Pharisees and the teachers of the law who belonged to their sect complained to the disciples, 'Why do you eat and drink with tax collectors and sinners?' Jesus answered them, 'It is not the healthy who need a doctor, but the sick.' ..."* They criticized the disciples and Jesus answered for them. Jesus often answers for us! It is safer to have Him answer for us. Jesus answer was deathless and redemptive; the disciples' answer would probably have been very evasive and unreal. Let Jesus answer for you!

Prayer for today: O Jesus, I do not know the ways to others heart, but You know and You come in ever so softly and oh, how redemptive! Help me to win others for you. Amen.

August 11   Matthew 5:11; Luke
                                   6:22; 1 Corinthians 4:13;
                                   Philippians 2:5-11

DON'T WORRY ABOUT YOUR REPUTATION

"Oh", but you say, "If I don't answer, what will happen to my reputation? I have to look after my reputation!" No, you don't. Anyone who is Living Victoriously has gained victory over anxious concern about their reputation. You do not have to look after it. **LOOK AFTER YOUR CHARACTER AND YOUR REPUTATION WILL LOOK AFTER ITSELF.** Be the kind of person about whom people won't believe bad things.

Besides, Jesus says: *"It is enough for the student to be like his teacher, and the servant like his master. If the head of the house has been called Beelzebub, how much more the members of his household! So do not be afraid of them. There is nothing concealed that will not be disclosed, or hidden that will not be made known."* (Matthew 10:25-26). In other words, don't be afraid concerning your reputation, if they call you prince of demons, there is nothing hidden – the truth will be known in the end. There will be justice in the end. You can wait.

Abraham Lincoln was one of the most loved persons America has ever produced. Most loved and most slandered. Nothing was too offensive to print about him. And yet no one believes it now. "There is nothing hidden." His slanderers slandered themselves.

Do people talk about you? How about you? Have you been a loose-tongued slanderer? Sew slanderous seeds and slanderous seeds you will reap. If so- "there is nothing hidden." Slanderers slander themselves. Think about it!

Prayer for today: O Jesus Christ, purest of souls, yet You were called Beelzebub, the prince of demons." Help me not to worry about my reputation. Help me to have faith here. Amen.

August 12   2 Corinthians 1:7; Philippians 1:29; 3:10;
                   2 Thessalonians 1:4-5

VICTORY THROUGH SUFFERING

Now we come to the question of pain and suffering. You can be sure we will meet them on the road to Living Victoriously; hopefully they won't be our constant companions on our way. But the question is: What shall we do with them and what will they do with us? First, note that pain has probably saved the human race from physical extermination. Had there been no such thing as pain, we probably would not have survived as a human race. For if we did not know that fire causes pain to us if we thrust our hands into it, we would let our hands be burned by that fire. If disease did not cause us pain, we probably would think little about it, and we would succumb to disease, because we would not have pain to warn us. Pain says, "There is something wrong – take care of it." So pain turns out to be our friendly watchman guarding us against dangers to life. Pain is God's preventive grace, built into the structure of our physical life. Nevertheless, there is much needless pain – it is in the world far beyond its biological uses in survival. We inflict this needless pain on ourselves and others needlessly. Much of this pain is curable and should be cured by individual and collective action. Suffering is a wider term. It may be caused by pain, but it has other and deeper causes. Suffering may be intensely mental and spiritual. Suffering also may be a part of God's preventive grace. It could be God's danger signal that something is wrong. If there were no mental and spiritual suffering, we, as a human race, might have committed mental and spiritual suicide long ago. Our first step, then, is to look on pain and suffering not entirely as enemies – they may assist us in gaining Victorious Life.

Prayer for today: O Christ, we thank You that through pain and suffering You have an authentic word to say to us. Amen.

August 13   1 Peter 4:1, 12-19

ARE CHRISTIANS EXEMPT?

Pain and suffering comes to us all. We are surrounded by nature, by other human beings, by our own physical bodies, and through these avenues pain and suffering comes to us. And the fact that we are Christians will not keep them from coming.

A young man was stunned by his failing in a final exam. He said, "I cannot understand. I prayed very hard before the exam and I live a very good life, (notice he didn't say anything about studying for his exam). Then why, oh, why, should I have failed? My faith in God is gone." He felt that if he lived good enough and prayed hard enough, he would be sure to pass his exam. When he was not exempt from suffering through failure, he felt his religion did not work – it should have made him exempt from failure. Now, suppose it had exempted him and others like him, what would happen to the human race? If it could be proved that if you lived a good life and prayed hard enough, you would be assured of passing your exam, then our classrooms would be deserted before exam time, and students would flock to the hillsides and other places for prayer and meditation, and in the process their minds would dry up. Mental suffering through failure, because of laziness in studying or incapability, is one of God's methods of keeping the human race mentally alive. It is mentally redemptive.

Christians as well as non-Christians suffer from wrong choices made by ourselves and others, from natural sufferings, sufferings through other humans, and through our physical bodies. Christians may even suffer from the very fact that they are morally and spiritually detached from the world. None of us are exempt from pain and suffering. Why should we be – Christ wasn't.

Prayer for today: O Christ, You are our way, our only way. Help us to learn that fact. Amen.

August 14   Acts 5:41; Romans 8:12 & 18; Colossians 1:24

WHAT IS OUR ATTITUDE?

We said yesterday that suffering happens to all of us – good people included. But while the same things may happen to all of us they do not have the same effect on all of us. The same thing happening to two different people may have an entirely different effect on them. It all depends on our inner attitude. **What effect life has on us in the long run depends on what life finds within us.** Sorrow and suffering makes some people resentful and bitter, others it sweetens and refines, same event, with opposite effects. What happens to us "without" does not determine the "outcome." That depends on what life finds "within" us. There were three crosses that day on Calvary's hill. The same event was happening to three people. But it had three different effects upon them. One thief complained bitterly and shouted at Jesus for not saving Himself and them; another saw this tragedy a result of his sins, repented, and through it saw an open door to heaven; the third through that cross redeemed a race. Here we have the same event, three entirely different results. **So the thing that matters is not what happens to us, but how we respond to it after it happens**. Your cross can become the most blessed of unlimited opportunities. The same "sunshine" falling on two branches of a tree – in one it causes decay; in the other it causes growth. It all depends on the responses the branches gave. One meets the "sunshine" with inner life and more life results. The other meets it with inner death and more death results. How will you meet the "Sonshine"? According to inner response, suffering leaves some people writhing in helpless despair, others it leaves stronger and more capable of encountering more suffering, capable of encountering anything.

Prayer for today: O Christ, transform our inner base metal attitudes of ordinary and extraordinary events into the gold of Living Victoriously! Amen.

August 15   Acts 8:3-8; 2 Corinthians 12: 7-10

DO YOU KNOW WHAT TO DO?

Most Christians understand from Christ example that we are not to escape suffering, nor merely to bear it, but to use it. We can take it into the purpose of our life and make it contribute to God's glory for which we really live. The raw materials of human life, the things that come into our life from day to day, can be woven into garments of character. All of this depends on what inner attitudes we take. Take two people, both of them intelligent and well-bred, suffering from the same illness. One, it is making bitter, resentful, and hopeless, the other it is making radiant, sweet and hopeful. The one mentioned last will emerge from the suffering as pure gold. And their very attitude will help them emerge. Nothing tones the body like a peaceful, hopeful, victorious spirit. The other one may not emerge at all, for they are handicapping their body in its fight to recover by dragging their body down with their despairing spirit. The difference is that one inner life is adjusted to the will of God, and the other is not, same circumstances, two very different results.

Two families each lost a son in death, one a true Christian family and the other was <u>not</u> a Christian family. A twelve year old boy talking to his Mother said, "It isn't so hard for the Christian family, for they know what to do. But these other people don't know what to do." The boy had hit the mark in the situation. He saw the same event happening to two families, each with a different result. Because the Christian family knew what to do – "depend on God." We can say to ourselves, "I cannot determine what happens to me but I can determine how it will affect me after it happens. It will make me a better person and more useful." That is what we call VICTORY!

Prayer for today: O Christ, help us to be determined to use our circumstances, whatever they may be, to Your glory. Amen.

August 16   2 Corinthians 4:8-12; 6:4-10

THE PAIN GOD IS ALLOWED TO GUIDE

(2 Corinthians 7:10) Paul says, "*Godly sorrow brings repentance that leads to salvation and leaves no regret, but worldly sorrow brings death.*" Some pain leads to life and some pain leads to death. And the difference is this: In one circumstance one person's pains were dealt with by their own hands on an entirely human level. This makes us bitter and cynical and full of complaints. It leads to death. On the other hand, a person takes God into their pain and allows Him to guide them. God then turns what would have been senseless suffering into a spiritual discipline. A better person emerges. It leads to life.

So in every circumstance that we face therein lies life or death. The common, everyday circumstances of life make us common – or Christian! A man's wife called his attention to a beautiful sunset – the sky was streaked with fluffy white clouds. "Yes," he said, "It reminds me, please see that my bacon is cooked with more fat in it." He turned a radiant sunset into a reminder of bacon! That comment made the glorious into commonplace. It is all the result of what is found within us. To the wife the sunset was a thing of beauty – life; to her husband, commonplace – bacon, with white streaks of fat.

The pain itself from which we are suffering may have come from some evil source, but the question is not where it came from, but were it is going! Where it goes is determined by whether we allow it to be guided to life or to death. And that is determined by whether we put God into the pain, and offer it to Him as we offer everything else, and make it a part of His redemptive purpose for us. The cross is an example of God-guided pain. It ushered in salvation. Our crosses may also usher in salvation, if God is allowed to guide the pain involved in them.

Prayer for today: O Christ, You turned Your cross into a throne, help us to wear our sorrows and sufferings with regal dignity. Amen.

August 17   Job 12:4; John 16:33, 17:4; Acts 3:14-15

WILL LIFE ALWAYS BE FAIR?

Yesterday we ended by suggesting that our sufferings might come from an evil source outside our own will. And you say, "This isn't fair." No, it isn't fair. But we all know life isn't fair. Christianity never taught that life would be fair. On the contrary, Christianity has the cross at its heart – and that is the world's supreme injustice, (unfairness).Don't ask for fairness from life – ask for power to turn unfairness (injustice) into a better life. Then you have more than justice, you have life itself. Life was not fair to Paul. He found life coming to him in the form of imprisonments, beatings, desertions, anxiety and seemingly there was no one to care. It wasn't fair. But Paul made it into something better than fair. (Paul explains in Romans 8:28). "*And we know that in all things God works for the good of those who love him, who have been called according to his purpose.*" The thing itself may not be good; it may have come from the very devil himself, but God throws in enough good to make it work together for good. God actually uses evil for the destruction of evil. He uses the devil-sourced evil for the making of God-inspired men and women. If we work with God, we can turn our very defeats into victories. That is what the cross itself is. There was a wonderful Christian woman who served God and others for many years, a beautiful character, and then she became blind. Life wasn't fair to her. No, but she made it more than fair, she made it beautiful. "It is all dark," she said, "but then it is all very lovely," she added, with a quiet heavenly smile. Don't offer that woman fairness; she has grace and that is more than fair. So don't ask that life be fair, ask that power be given you to make life's unfairness (injustices) into opportunities, life's very obstacles into instruments.

Prayer for today: O Christ, Your life was supremely unfair, yet You did not whine for fairness, but You boldly turned the worst into the best. Help me to know how to do the same. Amen.

August 18   Acts 16:22-34

SEIZING THE MOMENT

Doctor Vail was performing more operations, at the time, than any other doctor in India, among them thousands of cancer operations. Dr. Vail, himself, developed cancer and died with it. But – before he died he flew to Germany, and while not cured, he came back to India with a new treatment for cancer that would help thousands. Cancer struck Dr. Vail and he struck back with a cancer treatment. And he did so while he himself was hopelessly stricken. He seized the moment. So did Beethoven. Beethoven had gone stone-deaf. "Oh, if I were only free of this affliction, I could embrace the world." ...But "I will seize fate by the throat; most assuredly it will not get me wholly down—oh, it is so beautiful to live like a thousand fold." Fosdick quotes a biographer of Beethoven, himself a musician, who comments on the above statement: We are eternal debtors to Beethoven's deafness. It is doubtful if such lofty music could have been created except as self-compensation for some affliction, and with the utter isolation which the affliction brought about." Beethoven seized the moment. E. Staley Jones first Sunday school student became an engineer. An explosion left the man totally deaf and totally blind. At that time, there was no way to communicate with him except to spell out the letters with their fingers on the back of his hand. He was shut off from the world. Not at all! He gained more information and knowledge through other people's finger-tips and through his own meditations than ninety-nine percent of those who have open eyes and ears. Moreover, this man established a far-flung business for the blind. He seized the moment. We all can think of wonderful people who took bad circumstances of life and seized the moment to make marvelous results for Christ. Whatever the circumstances your life holds, do not wait, seize the moment. You'll be so glad you did.

Prayer for today: O Christ, help me to seize this moment and every moment and make it serve Your purpose –and mine. Amen.

August 19   1 Corinthians 4:9-13; 2 Corinthians 1:3-7

LIGHT ON LIFE'S DARKEST PROBLEM

Jesus said, "*I am the light of the world.*" (John 8:12, 9:5). In the book of (John chapter nine) we read the story of the man born blind, when the disciples asked, "*Who sinned, this man or his parents, that he should be blind?*" At this place of undeserved suffering – Christ is the light of the world.

Christ was and is the light of the world's darkest problem. The more we listen to various suggestions of philosophy and religion concerning the problem of undeserved suffering, the more we should be convinced that Christ is the light of the world at the world's darkest problem.

The undeserved blindness of this man was not from sin of his or his parents (verse 3). But happened in the ordinary course of Divine providence, and should now be an instrument of salvation to his soul, edification to others, and glory to God. (John 9:4), shows Christ could plainly see that to cure this man would draw down on Him the harmful intent of the Jewish rulers, yet as long as it was Day He must accomplish the work He was sent to do for the One who sent Him. Day representing the opportunity to do that work; Night, the loss of that opportunity. (Verse 5), "*I am the Light of the world,*" it was His business to dispense light; and neglect no opportunity that would offer to enlighten the bodies and souls of people everywhere.

Christ then showed us what He meant. He turned every single adverse circumstance, every single injustice, every single disappointment, every single betrayal, every single desertion, and every single cross and made it contribute to the end He had in view, the Kingdom of God. To be able to use pain and sorrow – this is LIGHT, and the Man who can give us power to do this very thing is "THE LIGHT OF THE WORLD."

Prayer for today: O Christ, You spoke the word of light when life seemed dark and mysterious, help us each day to take that light and live by it, and in doing so become light to others. Amen.

August 20   Luke 7:36-50; 10:25-37

FROM THE MASTER OF LIFE
LEARN THE MYSTERY AND THE MASTERY OF LIFE

The world desperately needs to learn these two things:

Light on the mystery of life, and **Life** for the mastery (superiority) of life. Jesus gives both, for He has both to give. Peep through this open door of the Pharisee's house and see if you see any light. (Luke 7:36-50). A Pharisee had invited Jesus to his house for dinner. And then for whatever reason, possibly to show his own authority and partial contempt for Jesus, the Pharisee omitted all of the courtesies he would customarily give to a guest. The Pharisee gave Jesus no kiss of greeting, no water for His feet and no oil for His head. It was a social snub. It is one of those things that send some people rushing to their bedroom with a terrible headache and a terrible hatred. Instead of Jesus acting in this way, something else happened. The discourtesy of the Pharisee gave not only the opportunity for Jesus to teach a valuable lesson, but it also gave the opportunity of a poor, stricken sinful woman to make up for what the host had left undone. And never was there such courtesy- - - tears to wash Jesus feet, her hair in place of a towel, and precious perfume – all of these came from the depths of the heart and not from mere courtesy. The Pharisee hardens his heart and criticizes Jesus bitterly. Then Jesus takes moral control of the situation. He points out to the Pharisee his discourtesy, and then proceeds to forgive him and the woman. He put them both in the same category of needy sinners and forgave them both. He, who did not receive the gifts that courtesy should have brought, turned and gave the gift of forgiveness. And by doing so was morally in control of the situation, so instead of being the snubbed guest, He became the giver of abundance. Jesus did not bear that snub, He used it. And the world sits at the feet of such a Master and learns how to live.

Prayer for today: O Christ, when I am socially hurt and snubbed, help me not to be resentful and bitter, but big and forgiving. Amen

August 21   Acts 26:29; Romans 8:18;
                                 2 Corinthians 4:17;
                                 Ephesians 3:13

LET THE GLORY OUT!

Hard circumstances will either make us or break us. We have all probably seen or heard of a man or woman who because of death of a spouse or divorce straightens up and becomes an oak, around which the growing children wrap their lives, and are forever grateful for such a parent. But this strength would have never come out and developed had it not been for the tears that watered the vine and made it an oak.

Edwin Markham wrote:

"Defeat may serve as well as victory
To shake the soul and let the glory out.
When the great oak is straining in the wind,
The boughs drink in a new beauty, and the trunk
Send down a deeper root on the windward side.
Only the soul that knows the mighty grief
Can know the mighty rapture. Sorrows come
To stretch our spaces in the heart of joy."

We will be struck by many blows of many sorrows and troubles, but only what is in us can splash out of us. Out of some of the blows of circumstance and trouble splash complaint and bitterness, out of others splash joy and victory. It brings out what is in us. An older Christian gentleman was standing on a train as it was pulling into the station, the train lurched and threw him from one row of seats to another row of seats across the isle, those near him heard him say, "Glory," and when he hit the other side, "Hallelujah." The jolting splashed out what was in him! Will trouble serve to shake your glory out? If so, then you have victory. This is what trouble did to Christ. It shook Him to death and scattered grace across the world.

Prayer for today: O Christ, help us to have such victory within that peace and joy will splash on those around us. Amen.

(Read with previous lesson)

THE GLORY SPOUT

If your religion is in doubt,
If your heart doesn't know
What your experience is about,
Then get under the spout -
Where the glory comes out.

If your religion, my friend,
Doesn't give you peace within
And joy beyond measure,
If it doesn't offer great pleasure,
Then get under the spout –
Where the glory comes out.

Is your religion dry and dull?
Is it boring and uneventful?
Are you in bondage instead of free?
If it is all these things, don't let it be!
Hasten – Get under the spout –
Where the glory comes out.

Now ask yourself another question,
Concerning this religion matter,
Are you living for Christ for -
What He can do <u>for you</u> OR <u>through you</u>?
If it is the latter,
Then you are under the spout –
Where the glory comes out.

By-MaryAnn Moore (May 21, 1979)

August 22

Habakkuk 3:17-19;
Luke13:1-5;
Hebrews 2:10

IS TROUBLE GOD'S PUNISHMENT?

Many feel that when they have trouble in their life, it is God's punishment for some sin. This attitude makes Living Victoriously impossible. We must admit that this is a world of moral consequence and sin does bring trouble. However, Jesus rejected the idea that great misfortune and sin were always connected. In today's scripture in (Luke 13:1-5), Jesus comment concerning the fall of the Tower of Siloam and those whose blood Pilate mingled with their sacrifices, the ones suffering *"were not sinners above the rest,"* He said. No, look on trouble as an opportunity to show what godly stuff you have within you.

"Why do I creep along the heavenly way,
By inches in the bright sunny day?
Then when darkness of night around me lowers
I run miles in one short hour!"

The darkness of night may only serve to hasten your pace toward Home – an old Indian proverb says, "The bursting of the petals says the flower is coming." So when your heart burst with pain and grief, it's the bursting of the petals to let the flowers out. The heartbreak of Gethsemane was the bursting of petals that let the Passion Flower out. And the world is filled with its perfume. It is wonderful and amazing what God can do with a broken heart **IF** you will give Him all the pieces. Let Him put your broken life together again, perhaps in a new glorious pattern. On a Mission Agricultural Farm they discovered that when the tops of an eggplant withered from frost, the plant had a second crop. From the frost they discovered something. They learned after the plants gave one crop they cut them back and the plants gave a second crop. So the cuts that we receive from life may not be God's punishments, but God's pruning and may those be used for greater fruitfulness.

Prayer for today: O Christ, prune me to be more fruitful. Amen.

August 23   John 16:7-8; Hebrews 12:3-12

GOD TAKES AWAY OUR CRUTCHES

Let's pursue the thought that our troubles may be God's pruning.

The true story is told about a woman who had been crippled for years with a spinal cord problem and could not walk without crutches. One day as she was coming down the stairs, she slipped and fell to the bottom of the stairs, her crutches being lost to her on the way down. She lay there calling for help, but no one was near to hear her call. With great effort she drew herself up by the banister, began to walk and has been walking ever since - without the crutches! The fall and the loss of those crutches was the best thing that ever happened to her. There are many things in our lives which we lean on heavily – family, friends, money, positions, etc. That may not be wrong, but they become crutches that weaken our moral fiber. **ANYTHING WE DEPEND ON IN THE PLACE OF CHRIST IS A CRUTCH**. Then when misfortune takes them away we are shocked and hurt. Our crutches are gone – what now? Oh Yes- our own feet, our own backbone and the grace of God! That is enough on which to build a new life.

Another true story: There was a young man, a cruel young man, a devout Pharisee, he hunted down and persecuted followers of Jesus, while still breathing out murderous threats against the Lord's disciples, and on his way to Damascus to take more prisoners for his cause against Christ, suddenly he lost his crutches! He lost everything, his standing in society, his position as a physician, family, friends, his appetite, his eyesight and even his very familiar name. This man Saul would never be the same, he would now suffer much FOR Christ name. (Acts 9:16). Saul did not weep over his lost crutches, though he was blind, now he could see and what he saw and felt was a new man with a new name, filled with God's spirit and ready to be used for God, not against Him, ready not to imprison people, but to set them free.

Paul was ready to stand up and be counted.

This is the message God has for our civilization that also has its crutches: "Throw away the crutches – stand up and be counted!"

Prayer for today:
O Christ, when You take away our crutches, whatever they may be, help us not to whimper and whine, but stand on our feet and be counted. Amen.

{USE THIS SPACE TO RECORD ANY CRUTCHES YOU NEED CHRIST TO TAKE AWAY}

August 24   Romans 5:3-5; 8:35-39

GOD'S INSULATIONS

We try to meet pain and misfortune in two ways: One by isolation, the other insulation.

A man said, "I am praying that either my wife will die or that I will die." He put her first, anyway he continued, "What else can I do, for we cannot get along together." That is being a moral coward, and a Christian has another way out. We can do what an oyster does when it gets an irritating grain of sand in its shell – it grows a pearl around it. It turns irritation into iridescence. There are many of us who turn our daily irritations into character, into patience, into beauty. Having withstood that lesser thing at home, we are ready for bigger problems outside the home. We are insulated. Small problems become the process by which we insulate ourselves against greater problems. It is nature hardening us for bigger stress.

Milo of Crotona, a weight lifter, bet that he could lift a bull into the air. He bought a calf and lifted it each day as it grew bigger, so when the calf became a full-grown bull he could lift it even then. So – God increases our strength by helping us conquer our daily trials, until one day we will be able to lift more than our regular load.

Prayer for today: O Christ, when sorrow eats at me, help me to remember Your insulations – and rejoice. Amen.

August 25   2 Timothy 2:12; 1 Peter 1:6-7; 5:10;
                             Revelation 2:9-10

SUMMING UP

Life brings sorrow to all of us. "Affliction really does color life,"
said a friend, to one who was suffering. "Yes," replied the suffering
one, "And I choose color." And so it was with a minister friend of
mine – he chose color. He chose to live through his long painful
years of affliction. He suffered with diabetes and the horrible effects
of that disease – dialysis, numerous surgeries where, through the
years, he lost fingers, toes, and eventually both legs, the breakdown
of other parts of his body, heart, stomach, eye- sight and much more.
He was completely incapacitated? **NO! Not at all**! Only his body
was. His room was the center of spiritual power. He had the most
heavenly smile – shaped with beauty and dignity. He chose to be
beautiful inside and out. When he died even the doctors and nurses
were amazed at the presence of God that was felt in his room as he
passed from this life to a greater one. My friend could not eliminate
his suffering, but he chose to use that suffering to God's glory. And
because he chose to live it with color we were all blessed.

> Our anguish cry goes up to God,
>   "Lord, take away pain!
> Take away the shadow that darkens our soul,
>   With its ever tightening chain,
> It strangles our heart; causes a heavy weight,
>   On wings that longs to soar.
> Lord, take away pain from the world you made,
>   So it will love You more."
>
> The Lord answered to the cry of His world:
>   "Shall I take away pain?
> And with it the power of the soul to endure-
>   That soul made strong by the strain?
> Shall I take away compassion that knits heart to heart?

And sacrifice you feel is too high?
Will you lose all the heroes that's been through the fire
   And lifted scorched faces to the sky?
Shall I take away love that redeems with a price?
   And yet smiles at its loss?
Can you spare from your lives that desire that longs for me?
   The Christ on His cross?"

Prayer for today: O Christ, we will fight beside You to take away suffering, for it is not Your will; but where we cannot eliminate it, help us to use it to Your glory. Amen.

August 26   Mark 6:30-32; Acts 1:3-4; Galatians 1:15-17

MUSIC IN THE MAKING

We have been discussing positive pain and suffering, but there are troubles which there are no positive pain or suffering. These troubles arise when we are rendered inactive, shelved, as we say. Some of these come from temporary indispositions, some through approaching old age. In all of these our work is suspended and we have to face life inactive. This sometimes is harder than positive suffering.

Someone has said that in music "pauses are music in the making." This momentary suspense produces music more lovely than before. The pause prepares those who produce and those who listen for the finer music.

It is possible that those pauses in our lives – these suspensions from activity – may become music in the making. Cannot the temporary periods of inactivity, be made into periods which, in fact, become music in the making.

It was so in the life of Jesus. The call to give His message must have burned in His soul like fire during those silent years in Nazareth. Possibly, Jesus was helping His earthly father, Joseph, to build earthly things, when He knew He was commissioned by His heavenly Father to build a heavenly Kingdom. But Jesus did not get annoyed or impatient. He could wait – yes, for thirty years. We are so glad He waited – the music is sweeter for the waiting. Those silent years are a pause which became music in the making. Thirty years of silence, three years of song, Oh, but what a song!

It is richer because of patient silence in it.

It may also be in your life and mine – silences that enrich the ultimate music.

Prayer for today: O Christ, may we be patient under restriction, that we may be richer under release. Let us not be impatient, but let us trust. Amen.

August 27   Matthew 14:13-14; Mark 6:33-34;
                                   Revelation 1:9-10

PAUSES ARE—
MISSED OPPORTUNITIES AND INTERRUPTIONS

Youth often get annoyed or aggravated under years of disciplined schooling. Many throw away the opportunity for higher education and when the opportunity never returns they live with the regret for the rest of their lives. They refuse the pause, so there is no music in the making. Can you think of an opportunity that has passed you by because you did not want to work it out, study it out, or dig it out by the opportune roots? And now life sings very broken music and we live to regret that that part of our life is ineffective.

One of the most distressing pauses that we meet is that of interruptions. During the day we plan our work our quiet study time, our prayer time, our rest, or whatever – and people upset our plans – and us. And we complain that our time was ruined. But could it be that those very interruptions are opportunities? Jesus made opportunities from interruptions. Trace through His life and you'll find that almost everything glorious came out of an interruption. Some of His finest teaching, His greatest deeds, the revelation of His Holy Spirit, it all came out of some circumstance or some person, upsetting His plans. Actually, interruptions did not upset His plans; they only set His grace off in new directions. Christ looked at them as God placing human need across His path. These interruptions were opportunities. Once when Jesus was so pressed for time, He and His disciples had not had time to eat, He took them to the desert for quiet time. But the multitudes followed anyway, and Jesus had compassion on them, spoke to them about the Kingdom of God, healed those that needed healing, and then He fed them all. He taught, He healed, and He fed the very ones who had interrupted His plans and His quiet time.

But those five words *"He had compassion on them"* (Mark 6:34), mean more to us than any books on patience and love. Those words throw open a window into the heart of goodness. That pause was music in the making, and Oh, what music!

Prayer for today: O Christ, as we encounter interruptions, even those by very trying people, let us use them as opportunities to reveal Your Spirit within us. Amen.

August 28   Job 19:29; Philippians 1:21-25; 2 Timothy 4:6-8

THE MOST SOLEMN PAUSE OF ALL – DEATH

None of the pauses mentioned can compare with the pause of death. Our work is stopped, our plans cease, our connection with others is snapped, and the pitcher is broken, broken just as we were about to pour someone a drink of cool water. This is the most devastating pause of all. Or is it? It may be the pause that turns out to be life's sweetest, happiest, music in the making.

This was so with Alice Means, one of the rarest missionaries ever in India. What an amazing life she was living – building, teaching, making leaders! And the cancer struck her. She wanted to get back to America before she died, but was stopped in Bombay by the doctors, who knew she would never reach America. This is her letter to E. Stanley Jones from the Bombay hospital, after knowing she would be denied the privilege of going home to die. Knowing Mr. Jones was writing a book at the time she told him to use her as an illustration in his book which he did.

"I haven't suffered much yet, and when I do, I may not be able to tell you how it goes. How thankful I am for all these years of perfect, abounding health! What a happy life I have had! Let me tell you of the experience of these last two months:

{With a host of others I am working along in a great field, digging, sowing, weeding, watering, never noticing I had reached the edge, till I heard, "Alice, that's enough, come over here and sit down a bit." I looked up and there stood Jesus smiling at me. I went over and sat down on the grass by Him, and He said, "You have been busy working and have not had time for all those intimacies that go with a great friendship, such as I want with you.

Come along and let us walk together here." He put His arm through mine and we walked along an avenue all covered with grass and flowers, and the birds were singing. Oh, it is beautiful! As I look down toward the

river it is a little misty. But I know He will see me through that.}

Even now I am forever with my Lord. His peace within me is wonderful. Nothing can separate us now. It is heaven. That's all. The doctors and nurses cannot understand how I can so calmly discuss my condition and outlook"

Who can say that this pause of death to her was not music in the making?

Prayer for today: O Christ, Even death can be music in the making, let us welcome it with joy. Amen.

August 29

Psalm 55:16-17; Matthew 6:6; 14:22-23; Luke 18:1

LIFE'S MOST FRUITFUL PAUSE

The most fruitful pause of all is the pause of prayer. There is more music in the making in prayer than anything we know, and yet how few of us really use it? Prayer is the most talked about and the least used force in the world. We aren't talking about using prayer to gain benefit from the reflective influence that comes to us from quiet time and meditation. We are talking about our spirit coming into intimate, personal contact with the Spirit called God, so we can come to a common understanding with Him, can adjust our will to His will and through this contact find our personality heightened, enlightened, re-enforced and used. Experience shows that those who think of prayer as only a reaction influence soon give up prayer. It is not possible to project our spirit continuously to that which is not responsive. If you believe it is possible for God to put a thought into your heart then you can believe in prayer. CAN God put a thought into our heart? Yes, Christ can re-enforce the very foundations of our being by our knowing His own life. Life flows into life, will into will, love into love – that is what prayer means. It all happens when we and our prayers are in agreement to the Eternal God.

If the computer can send clear pictures
Across a continent or the deep blue sea;
If the songs of birds and the mighty wind
Can be heard across the mountain glen;
If music can be heard through thin air,
Why should we humans wonder if God hears prayer?

Have you gone to your knees broken, defeated, and risen, new and victorious. And everything in us knows we met God!

Prayer for today: O Christ, this wonderful pause of prayer – what music in the making there is in it! Help us to use it as a working way to live. Amen.

August 30   Psalm 37:4-6; Proverbs 3:6;
                            Matthew 18:19-20; John 15:7, 16

WE PAUSE TO CONSIDER PRAYER

Let's free ourselves of certain notions about prayer. Prayer is not a lightning rod to save us from the lightning of God's wrath. Many think it is – if they don't pray something bad will happen to them. "We don't have prayer in our home and nothing has happened yet." You say. No, nothing has happened yet – nothing except deterioration of your home. And that is more than enough to let happen. However, deterioration is such a slow process that we scarcely see it taking place and so we are not alarmed. Prayerlessness means slow ruin, not sudden misfortune.

Again, prayer is not bending God to our will – it is bringing our will to God's will. If we were mountain climbing and we throw the rope up and catch hold of the rock above, do we pull the rock to us? No, we pull ourselves to the top. Prayer does not pull God to us, it pulls us to God. It aligns our wills with His, so that He can do things through us that He would not other wise be able to do. His almighty will works through our weak wills, and we can do things out of proportion to our ability. Prayer is, therefore, not overcoming God's reluctance; it is finding His will for our life. Those who pray link up with God's will. God leaves certain things open around us depending on our will – those things will not be done unless we act – is it strange then that He leaves certain things open, depending on prayer – things that will never be done unless we do them through prayer? In sincere prayer our will coincides with His will. That is what we mean when we pray "in Jesus name"- that is – we pray the kind of prayer He would pray.

Prayer for today: O Father, let us strive to make our will coincide with Your will that Your power can coincide with ours. Amen.

August 31   Psalm 109:4; Luke 21:36; Romans 12:12

PRAYER – (Continued)

If when we pray we learn to ask less and less for things, and instead ask more and more FOR God Himself, FOR the assurance that our will and His are not at cross-purposes, that we agree on all minor and major matters, then we will know that we will get all the things we need – not want – need. *"But seek first his kingdom and his righteousness, and all these things will be given to you as well."* (Matthew 6:33*).* If I seek **FIRST** His Kingdom and His righteousness, <u>then</u> these things will be given to me as well. God is interested in things. But we must not want the reality of prayer to depend on whether we get this thing or that thing. If we get <u>Him</u> in living communion, then the prayer is answered and is effective. Things are a side issue. But with many Christians things are central, like the little boy who said, "I love my daddy. My daddy gives me a dollar every day." Money – praying, like money – loving, belongs to immature children.

Some people only pray and say they love God out of fear of punishment or hope for reward. God knows our heart. Love Him just for Himself!

Prayer is the power to get through difficulties, to be at our best, to become effective. We can cross "un-crossable" rivers, climb impassable mountains, and do impossible things through prayer. For God, the Eternal God works with us and in us. So, we must pray, sincerely pray, if we want to live – and Live Victoriously.

Prayer for today: O Christ, thank You, for what prayer has done for You and through You. May prayer give us power to go forward. Amen.

September 1   Psalm 4:4; 24:3-5; Isaiah 64:4; 1Timothy 4:15

MAKING OUR DEVOTIONAL TIME EFFECTIVE

FIRST OF ALL HAVE PRAYER TIME. Keep your prayer time religiously. Make things fit into your prayer time, not your prayer time fit into things. Anyone who neglects prayer time saying, "I can pray anytime or all the time," will probably pray none of the time. But keep a scheduled time to pray, it will probably project its spirit through hours to come. In the beginning of your prayer time be silent, let your mind relax and let it roam across your life to see if it stops at anything wrong. **If so, tell God you want to make it right**. Let the first moments of your prayer time be a sincere moral search. If nothing is shown to be wrong and our heart does not condemn us, then (Hebrews 4:16) says, "*Let us then approach the throne of grace with confidence, so that we may receive mercy and find grace to help us in our time of need.*" Then let us bathe our thoughts in God's Word. It will wash the fuzziest from our mind. Then we will understand, have insight into His word. Through His Word our attitudes will become right attitudes, so then we will pray right prayers, our thoughts up beside His thoughts, our purposes up to His purposes. Take a pen and paper with you and write down what comes to you as you study God's word. That pen in your hand is a sign of faith that some insight, some understanding will come to you, and it will. Don't hurry through your study. Every word is precious, pause and absorb every one. When we hurry through the woods, we see few birds or animals, they hide. But if we sit down and wait, then they come out. It will be so with you, prayer is a time exposure of our soul to God. Take obedience with you into your study time, for you will know only as much of God, as you are willing to put into practice! For God will answer many of our prayers – through us.

Prayer for today: O Christ, I come to You to help me make my time of prayer and Bible study effective, that through this time my entire day will be effective. Amen.

September 2   Luke 24:15, 32; John 20:19-20; Acts 1:4, 8

COMMUNICATION AND COMMISSION

Prayer seems to have many sides. Actually there are only two sides – Communication and commission. The rest are phases of these two. These are the two heart beats of the prayer life. And a heart must keep beating in two directions, are death ensues. Communication without commission – death. Commission without communication – death. Together – LIFE.

First there is communication. Have you ever seen on television or maybe you've had the opportunity to see for yourself, sap being freshly tapped from a tree? Imagine holding a cup nestled up against the wound of a maple tree and taking the sweet sap from the heart of that tree, think of prayer in that way. We press our empty lives like cups up against the wounds of the Eternal God and take from Him life, power, and redemption. Everyday let us nestle up against His wounded side, for we are empty without it. And everyday let our cup be emptied in living help to others.

In calling the disciples Jesus appointed twelve that they might **"be with Him,"** that He might **"send them out"** to preach, and **"have authority"** to cast out devils.

1. *Communication* – **to be with Him.** 2. *Commission* – **sent out to preach.** 3. *Communication* + *Commission* = **Moral Authority.**

If the call to be with Him holds together then everything else will follow. Neglect one and the other fades fast. And moral authority depends on the other two.

Empty prayer closet – empty heart, empty hands – this is the spiritual history of many. "*Jesus often withdrew to lonely places and prayed.* (Luke 5:16).

If Jesus needed to pray how much more we need to pray!

Prayer for today: O Christ, You showed us by Your example the source of prayer, may we tap that power and communicate it to others. Amen.

September 3   Psalm 25:9; 31:3; 32:8; 73:24; Isaiah 58:11

DOES GOD GUIDE OUR LIVES?

Commission follows communication. In communicating we feel the hand of God upon our life guiding us to do certain things. We have organized our religious lives around certain services in the church, two on Sunday, one on Wednesday, etc. If we attend these services, we think we are very good, faithful Christians. But between these services there are great gaps in our lives, where we allow God to function very weakly or not at all. God's guidance needs to fill these gaps and make us, every moment, responsible to Him. He is no longer just a small part of our life. He is in the very fiber of our being. Guidance, therefore, brings God in from the occasional to the continuous. Every Christian should live a God-guided life. And when we allow God to guide our life, He will be in everything that concerns us – directing, controlling, and inspiring. The Christian that doesn't know this sense of guidance in their life is missing something vital.

For we know that if we are not guided by God, we are guided by something else, perhaps ourselves. We also know that **TO BE SELF- MANAGED IS TO BE SELF-DAMAGED.**

We are not good enough and we don't know enough to guide our lives. God must guide them.

Have we stood apart from Christ?
Apart from joy and fear of life?
Have we seen, by faith, His face?
Have we looked, if but a moment, at His grace?
Even by brief companionship have we grown, more true?
With more confidence to lead, to dare, to do?
Have we today found time to pray?
Have we put our hand in His,
To compare His will and ours?
Such contact will endure,
Of that we can be sure!

Through storms of life, it will help us walk erect.
Sins waste, its strain; it will help us detect.
O Father, steady my steps that waver, help me to see,
The footpath you have mapped for me.

Prayer for today: O God, help me to recognize Your touch upon my life and obey it. Amen.

September 4   Genesis 50:20; Isaiah 54:17; Romans 8:28;
                     Philippians 1:12

HOW DOES GOD GUIDE US?

God guides us in– not one, but <u>many</u> ways. Of the many
– here are six out-standing ways in which God guides us: (1) by
Circumstances, (2) by Enlightened Christian Intelligence, (3) by the
Spoken or Written Word of Others, (4) by a Small Group, (5) by
the Scriptures, (6) by the Inner Voice. Sometimes God guides us by
circumstances. Something opens before us, perhaps unexpectedly,
just when we are in a state of confusion, uncertainty, doubt, etc.
That Open door is matched against our perplexity; we walk through
it and find it was God's way. Or He may close a door before us,
and that closed door proves to be God's preventive guidance. Many
times God lets us fail in a secondary thing that we may succeed in a
primary thing. Many people are ruined by secondary successes. We
may get involved in them and never get to the really important things.
E. Stanley Jones says He is sure God prevented him from becoming
fond of game-hunting in India. As a young man he found the area
where he was living filled with black buck. It was a very natural
thing to take a gun along while he visited the different villages for
evangelistic purposes. He did, and he shot eighteen times at several
and never hit one. Bad marksman, he didn't think so, as a youth he
was the best marksman in his crowd. But he had a feeling God was
making him miss, so he took the gun home and sold it, concluding
that God had not called him to be a hunter, but an evangelist. He
says his conclusion was correct. He might have been crippled by
secondary success.

Many a woman, realizing she is beautiful, soon realizes she has
nothing else except beauty. The secondary success of beauty makes
her neglect the primary facts of intelligence and soul and usefulness. **God's preventive grace has saved most of us at the point of
beauty!** That's ok! Now for the open doors of intelligence, soul, and
usefulness! God shuts lesser doors to open bigger and better ones.

Prayer for today: O God, sometimes You do save us by hard refusals and sometimes by opening doors. Help us to see You in both. And help us to obey without complaining about hard refusals, or without hesitation before open door. Amen.

September 5 Acts 6:2-5; 1 Timothy 1:7;
2 Timothy 2:7; Hebrews 8:10

GOD GUIDES THROUGH ENLIGHTENED INTELLIGENCE

God guides through Enlightened Christian Intelligence. The development of Christian understanding is a necessary part of Christian development. (Hebrews 5:14) says, *"Solid food is for the mature, who by constant use have trained themselves to distinguish good from evil."* God wants us to love Him with all of our mortal existence, including the mind – Jesus said, *"Love the Lord your God with ALL YOUR HEART, and with ALL YOUR SOUL and with <u>ALL YOUR MIND</u>."* (Matthew 22:37). Any scheme of guidance that excludes the <u>MIND</u> is not of God, for we are to be perfected completely not partially. God wants to gently guide us, not overrule us to do a certain thing – He makes us to be free, upstanding, and understanding. God will make it very clear to us what He wants us to do. I believe that God does guide us by the Inner Voice, but to make that the ONLY method and to depend on that Inner Voice to dictate the minute details of our lives would be weakening to us. We must not take one method of God's guidance ONLY and exclude others. Suppose a parent would attempt to dictate every minute detail of a child's life, asking only for absolute obedience, leaving little room for intelligent growth and understanding of moral issues and free decision, would that be guiding or overruling? Wouldn't the child's personality remain undeveloped under such? Also if we ask for dictated guidance in every little thing, this would make for unreality. God will guide our mental processes if we are inwardly honest with ourselves and honest about all the facts.

Prayer for today: O Christ, we need the impact of Your mind upon our minds, for without it our minds are confused and perplexed. And help us to obey what Christian intelligence we have learned. Amen.

September 6   1 Samuel 3:9; Acts 9:11-17; Philemon 4-17

GOD'S GUIDANCE THROUGH OTHERS

Sometimes God guides us through the Written or Spoken Word of Others. Some passage in a book becomes luminous and speaks directly to our need. To us it is the very voice of God. Some word in a sermon seems to speak directly to our heart. Or it may be a quiet word with a friend that opens the door to the solution of a problem, or relief from a grief.

Everyone should have such a friend, a confidant, "a sharing partner," someone to whom you can open your heart to the depths, so that they truly know who you really are; someone to whom you can "show your ugliness," if necessary, or to whom you can share your deepest confusion, secrets, etc. This kind of communication cuts your grief dramatically. A grief shared is a grief greatly reduced. Give your grief words: if grief does not speak whispers to the heart filled with pain then that heart will surely break.

That's what true friends do; they share each others problems as well as our joy. The friend, who is free from your inner emotions, may see your problem in just that detached way so necessary to give you needed understanding. HOWEVER, EVEN OUR FRIENDS WORD MUST COMPLY WITH OUR OTHER TESTS OF GUIDANCE. DON'T DEPEND ON IT TOO IMPLICITY. TAKE THE WORD OF A FRIEND, BUT MAKE YOUR OWN DECISION IN THE QUIETNESS WITH GOD.

Prayer for today: O Christ, who did long for a human friend in the hour of Gethsemane's darkness – but found none. Help me to find a true friend, for I will need one. Amen.

September 7   Acts 13:1-3; 15:25-28

GUIDANCE THROUGH SMALL GROUPS

Over the past few years we have been introduced to what is referred to as "small group ministries." Numerous Christian writers have given us great insight into the ministry and success of small groups, within our church body. And I, for one, believe God is in this type ministry. God is speaking to this generation through the small groups. He spoke to the first generation through small groups. The fact is Jesus formed a small group and He and His small group (His disciples) fellowshipped and worked together.

In order to form a working relationship with Jesus and accomplish his goal they brought together their minds, attitudes, and methods of life to bring forth a body of common ideas and attitudes. These became the New Testament. Individual writers wrote them down, but the Christian groups produced them in their interaction with the Spirit of God and with each other. When the disciples said, "*It seemed good to the Holy Spirit and to us...* (Acts 15:28), they could have said this not only in reference to that particular situation, but in reference to the whole body of true believers which was growing. That group had become more than a small group of men, but an organized body of the Holy Spirit. He was expressing His mind and His redemptive purpose through that group. Today God guides the individual through such closely knit fellowships in small groups. Each individual needs the nourishment, care, connection, love, etc. which a small group provides. In small groups we bond with others in the group, we pray together, study God's word together, and when one needs help, we give encouragement, whatever, the situation is the group is always there for one another. So—God guides through small groups.

Prayer for today: O Christ, I pray that You will touch me through my fellowship with others and help me to understand when You speak to me through their voice. Amen.

September 8   Matthew 13:11; Luke 10:21;12:12;
                               John 16:13-15; Acts 16:7-8

GUIDANCE THROUGH THE INNER VOICE

By the Inner Voice does not mean the voice of conscience, for the Inner Voice gives guidance, not just where a matter of right and wrong is involved as in conscience, but where we are talking life directions, deciding confusing situations, and where we take up work and responsibilities. The Inner Voice is not contradictory to an enlightened conscience, but it is in addition to it and beyond it. It is the Spirit of God speaking to us directly and authentically.

When we study the early recordings of the Christian Movement, the New Testament, we find that guidance was moving directly from external to internal. The Gospels open with guidance through dreams and visions and the voices of angels, as in the stories of Zechariah and Joseph. With Jesus it was different: He saw no vision or dreams. JESUS GUIDANCE CAME THROUGH INSIGHT THAT COMES THROUGH PRAYER AND THE DIRECT VOICE OF THE SPIRIT WITHIN. In the beginning of the Acts of the Apostles – we find the disciples fumbling badly – casting lots to see who would become a disciple in place of Judas, and giving God the choice between only two at that! How often we narrow God's choices for Him! God didn't want either of the two – He wanted Paul! They never repeated this initial mistake of depending on outer signs. The guidance became more and more inward. This was the way God intended. And this was also in the direction of deeper Christianity. **For the true gospel of Jesus Christ produces people who are not compelled by external signs, but impelled by an internal Spirit – the Spirit and our spirit working harmoniously and therefore effectively.**

Prayer for today: O Christ, who lived so in the Father that His gentle whisper was like thunder to You, help us to have that same sensitive response – today and forever. Amen.

September 9   Exodus 33:13-15; Psalm 25:5 & 9;
                               Isaiah 30:21; 40:11; Acts 8:31

GUIDANCE THEN AND NOW

The guidance in Acts is directing toward less dependent on outer signs and more on the gentle pressures of the Spirit within us. A personality is being born within us that will naturally and normally grip the Christian attitude – just as a well trained horse doesn't need a whip, the slightest suggestion will do. But in Acts there are other methods of guidance other than the direct voice of the Spirit: there was the Christian exercising common sense – *"It would not be right..."* (Acts 6:2). They were led by the facts – *"When they heard this..."* (Acts 11:18). The group came to a conclusion by prayer and fasting – *"Paul and Barnabas appointed elders for them, in each Church and, with prayer and fasting..."* (Acts 14:23). And in the exercise of thought – *"While Peter was still thinking about the vision, the Spirit said to him..."* (Acts 10:19).

As we have just been shown, God guides us in <u>many</u> ways. Perhaps the highest form of guidance is in this verse, (Acts 15:28) – *"It seemed good to the Holy Spirit and to us..."* – thinking His thoughts and coming to the same conclusions. That is cooperative spiritual thinking. *"Having been kept by the Holy Spirit from preaching the Word in the province of Asia, Paul and his companions came to the border of Mysia, they tried to enter Bithynia, but the Spirit of Jesus would not allow them to."* (Acts 16:6-7). The "<u>Holy Spirit</u>" and the "<u>Spirit of Jesus</u>" were used interchangeably, for they felt that the universalized Jesus and the Holy Spirit were one, the accents of the mind of Jesus were heard in the voice of the Holy Spirit, and He was acting as Jesus would act. <u>This gives the key by which we can discern the Voice of the Holy Spirit – does the appeal of that Voice identify accordingly to what we have seen in Christ? If so accept it, if not question it.</u>

Prayer for today: O Christ, we thank You that we can belong to the sheep that hear Your voice and know it and follow it. Help us to have a keen ear to catch Your accents every day. Amen.

September 10   Isaiah 8:20: John 14:26; 2 Timothy 3:16-17

THE SCRIPTURES AND THE POWER OF GOD

The key to recognizing the Voice of the Spirit is this: Does that Voice speak according to the Word of God? If so, it is authentic, if not, we should question it. For instance, in (Acts 11:12), when Peter says, *"The Spirit told me to have no hesitation about going with them..."* Isn't this an authentic voice of the Spirit? This is just what we see revealed in Christ – a mind that made no distinction between people. God gave Peter a vision that was aimed at bringing together Jewish and Gentile believers. But if Peter, had refused to obey God just because it was against Jewish law, (Acts 10:28) and Peter had said, "The Spirit told me **not** to go with them," then we would have to say: "Peter, you are wrong." That was not the Voice of the Spirit. It was the Voice of Prejudice and Fears. Jesus said, *"You are in error because you do not know the scriptures or the power of God."* (Matthew 22:29). The way to keep from making errors is to know two things: The scriptures – the **past** revelations; and the power of God – the **present** continuous activity of God. Some know only the Scriptures – they do not link themselves with the creative activity of God here and now – today. That's a mistake, the Scriptures reflect the past. Some know only the power of God today – they do not know in any real sense the Scriptures. That too is a mistake. For we can not correctly discern God at work today unless we continuously check it out by that revelation we have seen in Christ. But **if we are in constant fellowship with the power of God now working in us and we constantly tests that working with Jesus revelations in Scripture we will not go astray. These are the two things that keep us from making mistakes. These are the two guard rails that keep us going safely straight; but take down one rail or the other and we land in the ditch.**

Prayer for today: O Christ, help us to know You in history and in ourselves, and help us to find no difference. Amen.

September 11   Genesis 12:1; Proverbs 8:20; Isaiah 42:16; Acts
2:43-47

GUIDANCE (Continued)

Our study concerning guidance continues. Guidance can be limited, or even controlled, by the society we find ourselves surrounded by. Our guidance often conforms to the established pattern of that society in which we live.

The thing that makes us feel the guidance in the Acts of the Apostles was real is the fact that it did not conform to the established pattern of that day's society. In a framework of exclusive Jewish society, the disciples broke away and established a fellowship based on brotherhood beyond race and class. In a competitive society they formed a society based on co-operation and economic sharing and equality. They broke the patterns of the society in which they lived and established new ones.

Now, much of our guidance doesn't break away from the pattern of the society we live in, we just conform to it and let it guide us to wherever and/or whatever. Where we get our guidance may give us an attitude of trying to hold together our present society by force. We should not want our guidance to be governed by such a society, one that seemingly does not want to see change for better that benefits everyone. We may need to strive to break the pattern of much of our present society. You would think that would be a normal Christian happening to strive to break the pattern of much of modern society.

Prayer for today: O Christ, open my eyes to my limited framework and help me to catch the unlimited capacity of Your mind. Amen.

September 12   Isaiah 58:11; Zechariah 6:15; John 10:3-4

THE INNER VOICE IS DEPENDABLE

Sometimes our guidance will be like the voice of Philip, *"Go south to the road – the desert road- that goes down from Jerusalem to Gaza."* (Acts 8:26). God often sends us seemingly into a desert. But if He guides us into a desert, He has work for us to do there and will show us why He needs us there. If we sincerely listen and follow God's Voice, it will never let us down. It will always prove right. We may sometimes misinterpret the Voice; but when it is clear, it will be consistent. An example: My husband who is a retired barber, not being happily retired, now works at a large church as a "set-up" supervisor. {In case you don't know what a "set-up" person does—it is his job to take down and set up rooms for different meetings and such every day, all day. In a large church such as ours many great and wonderful things happen every day, so there is a real need for this service.} About the time for my husband's shift to be over he was informed of a very important meeting to be held in room 104 that afternoon, <u>even though it was **not** on the daily schedule</u>. Immediately, he and others went to work and set it up according to instructions. Pleased with their work, my husband ended his shift and started home. He had an errand to run that took him in the <u>opposite direction</u> of home from the church. With his errand completed he then started for home. As he came closer to the church, an inner voice said, "Stop and check 104." He thought to himself, "I must be going crazy, why check 104, we just set it up to perfection." There are several entrances to the church from the street he was traveling, and just before he reached the last entrance the inner voice said, "Stop and check 104." Feeling a little foolish, he stopped and checked 104 and to his surprise, the men on second shift, who had just recently arrived for their work, had **taken down,** the just completed, set-up.

By listening to the guidance of God's voice, he diverted, if not a disastrous situation, at least an embarrassing inconvenience. Coincidence? He doesn't think so. He is convinced his heavenly Father, seeing the need of the church leaders, worked through him to meet their need. In our life if God's care extends to big things, why not the little things? Both the sparrow and the star are in His care – and so are we.

Prayer for today: O Christ, thank You that You have never let me down. Help me not to let You down. Amen.

September 13   Isaiah 50:10; John 8:12; Acts 10:9-15

CONTINUING THOUGHTS ON GUIDANCE

"He went in and stood before the Lord" – that is prayer, standing at attention before God to get His orders for the day. You may not get any suggestions right then. If you don't, carry on as you have been. You can trust God's silence. If He doesn't answer immediately, don't be discouraged. Jesus did not answer the Gentile woman at once, but He did answer her, finally, and more. (John 8), He filled the Gentile world with His voice and power. He answered her – **plus!**

But in regard to some important decisions if you aren't certain of God's will – do not proceed. Wait until the guidance is clear. Don't act when you are only half prepared.

At those times you are waiting for guidance, fill that space with spare-moment praying. Peter got the vision that changed his whole life in spare-moment praying. *"As they were on their journey...Peter went up on the roof to pray."* (Acts 10:9). There Peter saw the necessity of unity among God's human creation and Peter acted on it and was changed forever. **The difference in our spiritual life is what we do with our spare moments**. Some of us waste it – and ourselves with it. Others gather it up and make it contribute.

Have you changed your life or that of another through a spare-moment of prayer? Pray and then prepare to be guided by the answer to that prayer.

Prayer for today: O Christ, help me to have an open heart every moment, for I want to be your minute-person, ready at any time to do Your will. Amen.

September 14   John 7:37-39; 14:17; Ephesians 3:16-19

KEEP YOUR COMMISSION FREE FROM FAULT

Cultivate a listening attitude as you pray. And as you listen you will get direction. And when you get that direction, keep it free from fault. Paul speaking to young Timothy said, "*I command you before God who gives life to all, and before Christ Jesus who gave a fearless testimony before Pontius Pilate, that you fulfill all that he has told you to do, so that no one can find **fault** with you from now until our Lord Jesus returns.*" (1 Timothy 6: 13-14 <u>LB</u>). In light of two things: in the presence of the good life of Christ who is the Life of all, and in the presence of this life poured out in sacrifice before Pilate, keep your commission free from fault. From **fault** of what? Obviously, fault from emptiness and from a lack of self-giving, giving of ourselves to God's purpose for our lives.

Here is this life of God throbbing in every fiber of the world: in the light of that fact <u>be free from emptiness and be blameless</u>. If God commissions you, guides you to take up a task, however small, or however large, He will provide resources. <u>Commission and equipment go together</u>. If God commissions you to speak to a person, or to fight for a cause, He will equip you for that work. Draw heavily on that equipment; He will give you all you need to do what He has called you to do. You don't have to cry to Him for spiritual equipment it is there for the taking. Emptiness is now sin, for fullness is now your privilege. Keep saying to yourself, "*I can do everything through Christ, who gives me strength.*" (Philippians 4:13). You will be astonished at your ability to do things. Nothing now can make you afraid- absolutely nothing. God is your life, and God is your life-equipment.

Prayer for today: O Christ, **You** are the life of my life, help me to be ever open to You, that my life may not only be there, but be operative always. Amen.

September 15   Hebrews 10:38; 12:1-4; 13:13

THE FAULT OF PARTIAL FULFILLMENT

Yesterday we saw that we were to keep our commissions free from the fault of emptiness and from the fault of self-giving. Jesus gave His confession before Pontius Pilate at the place where witnessing meant a cross. Christ commission had in its itinerary to go the distance, and go the distance – He did! What Christ did was not half-way done, it was complete, no pretense at doing it, no holding back, and it was solid, well done.

POUR YOUR CONCRETE FOUNDATION AND STAND ON IT FOR CHRIST SAKE.

Carrying out the will of God is not always a pleasant thing in a messed up world like ours. At times we may have to wipe the blood from our lips after having to tightly close our mouth on our teeth of determination. The commission often means a cross. Our friends may misunderstand us and leave us, and we may be left to give our confession – alone. So be it, we will ask for strong inner strength to endure and see the thing through. For a friend or a cause would you put yourself in danger? If we would put ourselves in danger for a friend, then why not for a FRIEND and CAUSE – that FRIEND BEING GOD AND THAT CAUSE BEING THE KINGDOM. Let's not be tempted to compromise and "call it a day" just short of putting it into action. Let's not become compromised Christians –"rejecters" of the cross.

To try to put justice at the heart of human society will cause a cross, so we decide our commission reads to change ourselves and leave it at that. We refuse to witness before Pontius Pilate. That is not what Jesus did. He witnessed to His kingship before His individual disciples, He also witnessed it before the Roman governor and said He was King there also in the corporate relationship of His people. That cost Him a cross. But He said it nevertheless.

Prayer for today: O Christ, nowhere did You hesitate. Help me not to hesitate in obedience. Amen.

September 16   John 8:36: Acts 6:8-10; Galatians 5:1;
                                2 Thessalonians 3:1

AN INWARD STRONGHOLD

If habits in our life keep us from God's guidance, then we are not free to express God's will for our life. We have an inward stronghold. We must get victory over that sense of inward self-consciousness and shyness, or we will never be useful to the Kingdom of God. Once a group of mental health experts were asked the question as to what, in their opinion, were the most serious behavior patterns in young children. They included these: excessive modesty, suspiciousness, shyness, being withdrawn, selfishness, constant whining, fears, depression, daydreaming, showing no interest, hypertension, demands for attention, sensitiveness, and moody. These hinder the development of the child. Now note, out of the fourteen behavior patterns almost all of them refer to an inverted self, a tendency to become wrapped up in oneself. Obviously, this inhibited self must be unwrapped and freed before maturity. When Peter and John were before the Sanhedrin, it was said, *"When they saw the courage of Peter and John and realized that they were unschooled, ordinary men, they were astonished and they took note that these men had been with Jesus."* (Acts 4:13). Their outspoken fearlessness was a sign that they had been with Jesus. It was so then – it is so now. Once in the company of Jesus we are freed from cramped habits and self-consciousness. He has that power to give to us. *"For I will give you words and wisdom that none of your adversaries will be able to resist or contradict," said Jesus.* (Luke 21:15). Some have words and no wisdom, and some have wisdom and no words. Jesus can give us both – something to talk about, and He will help us talk about it. Strongholds in our lives **can** be broken and made victorious.

Prayer for today: O Christ, thank You that no fears and habits crippled You. Help me to be like that. Amen.

September 17   2 Corinthians 4:1-6; Ephesians 5:8

THROWING CAUTION TO THE WIND

A crisis had come in early Christianity. The Apostles had gone to the Jews alone and had acted as though this were a Jewish gospel, from Jews to Jews. But then the crisis came: *"When the Jews saw the crowds, they were filled with jealousy and talked abusively against what Paul was saying."* (Acts 13:45). *Then, throwing caution to the wind, Paul and Barnabas said, "We had to speak the word of God to you first. Since you reject it and do not consider yourselves worthy of eternal life, we now turn to the Gentiles. For this is what the Lord has commanded us: "'I have made you a light to the Gentiles, that you may bring salvation to the ends of the earth.'"* (Acts 13:46-47). They threw caution to the wind and saved themselves and their gospel. The gospel they had in their hearts was actually larger than that which they were proclaiming. They were proclaiming a gospel for Jews when it was a gospel for all mankind. Today a similar crisis in Christianity – we have a larger gospel in our hearts than we are actually proclaiming. We have a gospel which will cure our individual illness and our social ills as well. We've had reservations about one or the other. We have not acted on the situation. Now, this world-shaking crisis is forcing us to throw caution to the wind. **We must** act on the larger implications of our gospel. It is always safe to do so. It is always dangerous to minimize Christ, for that is always wrong. It is always safe and always right to act upon the larger Christ. The smaller view of Christ has always proven wrong, the larger always right. Now, some of us have reservations about sharing this gospel with individuals – we are tongue-tied. We are not spiritually contagious. We either don't have anything to give or we can't give what we have. Others have reservations about sharing to a group. They either haven't anything to give, or their fear is greater than their witness.

Prayer for today: O Christ, deliver us from fear and help us to throw all caution to the wind and go all out for You. Amen.

September 18   Matthew 13:44-46; Acts 5:19-20;
                                1 Timothy 4:15

MAGNIFICENT OBESSION

Yesterday we said that we must throw all caution to the wind in regard to proclaiming a gospel for the entire world, for there is a crisis around us. The "world" is setting up new standards. Shall we allow these new immoral standards as we have done in the past, or will we set the Kingdom of God on earth as the standard for the future? Let's choose the Kingdom.

We may be criticized as we seem to be "obsessed with the idea of the Kingdom of God on earth," but wouldn't we like to be guilty of that charge, for it would be a magnificent obsession!

Is anyone obsessed with the idea that immorality could end for everyone? We have the same means to stop it, that spread it, everything except a collective society, (a society united to change things). The Kingdom of God would mean that united we would be turned toward abolishing immoral behavior as a way of life. Are we obsessed with the idea that race hatred, and social class could cease and that we could all become equal toward one another? The Kingdom of God would mean just that.

So, are we obsessed with that Kingdom? We could add so many ideas we could and maybe should be obsessed with, but you get the picture. Above everything else, let's be obsessed with the idea that the Kingdom of God is the only workable procedure, and that this Kingdom is at hand.

We should therefore throw all caution to the wind and say so. Someone has said, "That some Christians fairly shout their answer to the world." Don't you wish we could do that and everyone would listen? Magnificent Obsession!

Prayer for today: O Christ, we pray that You will help us to shout our answer to the world's need. For we know that You are the answer – the only answer. Amen.

September 19   Luke 9:49; 1 Corinthians 3:16

THE KINGDOM OF OUR FATHER DAVID

Note two attempts to reduce the Kingdom. The disciples asked, *"Lord, are you at this time going to restore the kingdom to Israel?"* (Acts 1:6). After three years of teaching they saw in the Kingdom of God **only as** the restoration of the Kingdom to Israel. They did not reject the Kingdom – they reduced it. They made it into something less than it really was. And the second attempt we speak of – when Jesus came into Jerusalem in triumphal entry, the multitudes cried, *"Blessed is the coming kingdom of our father David!"* (Mark 11:9-10). – The Kingdom of our father David??

This has been the ruin of the gospel of Christ: He inaugurates something big and challenging and we interpret it as "our father David." Denominationalism has taken the Kingdom of God – a worldwide, universal Kingdom – and turned it into the Kingdom of our father David – Catholic, Methodist, Lutherans, Baptists, Presbyterians, Pentecostals (only to name a few) – as if the Kingdom of God weren't larger than any denomination you can mention. ALL are a limited version of a universal conception – the Kingdom of God – into a local one – the Kingdom of our father David, reducing the Kingdom of God.

And when we make the Kingdom Of God, which takes in the whole of life, into a means of our individual salvation alone, leaving untouched the social society am I not making the Kingdom of God into the Kingdom of Self?

We as Christians must throw all caution to the wind and give our answer to the world's need – without hesitation, without compromise. **For the world is sick unto death. Our silence now becomes a guilty silence – and deadly.**

Prayer for today: O Christ, forgive us that we have made Your Kingdom small and irrelevant, help us to now make it big and sufficient. Amen.

September 20   Jeremiah 20:9; Amos 4:8; 1 John 1:1-3

PERSONAL CAUTIONS IN PERSONAL CONTACTS

Many of us are free and direct until we come to the really important things, the inner things, and then we close up. We need to be free of binding cautions. You may say, "I am shy and self-conscious; I just can't do it." True, you can't do it alone, but you can become strong in that weak place. Repeat to yourself daily, "I can become strong in my weakest place." Or better still the all favorite scripture – (Philippians 4:13) *"I can do anything through him who gives me strength."* Jeremiah pleaded, when the call of God came to him, *"I do not know how to speak; I am only a child."* (Jeremiah 1:6). Jeremiah offered that trembling hesitation to God, but when he did speak, how mightily he spoke! When the call of God came to Moses he pleaded that he was unable, for he was *"Slow of speech and tongue"* (Exodus 4:10). But God loosened his tongue, and when Moses did get started, he made a speech that covered the entire book of Deuteronomy! Jeremiah and Moses became strongest at their weakest place. Some people look on Christian religion as something so **sacred** that it becomes **secret.**

Suppose a Mother said to her children, "Now children, food is such a sacred thing I cannot talk to you about it, nor can I allow you to take any of it." Suppose the teacher said, "Now, students, knowledge is such a scared thing I cannot talk to you about it. There will be no classes today." Absurd? Yes, but no more absurd than the unnatural attitudes we assume about the best thing we have – the good news about the power of Christ. There we should be natural and contagious. Walk the walk and talk the talk.

Someone has defined a Christian as one who speaks by word and by life. That is a great definition.

Prayer for today: O Christ, I pray that You will loose me from these binding restraints, and help me be free – free to recommend my Savior. Amen.

September 21   John 4:14; Acts 1:8; 2 Corinthians 3:17-18

THE POWER THAT GIVES FREEDOM

The only way to lose self-consciousness is through God-consciousness. We become so conscious of God's presence within us we forget about our self. (2 Corinthians 3:17b) *"Where the Spirit of the Lord is there is freedom."* – Freedom from strongholds, inhibitions, and paralyzing sins. This generation has lost touch with the Holy Spirit. We have taught this generation to follow Jesus as an example, and it has produced a pale, colorless Christianity. The gospel does not ask us to follow Jesus as an example – **it offers us the resources of the Holy Spirit in the inner life and then we follow Jesus because we have the desire to do so. This kind of Christianity becomes colorful and red-blooded. It has resources, therefore it has POWER.** A modern version of the Gospels spells the "Holy Spirit" – "holy spirit". That is symbolic of what has happened to **this generation**. It **has turned the Holy Spirit into a vague, impersonal influence with no power or strength. That is not the Holy Spirit of the Acts of the Apostles. There the Holy Spirit was no mere vague, impersonal influence – He was God meeting them inwardly, reinforcing, cleansing, bringing the soul forces into loving unity, and setting them ablaze with God.** Speaking of the men who were arguing with Stephen in (Acts 6:10) –*"But they could not stand up against his wisdom or the Spirit by whom he spoke."* Note the uppercase "S." You could **not** tell where Stephen's spirit ended and God's Spirit began, for the Spirit lived in his spirit, and was the wisdom of Stephen's wisdom. When the disciples got hold of that secret at Pentecost, they were immediately and decisively freed from any binding habits and spiritual strongholds and became flaming evangelist of the Good News. We need to rediscover the actual resources of the Holy Spirit. "FREEDOM!"

Prayer for today: O Christ, help us to rediscover Your gift to us and live by its freedom, and become effective by its power. Amen.

September 22   Luke 4:18-32; John 7:37-39

FREEDOM FOR YOUR RESTRAINED SOUL

Jesus said these remarkable words, *"Whoever believes in me, as the scripture has said, streams of living water will flow from within him." "By this he meant the Spirit..."(John 7:38-39)*. The King James Version says, *"Out of his belly"* instead of the translated words *"from within him."* The "belly" was considered the very foundation of life, the deepest part of one's nature. Today we would say, "From the depths of the subconscious shall flow rivers of living waters." The Spirit in the depths of the subconscious, cleansing, controlling, empowering, this brings the whole of life into a living unity, and in the flood of this new Life all compartmentalizing, inhibiting restrains are broken. Rivers of living water flow! This is a fact. The disciples knew it and it turned shy believers into irresistible apostles.

There are nine "rivers" that flow out of a life that is Spirit-controlled: *"Love, joy, peace, patience, kindness, goodness, faithfulness, gentleness and self-control."* (Galatians 5:22-23). It adds, *"Against such things there is no law."* If you have those things at the center of your life, you can act as you please, for you are not controlled by a law to do them, but impelled by an inner life. You can act naturally because you act supernaturally. Note, the first flow from a Spirit controlled life is 'Love" and the last is "Self-control" – You began with love and end with self-control. You control your lower self because you love the higher self. Also note that each quality of the fruit of the Spirit is a quality of moral character. Not one of them coming from without, all coming from within, and every one of them valid and vital today.

Prayer for today: O Spirit of the Living God, fall fresh on me. Break down the restrains in my life and make me free. Take over the depths and I will not worry about the surface. Amen.

September 23   Isaiah 57:14; Romans 14:13;
             1 Corinthians 10:32-33;
             2 Thessalonians 3:9

DO WE INTERPRET OR INTERFERE?

We are to interpret through our lives the purpose of God in the "here and now." We are to extend the Incarnation. Jesus Christ in His bodily form invested in God, we are to do no less. In a small village, long ago, a missionary doctor on an errand of mercy was stripped by robbers, but strangely, they did not take his camera, and he snapped their picture. Later, one of these robbers came to the doctor's hospital for an operation. They recognized each other. The robber was in the doctor's power – and helpless. The doctor used that power to forgive him and heal him, and, while doing so, **interpreted** the purpose of Christ. However, some of us interfere with that purpose. In (Mark 10:13), the disciples interfered when they tried to keep the little children from Jesus. They interfered with the spirit and purpose of Christ. Do we interpret Christ or interfere with Christ? We represent either the cure or the disease. Jesus interpreted the Father. (KJV John 1:18) *"No man hath seen God at any time; the only begotten Son, which is in the bosom of the Father, he hath declared him"* – literally, **"He has interpreted Him."** And what an interpretation! As we listen to His words and watch His acts and see His Spirit, God grows tenderly beautiful to us. And personally, I fall in love with such a God. Mark says, *"Jesus walked in the temple"* (Mark 11:27), and Luke says, *"Jesus taught daily in the temple"* (Luke 19:47). They were both right – His walking was teaching. Jesus walked the walk and talked the talk. His very walk and talk interpreted God. Once it was said He was *"teaching and journeying"*- (talking and walking) (KJV Luke 13:22), on His way to Jerusalem, where the cross awaited Him. He had inward freedom to teach the love of God to others – on the way to die! But even through that death He gave us a deathless interpretation of the Father. What an interpretation He was!

Prayer for today: O Christ, as You interpreted the Father, help me to interpret You. Amen.

September 24   1 Corinthians 1:17; 4:18-20;
                                1 Thessalonians 1:4-5

INCREASING OR DECREASING THE MESSAGE

Have you noticed how an interpreter can either increase or decrease the meaning of a message or speech? If you have watched a speech on television and immediately after a commentator will "interpret". Most of the time it is so misinterpreted you don't recognize it as the same speech.

Some even use the opportunity for self-display. It may be so obvious that the entire speech is ruined. Are we ever guilty of using the opportunity to interpret Christ into an opportunity to put ourselves on display? If so we become someone who interferes instead of one who interprets Christ. Self-display rather than Christ-interpretation.

Sometimes we decrease the message because we put too much of ourselves in it or sometimes because we are not in it at all. We treat it as "routine duty." It doesn't consume us; we do not burn with the message. We take the affairs of the Kingdom of God into our hands, but will not let them reach our heart.

We are dead channels of a living Christ. If Christ doesn't get into our blood and raise our blood pressure, why? Such a Christ, such a message, such a need! We decrease it by our inner lifelessness that should live and challenge and redeem.

Do we interfere with Christ message because we put too much of ourselves in it, or because we are not truly in it at all? Or do we truly interpret Christ?

Prayer for today: O Christ, forgive me that I have again and again become interference breaking up clear reception. Help me to become one who increases Your redemptive message. Amen.

September 25   John 4:3-42; Acts 28:30-31;
                               Philippians 1:12-14; 2 Timothy 2: 9

IS THE MESSAGE GETTING THROUGH?

Now see how to get the message through to human need, for it is not enough to live victoriously – we must help others do so as well. **Anything worth having is worth sharing.** A Christian has been defined as "one who makes it easy for others to believe in God." Jesus did that. God was with Him wherever He went.

Let's see how Jesus got His message through to an exceedingly difficult woman, the Samaritan woman. (Not that Jesus ever looked on a person as exceedingly difficult). You must **love** people to influence them. Let us study His method, for He was not only our example of how to live, but our example in helping other people to live. We will take His delicate dealings with the woman step by step and learn as we go.

First, the recorded event says, *"He had to go through Samaria."* (John 4:4). It was necessary that He go through Samaria. God had a plan. Jesus took this inevitable situation as an opportunity to get His message across. There are certain situations in our lives that are inevitable – we have to go to work, to school, home duties, etc., or we may be compelled by circumstances to sit on a park bench unemployed. Evangelize through that inevitable situation in your life; find your opportunity in the ordinary contacts of your day. Then your day will not be ordinary, for the contacts are redemptive. You are turning your common everyday situations into uncommon life – changing results. Your getting God's message out. Life – contacts become life-changing. There is absolutely nothing better than this.

Prayer for today: O Christ, help us to recognize and seize the everyday opportunities of contacts and make them live with meaningful results, as You did. Amen.

September 26   John 4:7; Acts 8:29-35; 17:22-23

OUR FIRST APPROACH TO CHRISTIAN WITNESSING

The first step in opening the conversation is most difficult. Many hesitate to take that first step for fear of being treated with disrespect. But even if they do treat you that way, be so spiritually filled with God's love that you don't know when you've been snubbed!

There were many reasons why Jesus should not have spoken to the Samaritan woman – He was tired and hungry; to talk to a woman in public was to risk His reputation; she was a woman of loose morals; it was mid-day and at that time in hot climates everyone rests. These are some reasons why He should **not speak** to her. There was one reason why he **should speak** to her – **she needed to hear what He had to say**. This one reason outweighed all the others. You will find many reasons why you should not share the wonderful life you have found. You may never speak to a person without having to fight past those reasons. But that one, all important, reason always persists – people need to hear it, need it more than they need anything else. Let that be the determining factor as we take the first step in sharing Christ.

Jesus began at the place of her greatest interest – water. He began with water and then went from water to living water, and then to fountains of living water in the heart. Try to find out the greatest interest of the person and lead them with that chief interest. If a young person's interest is in athletics, talk to them about a strong body, and the necessity of keeping it healthy if it is to remain strong, and the power in Christ to keep it pure as well. If a parent is wrapped up in their child or children, suggest that knowing they want to give them the best, they cannot unless they have the best themselves. You cannot give something you don't have.

Prayer for today: O Christ, help me to find someone's greatest interest and to lead them through that interest to you. Amen.

September 27   Matthew 4:19; 22:15-22; 22:35-40;
                                John 4:9-10

OBSTACLES AND THE WAY AROUND THEM

The woman threw up an obstacle: *"You are a Jew and I am a Samaritan woman. How can you ask me for a drink?"* (For Jews do not associate with Samaritans). (John 4:9). The human heart tends to shy away at the approach of an intruder. It is the instinct of self –protection. We do not easily let people into our lives. So many Christian workers stop right here at the obstacle of shyness. They stop before they even begin – discouraged. The casualties among personal Christian workers are very great at this point. Today as always there are many things that closely resemble the Jew-Samaritan obstacle. But if the first instinct is to **shy away,** the second should be to **share away.** We all need to share <u>our inmost selves</u> with someone, provided that someone is someone in whom we have complete confidence. For that confidence is to be absolutely kept, or else there can be no further sharing. Do not be intimidated because of "shyness" wait for the deeper instinct to take over – to reveal **who you are and who you are about.** How did Jesus get rid of the issue between Jew and Samaritan? He raised a higher issue than her lower one – He talked about "living water" and as He talked she forgot about the issue *she* had raised. That is the principle: When people raise lesser issues, bury those issues, get their attention on higher issues. Don't get hung up on irrelevancies; go straight to the main business at hand. Jesus showed amazing confidence in the woman: *"If you knew the gift of God and who it is that asks you for a drink, you would have asked..."* (John 4:10)—if you see the better of life you will want it. That was an amazing assumption to make in regard to such a woman. <u>To influence people you must believe in them no matter what or who they are</u>.

Prayer for today: O Christ, help me to believe in myself and others, so they may believe in You. Amen.

September 28   Matthew 15:1-11; Luke 22:32;
                                              John 4:11-14

OBSTACLES AND THE WAY AROUND THEM (Continued)

Jesus had an amazing confidence in the woman – He knew she would want what was a better life when she saw it. This leads to the third principle: **To influence people you must believe in them** – **no matter who or what they are**. The people who influence us for the better are not the people who tell us how bad we are, but tell us how much better we can become. **Nag** people and they **sag**, **believe** in people and they **achieve.** But the woman was not yet through with obstacles. *She said, "Are you greater than our father Jacob?"* (John 4:12). She was ready for a comparison. Now, Jesus could have said, "Woman, your father Jacob was a scheming liar who stole his brother's birthright." And it would have been absolutely true! She would have gone away angry and hurt. **We must be determined to win people, not arguments! To win the argument you need only to be clever, but to win people you need to be Christian**. Jesus dismissed Jacob from this conversation. Jacob slides so gently out of the picture we scarcely notice that he is gone. And how did Jesus accomplish that? Again, Jesus accomplished that by raising a more important issue. He replied in this most wonderful passage of scripture, *"Whoever drinks the water I give will never thirst. Indeed, the water I give him; will become in him a spring of water welling up to eternal life."* (John 4:14). As the woman's thoughts became fastened on that fountain of water in her heart she forgot Jacob and the controversy. The more important issue pushed away the lesser issue. This verse, one of the most beautiful in scripture, was given to an outcast woman. Christ did not hesitate to give His best to the worst. Our best is not too good for the worst. So lavish it on others as Christ did. The worst will become the best.

Prayer for today: O Christ, Your best is offered at the shrine of my worst. Help me to exchange my worst for Your best. Amen.

September 29   Matthew 14:4; Luke 5:8;
                                John 4:16-19; 8:7

A MOST DELICATE MOMENT

When Jesus spoke about *"the well of water springing up into eternal life,"* (John 4:14) the Samaritan woman said she wanted <u>this</u> water; for one thing she might not have to come all the way back to the well to draw water. Her motives were mixed – she wanted to be saved from her immoral life and she wanted to be saved from the trouble of drawing water from the well. People have mixed minds and mixed motives. Many of us would have given up on her right there. Why bother with her with such mixed motives? But Jesus has such infinite patience – He would purify those motives. A youth taking Communion as a "dare" from his friends, felt after taking that communion that he must stand by it – and he did. He became a wonderful Christian. Christ took the hand that was half-heartedly held out to Him and forever gripped it. But in order to purify the motive Christ must purify the person. So He must get to our moral problem. Take it as logic. "There is a moral problem in every life." Face that problem, or miss the point on which everything else depends. If we are not saved from sin, we are saved from nothing. How did Jesus get to the Samaritan woman's sin? He could have said, "Woman, you are living a bad, adulterous life." But had He said that, she would have stepped back in shock. It also would not have been effective; it is for better to lead someone to point out their own sins, than to point them out for them. Then, and only then, are they ready to free themselves of them. So Jesus led the woman to acknowledge her sin by making a delicate request. *"Go call your husband and come back."* (John 4:16). At the word "husband" a guilty flush went across her soul. *"I have no husband,"* she replied simply, (John 4:17). These words meant more than they said. Her guilt was exposed. She was inwardly broken before her newly discovered self-and Jesus.

Prayer for today: O Christ, give us the right words to say, that will point others from sin to You. Amen.

September 30   John 4:19-24; Acts 19:18-19;
                                      2 Timothy 4:3-4; Titus 3:9

FACING UP

Yesterday we left the woman face to face with her sins. We must be sure before we attempt to help others face their sins, that we have faced our own sins. Assuming we have done that then, no matter what this sophisticated generation may say, to help others recognize their sins is our responsibility. The first step in facing sin is to expose it. But how do we get people to uncover their sin? **Be free to talk about your own sins and your victory over them**. Never be shocked what you may hear. Establish confidence, and then tell them you know the ONE and ONLY ONE, who can help them through. To get people to face up to their moral need have the person to examine their life in the light of these five questions. 1. Am I truthful? 2. Am I honest? 3. Am I pure? 4. Am I selfish? 5. Am I loving? Repeat them again, very slowly, and ask the person to answer honestly so as to see where they are in this examination of their life. Many will feel to tell the truth about themselves is very therapeutic and glad for the relief. Others to save embarrassment will be uncomfortable and make excuses, or may try to change the subject. The Samaritan woman did. She said, "*I see you are a prophet. Now tell me where is the place to worship, Jerusalem or this mountain?*" (John 4:19). Why did she ask this question at this particular time? Because the Samaritan woman found the conversation very uncomfortable, and preferred to go to a practical religious question. It is easier to discuss practical religious questions than it is to face one's own sin – easier but deadly. Beware of the attempt to draw you away from the question of the moral problem. Stay with the moral issue. Life and death lie in this issue. But they do not lie in the question of where to worship.

Prayer for today: O Christ, Your straight-forward focus saves us, for we could go off course. Help us to stay focused today so that we may help someone. Amen.

October 1   Isaiah 1:11-17; Matthew 23:3-14; 25-28

"RELIGIOUS" BUT ROTTEN

This Samaritan woman was apparently a religious woman – she was interested in the proper place to worship and in the coming Messiah who would tell them everything. Don't be fooled when people talk religion to you, for we may be very religious – and be very rotten. She was. Or we could be religious in spots and rotten in spots. Someone explained it as being only half-awake: They feel sudden outburst of guilt because they are haunted by impure dreams, and yet are perfectly unconscious that their lives are one long expression of envy, maliciousness, hatred, and no charitableness. Others are sexually impure and yet haunted with deep regret over speaking unkindly to someone. We have two motives: The one we portray and the real one. Take no one and no thing for granted.

Did Jesus answer this practical religious question about the proper place to worship? Yes, but note how He answered it. *"God is spirit, and his worshipers must worship him in spirit and in truth."* (John 4:24) – God is a spirit – that makes Jerusalem and this mountain irrelevant. God desires people to "worship him in spirit and in truth" – that makes the moral life relevant in "worship" – "in truth" by living right.

The moral problem was still central. No matter how far you go off the point momentarily, bring the conversation back to the central issue. When you are trying to help someone see their sins, you yourself must guide the conversation – not the other person or other circumstances. As you are leading toward victory, toward release, so you must be in moral control of the situation. At every point Jesus guided the conversation with the Samaritan woman, and in the end He guided her to release.

Prayer for today: O Christ, thank You for pointing us to the door that leads to freedom. Help us to point others to that door. Amen.

October 2
Matthew 10:8; Mark 5:19;
John 1:35-37; 20:28-31;
Colossians 1:18

OUR PURPOSE

What was the purpose of the conversation between Jesus and the Samaritan woman? It was the words: "*I who speak to you am He.*" (Luke 4:26). The purpose of the entire conversation was so Christ could reveal Himself to her. He got her to see herself, that she might then see Him – SALVATION!

The purpose of our work and conversation is just one simple thing – to get people to see Jesus. If we fail in getting people to see Jesus, we have failed our purpose. Our business is not to be clever, but to be Christian, and we can only be Christian as we show others Christ. But it must not be an intellectual understanding of Him – it must be a moral understanding, a firm understanding of Christ as the power that can change and transform life. The person must not just look at Christ, but completely surrender to Him. That is seeing Him. Then that person is "firmly implanted" in Christ.

There is one other step, not only to get the woman to see Christ, but to fill her so completely with Christ vision that she would go and tell it to others. She left her water jar and ran off to the village and told what happened. The bottom line of evangelism is to produce other evangelist. It is satisfying to win people to Christ, but REAL satisfaction is when we see them winning others. Then we know we have started something that knows no end. Do you belong to the problem or to the solution? As we try to help solve problems we become more deeply rooted in Christ. (Matthew 28:8-9 KJV) tells us, "*And as they went to tell his disciples, behold, Jesus met them.*" On the way to tell others, Jesus met them – He always does. On the way to tell others you will sense His warm, living presence.

Prayer for today: O Christ, help us to know the purpose You have for our life and may we work toward that end. Amen.

321

October 3 Psalm 51:10-13; Acts 2:41-47; 11:22-24

IMPROVED SOCIAL LIFE — INDIVIDUAL CHANGE

When the disciples returned from buying food in town, they found Jesus in a very <u>exalted</u> state. He did not want to eat. When they urged Him to eat something He said to them, *"I have food to eat that you know nothing about." "My food"*, said Jesus *"is to do the will of him who sent me and to finish his work."* (John 4:34). Why should Jesus be so exalted over such a small incident? Small? Watching that individual spiritually change in that moment was the greatest thing on earth, something He identified with as the will of God. And that will, satisfied His hunger. **Doing the will of God absolutely satisfies our spiritual hunger!** If Jesus felt so excited about changing an individual, why should it be looked upon as of little consequence, as some of society does today? Is our world so small that we can't emphasize both social change and individual change? Can we not blend both? The Kingdom of God may mean changing of our social life but it also means just what happened to the Samaritan woman – a changed individual life.

Ten years after some grafted peach trees were planted they were not over two feet high. The reason is that deer came in at night and ate the growing tips as fast as they grew out. The trees had a good quality of life, but growth was impossible. Now, put a fence around those same trees and watch them grow and bear fruit. You could say the fence was an improvement in our social life. Now, graft into that life a spiritually changed individual and we will bear fruit. However, a fence around "un-grafted" wild peach trees will not bear fruit; neither will a life bear fruit until grafted with spiritual change. Individual change without amending our social life won't do. Both are needed. Jesus rejoiced that day when He put the graft of a higher life into a human soul. That was God's will for Him – it is God's will for us also.

Prayer for today: O Christ, keep my life grafted to You and give me power to put the graft of Your life into other lives. Amen.

October 4   Psalm 40:8; 119:16, 45,105,162,165; John 7:6

HIS WILL—OUR "SOUL" FOOD

Nothing excites the soul, gives it a great sense of peace and victory so much as the fact that we are being used to change lives of others. This is a very essential part of Living Victoriously, without it Living Victoriously will remain an unfulfilled dream. The battle of life is not won by defense, but by offense. The will of God is redemptive, and when we feed upon that will, we shall be redemptive. Jesus said that to Him the will of God was food, (John 4:34), it was something that satisfied His hunger, sustained Him, something that He lived by. To some of us the will of God is like medicine. We do it once ever so often to make us feel better. It's a bitter pill to take, but it is needed to get rid of our illness. This view of the will of God is very common and accepted. Actually the will of God is born, brought forth by our spiritual birth. Then when death and misfortune visit us, we can say: "Your will be done." Death and misfortune also are bitter pills, but with Christ as our doctor we will survive victoriously. To some the will of God is like sweets at the end of a meal – something to round off life, and give it taste. But we don't live by sweets alone. Neither do such people live by the will of God – except may be occasionally. Sweets give life flavor, but not its food. To Jesus the will of God was neither medicine nor sweets; it was "soul food" – the thing that sustained Him. This implies that we are made for the will of God as the body is made for food. It fits both our moral and our spiritual make-up. Everything else is poison – this is food. We live as we live by the will of God – we wither and die if we live by some other will, particularly our own will.

Prayer for today: O Christ, Help me to feed upon Your will as my "soul food." May that will within me turn to moral strength and spiritual victory. May it be life to me. Amen.

October 5   Matthew 19:21; Romans 8:5-8; 14:15

MY WILL—MY POISON

Yesterday we said that we are made for the will of God, (for His purpose), just as the body is made for food, that the will of God feeds us while everything outside of His will is poison to us.

Many people, some even in their later years of life, enjoyed success in their chosen profession, happiness in their families, perfection in their social lives, but are still seeking inner peace. They are intelligent, modern, and thorough, but – feeding on some purpose other than that of God. And still hungry. If you haven't found satisfying nourishment in your way of life, as grand as it may be, if you still feel dissatisfied, hungry –are you trying to live by the will of your natural desires? Paul says in (Romans 8:5-6) "*Those who live according to the sinful nature have their minds set on what that nature desires; but those who live in accordance with the Spirit have their minds set on what the Spirit desires. The mind of sinful man is death, but the mind controlled by the Spirit is life and peace.*" Sin is poison to us. We are not made to live by our lower sinful nature, but by our higher nature, that higher nature is led by the will of God. Anything that seems to satisfy you, outside the will of God, is a harmful drug, certainly not soul food. The will of God is food – soul food. When we feed on that we are not hungry for anything else, it is completely satisfying. We feel at the center of our being that we have resources, nourishment, re-enforcement, life not our own, and we live by that very life. Living victoriously is the natural, normal outcome of doing God's will (fulfilling the purpose He has for our life). We are immovably fixed in God, and immeasurably fed by Him. There is nothing that sustains us like knowing that God is feeding us as we live the life He has prepared for us to live. Is it any wonder that we share that same sense of excited joy Jesus had on this occasion?

Prayer for today: O Father, I put my life in Your hands, lead me and feed me, I pray. Amen.

October 6   Mark 9:27; Acts 3:6; 8:35; 9:34;
                             Colossians 1:14:20

SUMMATION

We cannot close this phase of Living Victoriously in which we share our Christian lives with others without summing it up with these words, "*they brought him*" (Mark 9:20a).

This phrase sums up the very meaning of our gospel. A human need, One who can meet that need – Christ, and the "brought" connected the two. "*Bring the boy to me*" (Mark 9:19) "*So they brought him.*" (Mark 9:20).

At one end there is a human need at the other end is the One that can meet that need.

Never has there been a time when our human needs have needed to be met more than at this present time. Detached, drifting, distracted and desperately wanting something – that is "us" in this modern world. Going – we don't know where! Feeling –we don't know what! Thinking –with no great confidence! Modern humanity is in deep need.

Christ, who can meet our every need, stands ready, able, and available. But He cannot reach that human need without a human connection. That connection is the Christian. The Christian life **"brings"** or **"brought"** the gospel of Jesus Christ to others.

As a Christian we are the vital connecting link between Christ and the sinner. We must get the message across. If we don't who will? You and I are to be in such close contact with Christ and human need that we convey his very life to that need. What a wonderful place to be.

Prayer for today: O Christ, we know that if we fail, we will have failed in Your purpose for our life. Help us not to fail You – and others. Amen.

October 7   Mark 9:43-47; 14:37-38; 1 Peter 1 6-7

LIVING VICTORIOSLY AND TEMPTATION

We have just studied the fact that Living Victoriously means to say "yes" to the will of God; and we are to say "no" to temptation. Christianity is not all prohibition, it is a privilege, but some things are prohibited. In Mark (9:43-47) Jesus said, if either our <u>hand</u> or our <u>foot,</u> or our <u>eye</u>, causes us to sin, free ourselves of it.(actually the **KJV** of scripture says "<u>cut it off</u>" when speaking of the hand and foot, and when speaking of the eye- it says "<u>pluck it out</u>"). In other words, <u>do not tolerate anything from head to foot that gets in the way</u> <u>of the main purpose of our life. From head to toe we are to belong to</u> <u>Christ</u>. Now, note the order of these three – hand, foot, and eye. The hand - doing evil; the foot - approaching evil, but not actually doing it; the eye - looking at evil with desire from a distance. We must cut out sin at any stage, whether it is hand-sin, foot-sin, or eye-sin. The place to cut it out most effectively is at the <u>eye</u>, the place of thought. Some people live too much at the stage between the <u>eye</u> and <u>foot</u>; they play with sin at the <u>hand</u> stage. They go beyond thinking about it, they actually approach it, come to the very edge of it and expect to pull back just before falling into it. In this way they get <u>some</u> plea-sure from getting up close to evil, feeling its burning warmth, but they also have <u>some</u> pleasure from the fact they were good enough to restrain at the end. It is called playing with fire! It is an attempt to have, what we think, is the best of both worlds. A foolish attempt, for it leaves you homeless. You are not at home in Christ and not at home in evil. Dissatisfaction is at the end of the attempt at double pleasure. Watch your step; don't let your feet take you to the edge, for you could fall in.

Prayer for today: O Christ, we thank You for Your decisiveness. We pray that You will save us from all double-mindedness – help us to be decisive. Amen.

October 8   Matthew 4:8-9; 5:28; 6:22; 1 John 2:16

EYE – SIN

The most effective place to kill sin is in the "eye" stage. That means the actual seeing of evil with the physical eye, or seeing it in our imagination with the <u>mental eye</u>.

When an evil thought comes to your mind, here are a few suggestions to draw your attention away from that thought. (1) Bat your eyes very rapidly, the thought is broken up. Since it is a voluntary act demanding voluntary attention the attention is drawn away from the thought. Then as soon as you can get back your equilibrium, pray, "O Christ, save me." It is a great plan because it works and it is always available. (2) Change what you are doing at once in order to get your attention on something else. Example – you are hiking in the mountains and you're troubled with an evil thought, pick up a very heavy rock or log and carry it or take off your shoes and walk barefoot, either would certainly draw your attention away from the evil thoughts. Usually these battles of the mind take place when our mind is not absorbed with mental or physical task, but when we have nothing in particular to involve our mind or ourselves in. You know the old saying – "An idle mind is the devil's workshop." This is <u>so</u> true! (3) If you are alone when an evil thought attacks you, immediately go, if possible, to a group of people. We sometimes talk about the temptation of crowds. However, crowds can save us from ourselves and our evil thoughts. We are ashamed to entertain evil thoughts in the company of some people. They also draw our minds to other interest. (4) Change the mental picture to a religious one. Train your mind to run at once to the cross. It is hard to think of evil and Christ at the same time. The two thoughts are not compatible.

Prayer for today: O Christ, give me purity of mind, for I want the kind of mind in which You can be at home. Amen.

October 9   Psalm 19:14; 104:34; 119:54;
                                         2 Corinthians 10:5

OVERCOMING TEMPTATION

We continue to look at the way evil thoughts may be overcome: (5) put your mind under a strict discipline. The mind is the servant of your personality and can be made to obey. You can turn off your thoughts just as you turn off your television. The mind soon begins to understand who the master is. Paul speaks of *"bringing every thought into captivity to the obedience of Christ."*

(2 Corinthians 5). But the mind will play tricks on you if it knows in the end you will give in. Refuse to yield or compromise when it comes to discipline of your self. (6) In order to determine your thoughts when you awake, think of the purest, finest thoughts just before you go to sleep. Those last thoughts just before you drop off to sleep are very determinative, for the door into the subconscious is opening and they drop into it to work good or evil.

Remember you are fighting the battle of your <u>day</u> dreaming and <u>night</u> dreaming life when you are fighting that evil thought. Do not let your last waking thought be an impure thought, for it will attach itself to your mind like a tick. Crowd it out by making your last thought of the day a thought of Christ. (7) Get plenty exercise. Play games and become interested in them. (8) Try to help someone else in their battle. The very sense of your responsibility for someone else will help you in yours, your thoughts will be of someone else instead of yourself and the fact that you do not want to let them down. (9) Breathe a prayer the moment an impure thought comes to mind.

Prayer for today: O Christ of the pure mind, make me pure in mind today – and always. Amen.

October 10   Matthew 13:23, Hebrews 2:1; James 1:19,
                               Revelation 2:7, 11, 17

CONSIDER CAREFULLY WHAT YOU HEAR

In our study of control of the mind, it will help us to look at a most important verse: *"Consider carefully what you hear. With the measure you use, it will be measured to you – and even more."* (Mark 4:24). Here Jesus says, "Be careful what you hear, for the measure of attention you give it, is the measure of impression it will make on you. The degree of attention is the degree of impression. In memory training it is not a matter of memory, it is a matter of attention. A bad memory is the result of bad attention. So we should **not** say, "I have a bad memory," but say, "I do not pay attention." Somewhere it was said that there are just three laws of learning: Concentrate, concentrate, concentrate. So - Jesus said, be careful the things you pay attention to. Because **the part of our surroundings to which we pay attention influences us.** People think about sex – that's good, but it is the thinking too much about sex – that's bad. If you concentrate your attention on sex, don't be surprised if it comes back to you in sex-impression. And then don't be surprised if you lose your sex battle in sex-expression. Be frank about sex, but after taking a frank view of the fact of sex, dismiss it from the center of your thinking. But if you are constantly wading through sex-entertainment in the name of frankness, you will soon be wading through filth, at least, in your mind. For you follow your attention. GLANCE at the fact concerning sex, but GAZE at the fact of Christ. But there are those people who GAZE at sex, and GLANCE at Christ, and then wonder why sex has the stronger hold on them.

So consider carefully what you hear and see,
for that attention determines your spiritual destiny.

Prayer for today: O Christ, we thank You that You have spoken this law so plainly. Help us to obey it just as plainly. Amen.

October 11   Psalm 73:2-3, 16-17; Romans 12:21;
                              Hebrews 12:3; 2 Peter 3:17

LOOKING AT PEOPLE INSTEAD OF CHRIST

We said that we must be careful to what we give our attention, **because how much attention we give to something will determine how much of an impression it makes on us**. Some of us pay entirely too much attention to what other people say and do. Our eyes are on people instead of Christ. And we wonder why we are so weak.

Peter once turned to Jesus and said, *"Lord, what about him?"* Jesus answer was penetrating, *"...what is that to you? You must follow me."* (John 21:21-22).

Many of us have our eyes on people, on their weaknesses in particular, and soon find ourselves stumbling – over people. A great many of <u>our</u> spiritual problems come from hurts stumbling over this insincere Christian, over that weak one. Don't let yourself become bitter and discouraged because this one or that one has given you grief. Think of what Jesus said to Peter, because He says the same to us, *"What is that to you? You must follow me."* We are on the wrong path and we know it, when we let others weaknesses fill our minds, then there is no room for thoughts of Christ.

You are not following that person – you are following Christ. To our own Master be true – stand or fall with Him. Christ is the only one who is always the same, dependable, sure, and true. Follow Him!! He will never let you down – People do.

So, if you are tempted to be up or down according to the way people treat you, resist it.

Prayer for today: O Christ, I pray that You will help me get my eyes on You and You alone, so that, no matter what people may do, or not do, I will follow You. Amen.

October 12   Matthew 26:38-39; Ephesians 6:11-13;
                                1 Peter 1:6-7

THE TEMPTATION TO GIVE IN TO OUR FEELINGS

Many of us stumble by having our eyes on people or we may stumble by having our eyes on our emotional self. We go up or down as our feelings go up or down. We do not want to minimize emotion, for it is the driving force of the soul, but those great ideals that have a strong emotional quality about them get to us. But if we pay too much attention to feelings, we won't have any. Emotion is the by-product of a great driving conviction – like the waves pushed up as the boat pushes forward. Think about your directions and if your power is sufficient to push forward then your feelings (the waves) – will take care of themselves. Our feelings are sometimes determined by our physical condition. It is hard to feel religious with a migraine! The light is still burning but it is dimmed by the pain. On a moonlit night throw a stone into the lake and destroy the moons reflection there. Though the moon sails sublimely on in the sky its reflection in the water has been disturbed. Our feelings are like the reflection on the surface of the water – subject to calm and storm and many changes. But our faith is like the moon in the sky, unchanged by what happens to the reflections in the water. If your feelings go up and down like a rollercoaster, when you look up you're up, when you look down, you're down, determine to keep looking up at Jesus, and not down at yourself or your feelings. Looking at your feelings is a sure way of being self-centered. Whether the moon shines with serene splendor on a mountain lake or the dark clouds of a storm is above us, this does not change our responsibility as Christians.

Prayer for today: O Christ, save me when I get my eyes on myself and the waves around me instead of on You. For among the flow of things You remain the same. Amen.

October 13   Psalm 26:1, 12; 2 Peter 2:9; 1 John 4:4;
                              Revelation 3:10

OUTGROWING TEMPTATION

Temptation has its advantages. As we struggle, we grow. Difficulties CAN make us stronger. When Jesus went into the wilderness, it is said that He went in, "*FULL of the Holy Spirit*," but He returned, "*In the POWER of the Spirit.*" (Luke 4:1 & 14). Simple fullness had turned to power under the influence of temptation. His spiritual tissues had grown tougher during the struggle. So it is with us. Two things happen as we grow spiritually: (1) Our temptations move on to a higher level, and (2) we outgrow many of them.

The temptations of Jesus were on a very high level indeed. In the wilderness He did not struggle with lust and passion, but with Satan's cunning temptations – and here light could have become darkness. Look at it as a compliment to be tempted at such a level. As we grow spiritually we find our temptations less extreme but still important. We outgrow temptations to be dishonest, lie, cheat, etc. and the battle of spiritual pride may take their place. Then there comes a time when we outgrow <u>most</u> of our temptations. This is the highest level of all – to be at a spiritual level where these things no longer touch us, or stir us. We have gone beyond them.

The last petition in the Lord's Prayer is, "*And lead us not into temptation.* (Matthew 6:13a). This is the highest petition of the prayer and the culmination of all: Lead me to a place where temptation has lost its grip, where there is literally no temptation. It will be so with us in many things. We will get the habit of victory over temptation. We become fixed in goodness. Habit is working for us now, and not against us.

Prayer for today: O Christ, I thank You that every battle now makes the next one easier. Help me to win every one today. Amen.

332

October 14   Acts 2:41-47, 4:32

PRINCIPLES OF LIVING PEACEFULLY WITH OTHERS

We have been studying the difficulties that result from temptations which mostly come from within ourselves. But many of our
spiritual problems do not come from us – they come from our relationships with others. It is not easy to adjust one's self to other people
and their ways. Christianity should teach us that very thing, for
Christianity is the science of living peacefully with others according
to Jesus Christ. Many of our attempts to live peacefully with others
do not obey the foundational principles of corporate living, for there
are principles or laws of corporate living that are as well defined
as those that apply to nature. We must attempt to discover them
and live by them. All of us have to live in relationship with others.
Many try to do it without any foundational principles, and it ends in
disaster and results in bitterness and conflict. If we depend too much
on emotion, and not enough on intelligent planning, the result will
be disastrous.

A great definition as to what our work as <u>a Christian is</u>: "<u>A person
sent from God to persuade others to put Christ at the center of every
relationship</u>." What are some of the principles we should conform to
if we are to live peacefully with others?

(1) We should recognize that life is corporate. Life cannot be
looked on as an individual thing, for doing so will bring consequences that have us continually in trouble with others. We tend
to turn the entire situation, whatever it may be, to ourselves, rather
than relating the situation to include others. A cancer cell is one
that demands that it be ministered to rather than being permitted to
minister to the body. It is destructive rather than constructive. There
are many people who are cancerous in society. They look at what
they can get from society rather than what they can contribute to it.

Prayer for today: O Christ, teach me how to live peacefully with
others, for I do want others to live peacefully with me. Amen.

October 15   Psalm 34:13, Isaiah 29:21;
                                   Matthew 6:33, 7:1-15

PRINCIPLES OF LIVING CORPORATELY – (Continued)

(2) After we realize that living in this world means living corporately we must proceed to be loyal to the group in which we are in immediate contact. Of course there are degrees of loyalty. There is the loyalty to one's self, to our family, to our group, to our country, to our job, to God. Our first and final loyalty should be to God. Where loyalty to God and His purpose conflicts with any lesser loyalties then the lesser loyalties must give way to God and His purpose must remain supreme and final. While this is true, there must be a degree of loyalty to the other groups where we work out the principles of God's purpose and make them operative with those groups. If we do not learn to be completely loyal to the smaller, we will never learn to be completely loyal to the larger.

(3) Loyalty to others should mean that we will never criticize them behind their back. There is bound to be criticism, because this is an imperfect world of imperfect people. But criticism should always be open, frank and constructive. **Fellowship is based on confidence, secret criticism undermines that confidence, and therefore there must be no secret criticism**. You cannot have fellowship, if you know or suspect that secret criticism is taking place. But when you know there is no open or secret criticism, then the situation is filled with confidence and freedom and fellowship. When about to voice criticism of another person, ask yourself these three questions: 1. <u>Is it true</u>? 2. <u>Is it necessary</u>? 3. <u>Is it kind</u>? If the criticism can pass these three tests, then it should be given openly and frankly. Christians in trying to be good are sometimes tempted to point out the faults of others, so that they themselves might look better. That is a miserable mistake!

Prayer for today: O Christ, save me today and everyday from the disloyalty of secret criticism. May the words die upon my lips and my heart because of Your love. Amen.

October 16   Proverbs 17:9; 1 Corinthians 13:4-6;
                              Hebrews 12:5-11; James 4:11-12

CONTINUING TO LOOK AT LIVING CORPORATELY

As we continue our study of living corporately: (4) Not only should we be able to give good constructive criticism to another person, we should also be willing to accept constructive criticism. And rejoice in it. (OUCH) Many of us are very willing to give it, but very unwilling and may even refuse it for ourselves. No one earns the right to criticize others unless you welcome criticism of yourself from others. The principle of give and take must be understood here. (5) However, we must guard against becoming petty, always looking for something to correct in someone. **We should be more inclined to compliment and encourage than to correct**. Do not be afraid that you will make people proud, **for sincere hearts are usually more humbled by compliments than by criticism**. If we are always looking for something to correct in others, we become dangerously close to looking for that speck in our brother's eye, while ignoring the plank in our own eye. (Matthew 7:3-4).

Our attitude should be that of finding the better things in people's lives, but now and then faced with the necessity of pointing out weaknesses. **But the emphasis should always be on the search for the good in others, for people are made greater by compliments than by corrections.**

Prayer for today: O Christ, You who find good things in me when I cannot find them in myself, help me to find the good in others, and to tell them so. Amen.

October 17   Matthew 5:25; Romans 14:13-16;
                               1 Corinthians 13:5; Philippians 4:5

LETTING GO OF SMALL THINGS

Continuing from yesterday: (6) We must be willing to let go of small things that do not involve principles. There are many tiny things that become huge because we insist on making an issue of them. It is much better to let go of small matters, so we can stand on the big ones. Our character can be judged on the size of the thing upon which we take our stand. One of the great things in life is to learn to keep small things small and great things great. We often reverse these things in our relationship to each other.

(7) Another principle is to refuse to look for discredit or belittling of ourselves by others. There is no person more difficult than the "touchy" person – always looking to get their feelings hurt and usually they do. If we spend our time looking to be overlooked or slighted, it shows that we are on the defensive, and to be on the defensive, shows we are dominated by fear. The defensive attitude shows that either we have an inferiority complex or a fear complex working within us.

(8) We should be more aware of our duties than of our rights. If we are always looking out for our rights, we will throw the emphasis on the wrong side of things. If we will think about privileges of service then we will have more rights than we know what to do with.

(9) Meet issues head on before they get cold. If you keep something in your heart it will turn ugly. Get it out immediately. The time element is very important. Don't put it off for any reason. Jesus says, *"Settle matters quickly with your adversary...while you are still with him..."* (Matthew 5:25). Don't separate and let the issue grow cold. Cultivate the habit of spiritual decisiveness. Get the unpleasant out of the way quickly!

Prayer for today: O Christ, we thank You that when meeting issues You did not hesitate. Give me that same boldness. Amen.

October 18   Ecclesiastes 3:1-4; 7:16; Acts 6:1-7;
                              Romans 12-16

GOING AGAINST YOURSELF

Continuing our study: The Christian way to live peacefully with one another: (10) We will often have to decide with others against our own wishes, desires, plans, etc. A little boy whose Mother was trying her best to give him proper guidance in life, found that he had taken the scissors, cut off one side of his hair and left a few other things in shreds. When she discovered what he had done instead of losing her temper, she suggested a "quiet time" to think over what he had done and what punishment should be given. After the "quiet time" she asked if he had any ideas as to what should be done. "Yes," he said, "I think we had better not let me have the scissors again." Sound advice! He had gone against himself and his desires to side with his Mother. This is something we will have to do often –decide that to side with others is better than holding on to our personal desires. (11) Have the power to laugh at yourself. Look at yourself in the mirror and burst into laughter. It will keep you from taking yourself too seriously. The capacity you have to laugh at yourself determines how high you have risen. There are these stages: the lowest – the person who doesn't laugh at all; then the one who laughs at their own jokes; then the one who laughs at the jokes of others; and highest of all is the person who can laugh at themselves. For the power to laugh at your self shows the power to look at yourself objectively. (12) In your relationships with other people, if you find a basic unfairness in your heart, then don't try to counsel someone else until you are doing your best to right any wrong that is still lingering in your heart. For that basic wrong will poison relationships and will show up again and again until you make it right in your heart. Build relationships on fairness and everything else becomes easier.

Prayer for today: O Christ, help us put Your mind into our relationships, and then we will know how to live together peacefully. Amen.

October 19   1 Corinthians 12:12-13; Galatians 6:2;
                       Ephesians 2:19-22

"ORGANS OF ONE ANOTHER"

We come to an important principle in living corporately: (13) Remember what Paul says in (1Corinthians 12:12-19)? Paul's point has nothing to do with our human anatomy. He wants to ensure that every follower of Christ feels important, and knows that his or her contribution is crucial. None of us has the right to act as though we are separate from the body. "We serve as organs of one another." So this thought should keep us from being jealous of one another. If a member of the body excels in singing, then it becomes the organ of song for us. We should therefore rejoice that our organ of song is so beautifully efficient. Another may excel in executive ability. We should be happy that our organ of executive power is functioning. The point is, we are striving to get a corporate job done, and the strength of any is the strength of all. You will have something in you which will be the organ of others, something where you are strong and they are weak. <u>None of us has everything, but we all have something</u>. Take an inventory of your strong and weak points, and see how your weaknesses can be supplemented by the strength of someone, and how your strong point can supplement the weakness of others.

(14) Keep a strong prayer life, and along with that prayer life keep a surrendered heart, when we are inwardly surrendered, we don't expect anything, and if anything comes to us, it is pure gain. Also, **when we are truly surrendered to Christ, we become immune to many of the hurts and conflicts that come in our everyday ordinary contacts with others. Pray for each other, prayer taps into the power of Christ. It will do it for you.**

Prayer for today: O Christ, Your power, and Your power alone can sweeten relationships and make impossible situations not only possible but glorious. Give me that power, I pray. Amen.

October 20   Acts 4:32-35; 1 Peter 2:17; 3:8 John 1:7

A CROSS SECTION OF A CHRISTIAN SOCIETY

We have been studying the principles of living corporately; now let's look at a cross section of a Christian society in the first century. (Acts 2:43a-47) *"Everyone was filled with awe...All the believers were together and had everything in common. Selling their posses- sions and goods, they gave to anyone as he had need...They broke bread in their homes and ate together with glad and sincere hearts, praising God and enjoying the favor of all the people. And the Lord added to their number daily those who were being saved."* Let's look at what was there: (1) AWE – the supernatural was working down through human relationships and was forming a new society. God became an incarnate fact. (2) UNITY - "all the believers were together." Many shades of belief, class and color among them, but they had a living unity that transcended difference. (3) That unity included the social and economic life. They were not only one in spirit, but also one in social and economic life – their whole life was one unit. They held no difference between the sacred and the secular. (4) Need was abolished. Good news for the poor – the first item in Christ's program was fulfilled. (5) Community, family, and indi- vidual life were preserved. The community was "meeting together in the temple courts everyday" –the family at bread at home –family was intact; the individual was filled with glad and sincere hearts — preserved and excited. (6) Single-heartedness. Divisions were gone on the inside, and also on the outside in their relationships with each other. Life was reduced from complexity to simplicity. (7) Life became sweet and contagious. "Enjoying the flavor" – sweet; "daily the Lord added" – contagious. These are the seven colors into which the white light of God's society breaks into. We MUST rediscover this light for our darkened age and put it not just in our churches but into our society as a whole. For this is God's will – His purpose.

Prayer for today: O Christ, may everyone share that victory. Help us to exemplify that victory in our total life. Amen.

October 21   Matthew 21:12; Mark 14:11;
                                    Luke 22:24-27; Acts 5:1-9;
                                    1 Timothy 6:10

DANGERS TO THE NEW SOCIETY

The two greatest dangers emerging in this new society, the Kingdom of God: Love of <u>money</u> and <u>power</u>. The new society was threatened when Judas gave in to the love of money, and when Ananias gave in to the same impulse. It was also threatened when the disciples began to argue over the places of power, and it was more than threatened from outside the new society when the authority of the Kingdom of God, as represented by Jesus, came into conflict with the Jewish religious authorities and the Roman secular power. They saw their power challenged and threatened as they fought back with a cross. <u>Love of money and power crucified Christ</u>. It is strange that sex had nothing to do with it, though we usually consider sex as the greatest center of moral danger. **Love of money and power held first place <u>then</u>, and they still hold first place <u>today</u>!** And if you think sex is running money and power a close race, consider just how often sex **IS** used for money and power. It is said that, "*Jesus sat down opposite the place where the offerings were put and watched the crowd putting their money into the temple treasury.*"(Mark 12:41). It is a serious and awful moment when Jesus surveys the money side of our religion and our civilization. He sees how we make money, how we keep it, how we spend it, and the hypocrisies and conflict that surround it all. He may be searching that side of our civilization as never before. He is probing to the roots and exposing the fact of the absolute unchristian basis of the money side of our civilization. His eye of judgment is upon that central moral fact.

We will not be able to obtain complete victory in human living individually and collectively until we obtain it at the place of money.

Prayer for today: O Christ, become our conscience at this point, we need Your light here to show us the way out, and we need power that will deliver us from the love of money. Amen.

October 22

Mark 12:15; Acts 4:36-37;
1 Corinthians 6:12;
Philippians 4:11-12

VICTORY OVER THE LOVE OF MONEY

We see that the love of money and power are the two sources of greatest temptation in life. How can we have victory over the love of money?

There is the individual aspect and the social aspect. Money must be individually surrendered. We all need money in this world of ours, but we do not need to be obsessed with it to the point it means more to us than Christ. **Don't let money be your master, master your money.** Make your money minister to both your needs and the needs of others. If money makes me more mentally, morally, physically, and spiritually fit for the purposes of the Kingdom of God, then it is legitimate and right – a servant of God.

In the social aspect we should inwardly renounce a system where money use is based on competition which turns society into "a scramble of pursuers and pursued." We should not be happy with a society based on the unchristian principle of selfish competition but work toward the making of a society based on the Christian principle of co-operation. Of course we know we can not do this all at once. Society is not prepared for it. And <u>all we as Christians can do is do it God's way, knowing we have renounced the old society and are working on a new one.</u> **On that base principle we can live victoriously both individually and collectively, because we are acting as though the victory is already won. It is, as far as we as an individual, is concerned.**

Prayer for today: O Christ, help me to renounce money as master and to realize it as servant by Your power. Amen.

October 23   Matthew 20:26-28; John 9:14;
                              Philippians 2:5-9

VICTORY OVER THE LOVE OF POWER

Let's look how power, which usually corrupts people, may serve people. <u>Power is the expression or projection of personality</u>. When the personality is converted, power must be converted along with it. Since the matter of power has both individual and social aspects, it must be doubly converted. Picture this: Jesus had just finished over-turning the tables of the money changers and cleared the Temple of all illegitimate use. Now, "He is sitting on the Mount of Olives oppo-site the temple," surveying the scene and thinking how the power represented in that Temple had turned from service to exploitation. It was given to serve the people; it now had the people serving it. It must now be cleansed, and if it isn't it must be torn down. **Jesus is surveying the power side of our civilization today**. His searching eye rests on the exploitation taking place through power. Can you feel His burning condemnations? Again, victory will only come through surrender. Jesus said: *"You know that those who are regarded as rulers of the Gentiles lord it over them...not so with you. Instead, whoever wants to become great among you must be your servant, and whoever wants to be first must be slave of all."* (Mark 10:42-45). <u>Therefore, we must give up all power over others in our life that is not gained by service to them</u>. **All power based on money, prestige, class, race, or sex must go, and only retain that which is gained by actual <u>self-giving service</u>**. This is personal. However, in regard to the social we must do the same. We must inwardly give up all power in the social and political arena that does not <u>**serve**</u> the people in their needs, and we must influence as many others as possible to do the same. Society is not ready to make that the criteria and test of power. In the meantime we are living victoriously **as far as it depends on us.**

Prayer for today: O God, help me to know no sovereignty but You! Amen.

October 24   Matthew 10:28; Luke 14:26; Acts 20:22;
                    Galatians 6:14

THE CROSS BECOMES INEVITABLE

Out of these social contacts a cross appears. If we are sympathetic to people and situations around us, we suffer inwardly to see what is happening. The effect of the gospel of Jesus Christ deepens and widens our sympathies. This means that we now sympathize more deeply because we are more deeply touched. So the process of our growing spiritually is the deepening of our capacity for the suffering that surrounds us. Each new friendship we form, each new person we lead to Christ, each new injustice in the social society we come in contact with, each new sin in others which we encounter, each new task we take upon ourselves, will become a "possible" suffering point. Through the gospel of Jesus Christ our soul becomes sensitive to others suffering and our sympathy reaches out to that soul. The cross then becomes inevitable.

In Jesus situation, His sympathies were far reaching in range and immeasurable in depth. He was the Son of man, so the cross that came as a result of that fact was universal and infinite. He touched all life in love and out of that love for us – He suffered. The cross is the focal point of that suffering. That suffering was there before and is still there and will be there until evil is banished. The actors in the terrible drama unwittingly bore witness of this universal cross when they inscribed upon the cross in Latin, Greek, and Hebrew. That was unusual. Did they dimly sense the fact that here was suffering breaking out into all languages? Or was it that they expressed His guilt in all these languages? It doesn't matter, for it was all the same – His guilt was His love – the guilt of loving us all, and therefore suffering for us all.

As we become personally and socially a Christian, a cross awaits us. It is inevitable.

Prayer for today: O Christ, Your cross is not an isolated thing – it continues in us. Help us to be faithful cross-bearers. Amen.

October 25 Matthew 25:34-40; Romans 9:1-3:
Galatians 4:19

THE CROSS IN ACTION

We saw in yesterday's study that our Christian sympathies become our Christian crosses. Once at a Christian school a teacher was striving to make good citizens of his students. One day he dug a grave in the school yard, and as the astonished students looked on he stepped into it and said, "Now cover me up and bury me. I cannot bear to live and watch as you continue your life doing the awful things that you do. I had rather die." The students decided to bury their sins, not their teacher.

Going out into life as a Christian, hopefully not to face evil so dramatically as that teacher, but your contact with evil will turn into a cross for you. Someone wanted to build a house with no windows or doors, only slits of a cross as the only opening, so they could look out at the world through a cross. Beautiful sentiment! But we must not only <u>look</u> out on life through a cross – we must <u>touch</u> life through a cross. Our contacts must be felt through participation in the experience of others. We must deliberately involve ourselves in what really doesn't belong to us, since as Christians we belong to every body, and, therefore, everyone's sorrows belong to us. When anyone is called deceitful, we tense; when one is an outsider, we feel lonely for them; when one is hungry, we suffer their hunger pangs; when children are abused, they become our own children; when race, color, or class, suffers because of their station in life, we suffer; how can we be free unless we suffer with them. Our love bleeds into sacrifice as it meets the world's sin. In a world of this kind a Christian without a cross is a Christian without Christ.

Prayer for today: O Christ, make me willing to open my heart to its deepest depths to the world's anguish and turmoil, and may my heart become a place of healing. Amen.

October 26   1 Corinthians 2:1 & 12; Galatians 2:20;
                          Colossians 1:19-20

LIFE LOOKED AT THROUGH A CROSS

My husband and I had three children, a daughter and two sons. All three children were and are children to be proud of, but here I need to tell you about the older of our two sons. He was a special personality, a great Christian, outgoing, fun, and loved by young and old alike, his number of friends were endless. Before he was three years old he had cancer – retinoblastoma. Twenty-one years later he was diagnosed with Ewing's sarcoma, he died two years later at the young age of twenty-three. Oh, God, why?

No one can face this kind of tragedy without having questions – is there a meaning and purpose to this? Does God really care? I had no answers then and I have none now – **EXCEPT** as I look at life through the cross. There I see a God who is there through every struggle and suffers all that I suffer and more. God goes with us – *"Never will I leave you; never will I forsake you."* (Hebrews 13:5). **(This is my favorite verse in the entire Bible, and I know every word of it is true.)** He lets everything that falls on us fall upon His heart. I love a God like that! For two long years as I watched our son suffer and then die, and saw his love for God never waver, I see hope and light only in a cross. My world holds steady. The cross saves me from bitterness. The way to be saved from bitterness is this: since this is a world of pain and sorrow and tragedy, let the cross save you from bitterness by using that pain and sorrow and tragedy for redemptive purposes. Through it all it shows the very love of God seeking, redeeming, healing, saving. THE CROSS IS LIGHT – THE ONLY LIGHT!

Prayer for today: O Christ, we thank You that we can see life through Your wounds and that through them we can see light – the very light of life. Amen.

October 27   Mark 14:41-42; 1 Peter 2:19-24; 3:14, 17, 18

THE "FOUR" WHO BORE CROSSES

That <u>DAY</u> there was four who bore crosses. They represented four attitudes. **The first** was the impenitent thief – his was a cross of unrelieved gloom. He blamed Christ for not saving Himself and them. He died blaming everybody but himself, and therefore bore a cross that had no light. Some bear that kind of cross to the very end. No repentance, no reconciliation, no release. **The other** thief bore a cross with light in it. He looked through and beyond the shame of it all and saw that Jesus really was a King, and asked to be remembered when He came into His Kingdom. This connected him with Jesus. On that cross the man lifted up his head and saw forgiveness open to him, for he had a repentant heart. That was the cross that started in gloom and ended in gladness. **The third** cross was laid upon the shoulders of *"Simon of Cyrene, who was on his way in from the country, they seized Simon and put the cross on him and made him carry* it *behind Jesus."* (Luke 23-26). They put on Simon an underserved cross – "they <u>made</u> him carry it." Life is like that – it grabs us and puts on our unwilling shoulders a cross. It changed the whole course of Simon's life and the life of his family, for his two sons, Alexander and Rufus, became well-known Christians. Simon did not **bear** his cross – he **used** it. When Life lays its cross on us, we can let that cross connect us with Christ – and be forever changed. It is not suffering that distinguishes us; it is the way we bear that suffering. Simon bore it well and it made him. **The last or fourth** cross was that of Jesus – a chosen cross. The others were involuntary – this was chosen. That is the highest attitude of all. Since life is bound to give us a cross it is better to expect it, accept it and <u>use</u> it to help others. The chosen cross is the cross of Christ and the Christian.

Prayer for today: O Christ, help me to take that chosen cross and make it redemptive for myself and others. Amen.

October 28   Exodus 16:20-21; 1 Samuel 2:1; Isaiah 55:12

THE CHRISTIAN'S JOY

Now that we have spoken about the cross, we can speak of the Christian's joy. For the Christian's joy is a joy won out of the heart of suffering. It has a certain quality that distinguishes it from lesser joys. Revelation speaks of those who *"sang the song of Moses the servant of God and the song of the Lamb."* (Revelation 15:3).

The song of nature is the song of the triumph of the strong over the weak. You've heard the bird singing happily with a quivering dragon fly in its mouth, or the grizzly bear growling satisfaction as he tears the fish apart, or the roar of a lion as he captures a helpless deer. The ghastly killing interspersed with happy singing. That is the song that comes from lower nature – it is a song mingled with pains of others. Hunger (greed) and power are satisfied even though it cost the lives of others.

Many sing that song. Their joy is the joy of personal advantage, no matter what it may cost others. They rejoice over their gain, even though their gain may have been someone's loss. They rejoice in success, even though they know that by ruthlessness they have pushed someone to the wall. It is the joy of knowing the head of John the Baptist is off, even though they do not like the sight of it on a platter in front of them. <u>We have won, that is all that matters</u>. It is the song of unlimited rights over the weaker.

There is a slightly higher joy. It is the song of limited rights, and eye for an eye, and a tooth for a tooth. We rejoice that we got even with someone. Our sense of rough justice is satisfied. We go through life getting satisfaction out of strict justice. That too is a superficial and precarious joy.

Prayer for today: O Christ, save us from the satisfaction of lesser joys that leave their sting, and help us to know Your joy, because we know Your cross. Amen.

October 29   Luke 6:22-23; John 16:20-22;
                               2 Corinthians 12:10; 1 Peter 4:13

THE SONG OF THE LAMB

We saw yesterday <u>the song of nature</u> – <u>the song of unlimited rights</u> over the weak. Let's look now at **the song of the Lamb** – <u>the song of unlimited love</u>, the song of doing good to those who despitefully use us, the song of One who died for those who crucified Him. This is life's deepest song. Anyone who can sing this song is in the highest element of spiritual evolution. That soul really has victory.

We've heard or known of those who have had loved ones murdered, raped or were victims of other criminal circumstances, and then we've heard how the family of the victim not only prays for the forgiveness of the criminal, but forgives the criminal. That is the song of the Lamb. We have that song in our hearts when tragedy strikes us and yet we carry on helping others and rejoice in the opportunity.

Someone told of having a canary that would not sing until after it had taken its bath. Then it would sing deliriously. We have a heart like that. It will not sing until all bitterness, all revenge, and all hate is washed away. When it is cleansed from these, then it can really sing – deliriously. Don't be ashamed of your stand for Christ. Bubble over with joy – our Lord is always there with us to save, to comfort, to guide and to cheer. Don't make light of that joy in the name of modern sophistication, for this joy is the most cleansing, the most energizing, the most service-inspiring and the most melody-producing fact on earth. It is salvation by joy. One drop of Christian joy puts more oil in the machinery of life than any other known thing.

Prayer for today: O Christ, we thank You for this exquisite joy, when we have tasted it; we know that we have tasted life itself. Help us to share this joy. Amen.

October 30 Isaiah 25:8; 26:19; Philippians 3:8-10;
Colossians 3:1

THE POWER OF THE RESURRECTION

We spoke of the exquisite joy of the Cross – the song of the Lamb. But there is more. There is the joy of realizing "the **power** of His resurrection."

The resurrection means that the worst is done and has been conquered. This puts an ultimate optimism at the very heart of things. The resurrection says that no matter how life seems to be falling apart around us - think of Jesus and His love. And that includes the physical, here and now. Had it been a spiritual resurrection only, it would have meant that victory is beyond physical, not surrounded by it. Just as the battle was physical, so the victory is a physical victory. This sweeps the whole horizon, and says that now, today, we can conquer anything – everything. No wonder the Christian in the midst of a decaying society is optimistic. We have solid ground for our optimism.

When Paul came to the Athenians and preached "Jesus and the resurrection," they said he was proclaiming "foreign gods" – they thought the "resurrection" was a separate "god," because of Paul's emphasis. There is no danger in that happening in today's world, for the resurrection has been dimmed, and with it a great sadness has come over us because of it. However, as Christians we will not make a god of the resurrection, neither will we make it dim, but we will declare it as the most amazing and transforming fact of human history. Nothing else really matters now – except this one thing: **CHRIST IS ALIVE**! Related to Him, realizing Him, drawing life from Him we are fellowshipping with ultimate Life, and nothing again can dishearten us or make us afraid. **When we know in the end we win, then what happens to us on the way shouldn't matter. HE IS RISEN!!**

Prayer for today: O Christ, I thank You for the joy of knowing that nothing need defeat me, since nothing defeated You. Help me to hold to that fact and live by it. Amen.

October 31

Psalm 16:11; 51:11-12;
Ephesians 3:16-19; 1
John 4:12-13

THE JOY OF HIS PRESENCE

In many worship services the worship leader says, "The Lord is risen!" And the congregation responds, "He is risen indeed!" In that strength we go into our day knowing the power of His resurrection. But we must not depend on the resurrection, but on the resurrected Christ, and certainly not on a resurrected Christ of the <u>PAST</u>, but on the actual, living, present Christ through whom and in whom we meet as our God NOW, TODAY AND EVERY DAY!

The deepest joy is the communion of Person with person. Sometimes our earthly bodies can barely contain the weight of that exquisite joy. It is more than a wonderful feeling. It is Life, Real Life. In tasting this new Life we feel so cleansed within. And why not? In the very center of our being we commune with Life – our thoughts are washed in His thoughts, our wills are strengthened by His will, and our affections are bathed in His. Some perceive the presence of His Spirit in different ways, but one moment of His sweet presence is worth everything. Life can never be the same.

To us it is no longer strange that God speaks to Moses out of a burning bush, for our hearts have become in fact a burning bush, out of which God speaks to us in tender tones – and directives. For out of this fellowship with the fire comes the call to redeem, to bid my people go. So this communion ends in a commission. And that commission in turn feeds upon the communion.

The wonder of it all is not that we should speak of His presence, but the wonder is that we would speak of anything else.

Prayer for today: O God, my Father, thank You for Your presence in my heart where I can commune with You there, what a blessing! Amen.

What is meant by **CERTAINTY** and **THE OPEN ROAD**?

CERTAINTY – Knowing **without a doubt** that we are God's child, fulfilling His purpose for our lives and certain that we will be with Him in heaven.

THE OPEN ROAD—The road to learning more and more as we study God's Word, pray, and follow His leading, always open for new ideas, new ways, not set in our own little world of staleness.

(Next page, please)

November 1   Romans 8:15-16; Philippians 1:6;
                              3:12-14; Hebrews 12:1-2

THE JOY OF CERTAINTY AND THE OPEN-ROAD

There is not a joy more wonderful than the joy of being in touch with Christ, and **knowing** without a doubt that we are His and He is ours. With that ultimate certainty life becomes permanent and centered. Life is no longer controlled by the changes around it. A certainty that is with eyes wide-open and still remains certain is indeed certainty. The Christian can have that.

Sometimes we have spiritual certainty, without an open road. We may be afraid of open roads. So we cling to our spiritual certainty and ignore everything else. Along the way we may discover the open road, but be careful when you find the open road that you do not lose your certainty. We can have both, certainty that we belong to Christ and an open road, where our ideas, mind and theological system can take in new and exciting things.

If we have the open road but no certainties, we know the quest, but no rest. We continue to travel and travel but never arrive. This is called empty righteousness. We think we can't be certain, but we know better. We travel with a new excitement when we have certainty within. It is a certainty that makes us excited to know more. We realize we cannot live on the after-glow of some past experience; there must be fresh discovery every day. And there is! The best sign is that we want more of Christ. A sure sign that we are on the Right-Road is when we feel we are on the Open-Road. There is eternal progress before us. The joy of spiritual growth is one of the deepest joys of life. Living victoriously means certain, but also adventurous living. Experience and exploration sum it up.

Prayer for today: O Christ, You have touched us, and our hearts are on fire to know more. Feed us "more" until we are satisfied. Amen.

November 2   2 Corinthians 3:17-18; Galatians 5:1;
                              James 1:25; 1 Peter 2:16

THE SPIRIT'S LAW

We have been looking at certainty and the open road. A scripture which sums up this combination of our spiritual certainty and freedom is this one, *"because through Christ Jesus – the law of the Spirit of life – set me free from the law of sin and death."* (Romans 8:2). Paul puts them together and says, *"The Spirit's law is life in Christ Jesus."* Someone divided religions like this: "Religion of the Spirit" – is directed from within.

"Religion of authority" – is directed from without. One depends on inner life, the other on outer law. Paul puts them together and says - the Spirit's law is life – Life in Christ Jesus.

Life in Christ is the fixed norm. We are not wondering – we **know** what life is, for we **know** who God is. God was transformed so He could become available. A high voltage wire sends a mighty electric current. We cannot use it. It is too powerful for our appliance. It would melt the thing, explode it, or at any rate it would ruin it. The current goes through a resistance box and transformer and into voltage which is usable, (or something like that). Our electric appliances are empowered, not destroyed. God becomes assessable. We now see what He is like and what we can be like. We have a fixed point in our world. You can't know how much that means to your life and the significance of it until you have seen it in contrast with systems where there is nothing normal, no fixed point. Whole systems drifting! But God has met us in history and that meeting is Christ. "Life in Christ Jesus," that gives us a fixed point.

Prayer for today: O God, we thank You that we have seen You in Jesus face. And now we can never be satisfied until we are like Him. Our heart glows with gratitude. Amen

November 3   John 16:7-15; 1 Corinthians 2:9-13

THE SPIRIT'S LAW REVEALED

The Spirit reveals what is unrevealed in Christ. He will not guide us contrary to what we find in the life and teaching of Christ. This is as permanent as law. But the extent of revealing is immeasurably great.

In (John 14:26) we see again the combination: *"But the Counselor, the Holy Spirit...will teach you all things and will remind you of everything I have said to you." "**He will remind you of everything I have said to you.**"* – This is concrete facts. *"**He will teach you all things**"* – this is the Spirit's direct, immediate voice to each generation and to each individual. This is progressive revelation!

And what is the Spirit's voice for this troubled and distracted generation who are searching for a way of life and plans for the future? The Kingdom of God on earth! Can we see the possibility of a new world in God's plan? God's plan scares governments and groups where other plans are being made. We are not ready for God's plan yet, for we are not ready for salvation. We will stumble along until one day we will fall on our knees and take God's plan seriously and then — — ! A new generation, a new fellowship, new people! Is it just a dream or is it a possibility? Do you hear the Spirit's voice among the clamor of voices, reminding us of the fact that our Master proclaimed the Kingdom as His message, and He does not change. The Kingdom is at our door – our one open road, our one hope. GOD'S PLAN IS SALVATION FOR ALL – *"He who has an ear, let him hear what the Spirit says to the churches."* (In other words, let every intelligent person and every Christian; listen carefully to what the Holy Spirit says). (Revelation 2:7, 11, 17, 29, 3:6, 13, 22).

Prayer for today: O Spirit of the Living God, You are speaking to dull ears and Your voice calls us anew to the Kingdom. Help us to listen. Amen.

November 4   Luke 22:32; Acts 13:1-3;
                              Ephesians 4:12-16; 2 Peter 3:18

PRACTICAL SUGGESTIONS FOR GROWTH

We have seen where we exist under a Living Mind – God's. And under His Law that is revealing Life. We must therefore grow to remain Christian.

1. **Grow by your mistakes**, even by your sins. Many people when they fall collapse and stay down. But losing a battle does not mean losing the war. Many have won wars though losing a few battles; it has made them more watchful, more humble, and more determined. When you fall, fall on your knees – a very good place to fall! Then get up and say well that was a jolt, but I have learned my lesson. Ask and you will receive re-enforcements for that weak place. You become strongest where you are weakest. Paul was a converted Pharisee and he became strongest where he was weakest – he became a man of humility who depended on grace. If you fall don't give up, get up.

2. **Grow by taking on a task beyond your powers**. That will cause you to depend on God's grace. Don't limit yourself to things that you can do – that won't stretch you. Do something that you can do only with God's help, in doing it you will grow. I know this from experience, leading my first Bible study, doing a rewrite of this book, I attempted these things at Christ's insistence, and truly there is divine re-enforcement in the attempt. Paul grew with the size of his task – the opening of the Gentile world meant the opening and enlarging of his whole nature, including his mind.

Don't ask for task suitable to your powers, but ask for powers, suitable to your task. And make them big! When God called Mary, she did not shy away, nor did she become proud, she simply said,

"I am the Lord's servant, may it be to me as you have said."(Luke 1:38). She was ready for anything. And how amazingly she grew spiritually under the greatest of her task!

Prayer for today: O God, my Father, give me spiritual task which go beyond me, so I may draw heavily upon Your resources. Amen.

November 5   1 Chronicles 4:10; Acts 1:8, 16:9;
                              1 Corinthians 16:9;
                              Revelation 3:8

GROW BY EXPANDING YOUR TERRITORY

3. **We must not only take on greater task <u>in order to grow,
    we must expand our territory</u>**. Christianity has grown to
    the limits of many of its concepts. It needs larger concepts
    – (ideas, images, etc.). Christianity has gone as far as it can
    go under the idea that religion has only to do with personal
    freedom and your personal culture. In finding the roots of
    our personal life we see it flow straight into our social life.
    This is the area of growth in the future for many of us, for
    we have been like potted plants, confined to the cramped
    ideas of a personal gospel. We must be transplanted to the
    garden of larger social ideas and endeavors, and then we will
    grow. We have reached the limit of potted growth. We need
    to expand our territory.

In planting trees someone was told after digging a deep hole
for the tree, to put in a layer of fertilizer, then a layer of dirt, and
continue to layer this way until you reach the top. This gives the
growing tree something to reach for. The trees roots get to one level
and they feel the call of the deeper level of richness. The call of what
is beyond is always there.

Christianity must put its roots into the total life of humanity, or
else it will die, root-bound. Or Christianity will remain a stunted,
pathetic thing in this modern world. But let's not talk about
Christianity in general, let's talk about ourselves. We <u>cannot</u> wait
until everybody else is ready to act. In the parable of the mustard
seed (Luke 13:19) it says the man planted a seed, "*in his garden*" –
{in his **own** garden} we must begin there. Jesus announced His own
program for the disciples in the Sermon on the Mount (Matthew
5:1-12). He expects from us the same.

Prayer for today: O Christ, help us to expand our territory and claim it for Your redemptive purpose. Help us not to be afraid, but begin now. Amen.

November 6   Isaiah 54:2-4; Luke 12:50;
                                    1 Corinthians 15:13;
                                    Ephesians 5:8-11

INTENTIONALLY PLAN TO GROW

4. **We said that we must expand our territory in our social life in order to further our own spiritual growth**. Of course our motive should not be just to save our own soul, but we should strive in whatever we do to help save humanity, because it is the right thing to do. Our all belongs to Christ. Anything less will result in <u>our</u> <u>own</u> expansion. So how shall we expand our territory for Christ? (a) Do it mentally. Renounce in the depths of your heart an unchristian, selfish, competitive attitude and give yourself inwardly to a principle based on co-operation. Refuse to give your approval to anything that breeds hate, poverty, disaster, etc. (b) Figure out how you can apply that inward ambition in positive action in your circumstances. Whatever your situation in life always endeavor to be co-operative instead of competitive. (We aren't talking playing competitive games here). <u>We are talking about spiritual growth</u>. In whatever circumstance you find yourself in, begin to build co-operative work ethics. (c) Break down any race or class barrier that may exist in your social or work circle. Do not patronize people of another race or class – they will sense it at once. The will to be a true and sincere friend is as important as the will to believe. <u>You must truly act like a</u> <u>friend before you can be one</u>. (e) Influence as many others as possible. **One thing we all possess is influence**. **We may use it for good or bad**. **But use it we do**! <u>Let's use it unashamedly to win people to Christ</u>.

(f) Become charged with the idea of "the Kingdom which is the Supreme Power of our Christian Socialized personality," and "the rule of Sovereign Love."

Prayer for today: O God, our Father, help me to begin the Kingdom Program and to know the Kingdom Power in every single one of my relationships. Amen.

November 7   Psalm 40:6-8; Matthew 23:4; James 2:16

BEWARE OF SATAN'S ATONEMENT

We said we should act as though the Kingdom is already operating in our heart. We must anticipate the full coming of the Kingdom. That anticipating of a new day will cost us. It will mean a cross. You will find your cross at the point of stress between your new life and your old life.

5. **At the point of stress is where temptation steps in:** You will be tempted to plan other people's sacrifices rather than your own. That is Satan's atonement. When *Caiaphas, the one who had advised the Jews that it would be good if one man died for the people* (John 18:14), he was practicing Satan's atonement, for he was not preparing to sacrifice himself, but someone else to save the people. That is Satan's atonement. When terrorist get people to sacrifice for the sake of a cause and then will not sacrifice themselves – again it is Satan's atonement. When ministers place burdens of moral responsibility upon others and feel their duty is thereby discharged, not touching the burden in the least, is this not Satan's atonement? If you preach it don't breach it.

I think the message here is if we see something that needs to be done, unless we plan on rolling up our sleeves and pitching in to get it done, don't promote it for others to do if you feel too important to do it yourself.

Therefore if we take our cross in order to bring God's message to others, let's be sure we do not take it and place it on someone else shoulders and walk away.

Prayer for today: O Christ, we pray that we may fulfill Your word, that each one of us will take "our own cross" and come follow You. Amen.

November 8   Ephesians 4:23-24; James 1:5-8;
                                    1 John 3:16-18

UNIFYING OUR MIND

For real spiritual growth there must be a unity between the conscious and the subconscious minds. The subconscious mind can be taught the purposes of the conscious mind. It can be educated. But the subconscious will not listen to what you say – only what you do. As the subconscious learns from the conscious they are both slow to forget. And the lessons the subconscious learns and takes to heart most deeply are not the purely intellectual notions of the conscious mind, but the values and emotions associated with them. For instance, a person may believe with their conscious mind that God is good and that all people are equal, but only if that person **ACTS** as this is true will their subconscious mind believe them. If our conscious mind affirms the principle of love, but we scheme to injure others, it is the attitude of hate that the subconscious mind learns. Therefore you cannot teach the subconscious mind anything that is not real. It will not learn it. What this says to me is – **no matter what we pretend to be – our subconscious knows the truth about us.** Jesus put His finger on it when in (Mark 6:8) He instructed His disciples, *"Take nothing for your journey except a staff – no bread, no bag, no money. Wear sandals but not an extra tunic."* Note: (KJV verse 9) says, *"And not put on two coats."* All right, you can see I have on only one coat, an outward sign of obedience as well as a message to all who sees me that I believe in God's faithfulness to take care of my needs, - no money, no bag, and no food. But **I have put on an extra, secret inner garment**. My subconscious mind will learn from the secret inner garment rather than the outer obedience. We should not pretend to be someone or something we are not. Go over your life and ask yourself if you are wearing any extra inner garments. **Growth is growth in reality – not in pretending.**

Prayer for today: O Christ, help us to tolerate no unreality, no make-believe. Help me to be real. Amen

November 9   Isaiah 40:27; Matthew 6:11;
                               James 4:13-15

LIVE TODAY!

6. **In our spiritual growth we must learn to live today – not tomorrow, "today"**. One of the most important things Jesus said was, *"Don't worry about tomorrow...Each day has enough trouble of its own."* (Matthew 6:34). Many of us ruin today by bringing the troubles of tomorrow into it. **Worry is the advance interest we pay on tomorrow's troubles.** Many of us go bankrupt paying interest on troubles that never come. So worry becomes sin – sin against God's goodness and love. A Doctor Worchester said, "You could pack all the actual misfortunes of your life into a moderate-sized closet, while your whole house, no matter how big it is, would scarcely hold all the unrealized evils and misfortunes you have feared and looked forward to." I had an uncle who was a building contractor. Sometime early in the successful years of his business he built a beautiful large office building, it housed his business as well as offices of others. With retirement approaching my uncle began to worry as to how he would make the final large payment on that building. I remember him worrying about it a year or so before the last payment was to be made. He worried needlessly. One month before the final payment was due, he died. I'll never forget the lesson **I** learned from his worry. It is reported that nine tenths of our worries never come to pass, the one tenth we can handle. Do today's task, fight today's battles, and don't be distracted by looking to tomorrow for things you cannot see and could not understand if you could see them. LIVE TODAY! Remember you do not have to win tomorrow's battles today. Win the battles you face today and tomorrow will take care of it self. Christ Power keeps you this very moment; that keeping power will extend to the next

moment, and to the next, and at the end of the day you can whisper to yourself, "**VICTORY**!"

Prayer for today: O Christ, I thank You that You have called me to today's adventure. Help me to make today eternal because I have put eternal worth into it. Amen.

November 10   2 Thessalonians 1:3-5; James 1:3-4;
1 Peter 1:7

GROW THROUGH OBSTACLES

7. **We will learn to grow through our obstacles**. When Beethoven, going deaf, said, "I will blunt the sword of fate." He meant it and he did. He grew by that very obstacle. When the Samaritans refused to receive Jesus and His disciples, (Luke 9:54-55) tells us that Jesus turned and rebuked the disciples for wanting to retaliate and then, *"They went to another village."* If you are blocked from the one, go on to the next. There is always a "next". And that next village was closer to Jesus' final destination. He didn't have so far to go the next day. He advanced toward His destination by the obstacle that the first village presented. Thank God, life always has another village. When we are disappointed in something, pass on to another village. The early impact of Christianity produced this fact: *"Philip had four unmarried daughters who prophesied."* (Acts 21:9). The fact that they never married was because of their Christianity. Spinsterhood emerged as the result of Christianity. At that time the unmarried felt the call to be married to the sorrows and sufferings and ignorance of the world. Like the daughters of Philip, unmarried status became prophetic. Have you been disappointed in your life's work? Grow with that disappointment. Henry Martyn, after years of patient work, translated the Bible into Persian and traveled to present it to the Shah. He went into the court to make his presentation. As he placed it before them and they began to realize what Book it was, they walked out one by one, including the Shah. Henry Martyn was left alone with his Book, rejected. His comment: "I refuse to be disappointed." And he passed on to another village. "I refuse to be disappointed," for the disappointment can be a spiritual growing place. It may put us on a new path,

368

jolt us out of old ruts, deepen our sympathy, and altogether make us a better person. Grow by your obstacles!

Prayer for today: O Christ, I thank You for making my frustrations fruitful. Help me to continue this way. Amen.

November 11   Genesis 32:24-29; Luke 18:1;
                                     Acts 12:5; 1 Corinthians 16:9

GROW THROUGH OBSTACLES – BY PRAYER

These enlightening verses say, "*But they were furious and began to discuss with one another what they might do to Jesus.*" (Luke 6:11-12). "*One of those days Jesus went out to a mountainside to pray, and spent the night praying to God.*" Here was an obstacle – the madness of His opponents which drove them to ask what they should <u>do **to** Him</u>, and He asked what the Father should <u>do **through** Him</u>. Prayer made it possible that Jesus would not be a victim of circumstances. He met His circumstances from above. What will my circumstances do to me today? Rather, what will I do today through my circumstances by prayer? Again here are my limitations; do they plot to restrain me, to keep me from being effective? Is the last word with the obstacle? NOT AT ALL! I decide through prayer, and the power that comes through that prayer, what I will do with my limitations, my obstacles. Many people have pressed forward by a limitation and have become great through that limitation. Sometimes the feeling of inferiority because of a limitation or obstacle gives that inward determination to advance. When coupled with prayer it gives us power to go forward.

What shall my enemies do with me? Rather, what shall I do with my enemies through prayer? I will have power to forgive them.

A Roman judge said to a martyr, "I have power to kill you." And the martyr replied, "But I have power to be killed." That was the greater and final power.

We grow by meeting our obstacles, but not through the obstacle alone, but through prayer brought on by that obstacle.

Prayer for today: O Christ, Thank You that the last word, even on the cross, was not with Your enemies, but with You. Help me to turn every obstacle into opportunity through prayer. Amen.

November 12   Acts 20:28; Hebrews 12:1;
                                               1 Timothy 4:16; 6:11

GROWING SPIRITUALLY

We have learned that our circumstances do not decide our destiny, prayer and God's Word does. Our spiritual lives are determined by the power we receive through prayer and studying God's Word. There is no substitute. **Prayer is our <u>communing with God, and God's communing with us</u>**. This will determine our spiritual growth. We can know we are growing spiritually when we can feel free and unafraid to share Christ with others. God says to Paul, "*Do not be afraid; keep on speaking, do not be silent. For I am with you, no one is going to attack and harm you...*" (Acts 18:9-10). Notice that God doesn't say that, no one is going to attack you (period), but He says, "*No one is going to attack <u>and harm you</u>.*" **No attack from without can harm us within. We can only be harmed from within by wrong choices. We are absolutely safe within as long as we are right with God.**

8. **Grow in your victory over "half-sins", things that may be lawful to you, but are not suitable for God's purpose**. Paul suggests in (Hebrews 12:1) "*...,let us throw off everything that hinders and the sin that so easily entangles...*" "*Everything that hinders*" – things that bring no condemnation, but also bring no contribution. Do not ask, "Is it wrong? But ask, "Does it contribute?" Then if it does not contribute to our life's purpose let it go. Jesus says to His disciples: "*You must be on your guard.*" Why? So that you might escape coming disaster? No. But be on your guard so you will be prepared to give your witness. (See Mark 13:9). Be spiritually prepared, He says, so that you will be prepared to stand before governors and kings as witnesses to them. For that hour does not depend upon your circumstances but upon you. Grow in quality of spiritual preparedness.

Prayer for today: O Christ, help me to let go of every hindrance that might slow my pace. For I desire to be spiritually prepared. Amen.

November 13   Matthew 21:21-22; Mark 9:23;
                               Luke 8:50; Acts 3:16

GROW IN CREATIVE FAITH

Jesus talking to His disciple, said in (Luke 17:3-6), *"So watch yourselves. If your brother sins...seven times in a day, and seven times comes back to you and says, 'I repent,' forgive him."* And *the Apostles said to the Lord, "Increase our faith!"* And *the Lord replied, "If you have faith as small as a mustard seed, you can say to this mulberry tree, 'be uprooted and planted in the sea,' and it will obey you."* He suggests that they "watch themselves" – about what? About having an uncreative faith in people, create faith in them even when they have sinned against you seven times in one day, after all, they did repent seven times, and seven being a lucky number believe in them that there will not be a sin number eight. That's creative faith. When the disciples asked that their faith be increased, it wasn't so much faith in God as faith in people, in unsteady, unwavering people.

Jesus says that if you have enough faith you can make a mulberry tree be planted in the most unstable soil in the world – the sea! You can make souls stable by creative faith. We need people with creative faith now, because a vast cynical attitude has crept across our spirits. We lack people of creative faith. Christians must hold the world together by their faith. We must hold society and individuals from going to pieces by our creative faith.

Grow in your belief in people, in their possibilities, in the fact that the worst can become the best. *"Watch yourselves,"* and let nothing weaken your faith. For if you lose your faith in people, you lose your faith in God too.

Prayer for today: O Christ, help me to believe in people as You believe in them. And help me to have creative faith. Amen.

November 14   2 Timothy 2:15; 2:20-21; 3:16-17

A PEOPLE PREPARED

9. As we continue to discuss this subject of being spiritually prepared to carry out God's purpose let's look at this remarkable statement concerning John: *"for he will be great in the sight of the Lord. He is never to take wine or other fermented drink, and he will be filled with the Holy Spirit even from birth...And he will go before the Lord, in the spirit and power of Elijah...to make ready* <u>*a people prepared*</u> *for the Lord.* (Luke 1:15-17).

A people prepared! If we ever needed a people prepared we need them now? A world seeking security, stability, a world in turmoil. Are we as Christians a "prepared people"? What kind of people can be a prepared people? The scripture tells us: John was extremely solid in three ways – **toward God, toward himself**, and **toward the people**. (1) <u>**Toward God**</u> – John was "great". We need people who are "great in the sight of the Lord" and don't care in the least if they are great or small in the sight of people. (2) <u>**Toward himself**</u> – he could put himself aside: he drank no wine or other fermented drink. But positively – he was filled with the Holy Spirit. We need people who can give up <u>things</u> for a great cause and who are filled with the Holy Spirit. (3) <u>**Toward others**</u> – he acquired the best and finest of the past – he came in the spirit and power of Elijah. We need people who will hold to every fine gain in the past. They must be conservative. But they must also be radical: *"And he will...'turn the hearts of the fathers to their children...'"* (Luke 1:17b). We would think it would be reversed here. But no, the older generation must turn its heart to the children, must think in terms of making the world safe, secure, fair, and loving for our children. We must therefore be radical. **Let us be extremely <u>solid</u> people in these three ways, toward God, toward ourselves, and toward others and we will be a prepared people.**

Prayer for today: O Christ, make me a person prepared, that I may help produce a people prepared. Amen.

November 15   Isaiah 26:3; Matthew 22:37; 2 Timothy 1:7;
                     1 Peter 1:10, 13

A PEOPLE PREPARED – IN MIND

(10) **In our study of growing spiritually, we must face the necessity of growing in mine**. No people can be prepared unless they are growing mentally. Religion today is up against the most complex problems both within us and within society, for our faith is being challenged from all sides. As Christians we must be able to show how God is great enough and dynamic enough to meet our worlds need. Today Christians are being forced to rethink how we represent Christ to a world that is in deep need. Our religion must function there, or it will be discarded as irrelevant. I know it seems this is already a fact, but a Christians we cannot believe this way. **The Kingdom concept demands we must function and function <u>strongly</u> in today's world. We must be relevant.** We are grateful for what unlearned Christians have done, but this is no time for ignorant belief. For the world suffers almost as much from wrong ideas as from wrong wills. Wrong ideas in history have produced as much havoc as wrong intentions. Christians therefore must think straight and act straight. Therefore, grow in mind. Try to read at least fifty pages of an inspirational book each day. If your mind stops growing, so will your soul. You will become the victim of set phrases and stereotyped ideas – caught in a mental rut. A new book will help jolt you out. We speak of an intellectual love of God, and Jesus spoke of loving God *"with the mind."* – A portion He added on His own accord to the Old Testament command and law. (Deuteronomy 6:5). New Testament (Matthew 22:37, Mark 12:30, Luke 10:27). It must have been important. IT IS! *"For the spirit which God has given us is not the spirit of fear, but discipline, and of love and a <u>sound</u>*

mine." (KJV 2 Timothy 1:7). Did He put "*a sound mind*" last for emphasis?

Prayer for today: O Christ, help us to conquer new worthy ideas and use them for the purpose of Your Kingdom. Keep our mind from getting into ruts. Amen.

November 16   Ephesians 3:17; Philippians 1:9;
                               1Timothy 1:5; 1 John 2:5

GROWING IN LOVE

11. **In all of our spiritual growing we must grow in love.
Unless we grow in love we are not growing at all**. "Jesus
knew that the time had come for him to leave this world
and go the Father. *Having loved*..." (John 13:1). It was
the greatest thing He had done in life and it would be the
greatest thing He would do in death. Nothing greater in life
or death for Him, nothing greater for us. <u>So</u> – <u>make LOVE
your pursuit</u>. But let it be an intelligent pursuit. Go over your
life and see if there are unloving and, unlovely places there.
Perhaps you may find a tinge of jealousy toward someone. If
so say something nice about that person today. Of course the
rule is if you can't say something good about that person say
nothing at all.

My husband has often told the story of his grandfather who was
known for never saying anything bad about anyone. When an older
man in their community died absolutely no one knew anything good
to say about him; they waited with great anticipation to see what Ben
Moore would have to say as he looked at the man in the casket. And
true to Mr. Moore's reputation he said, "Old John sure was a good
whistler." If we try we can always find the good in others. It is there
– look for it. Perhaps you find that your service to Christ is becoming
mixed with motives other than pure love. A little boy placed beside
his Mother's breakfast plate a note she hardly believed: "Mother
owes Bradley – for running errands-$2.00, for taking out the trash-
$1.50, for being good-$1.50, for taking piano lessons-$1.00, extras-
$1.00. Total $7.00. His Mother smiled, but did not say anything, and
at dinner time she placed the note on Bradley's plate with the $7.00.
Bradley was so excited.

But there was a note for Bradley that read: "Bradley owes Mother
– for being good, $0.00, for nursing him when he is sick, $0.00, for

all his meals and beautiful room, $0.00. Total: Bradley owes Mother $0.00."

Tears came into Bradley's eyes, he put his arms around his Mother's neck, thrust his little hand with the $7.00 into hers, and said, "Take this money back, Momma, and let me love you and do things for nothing!"

Prayer for today: O Christ, cleanse my heart from the will to bargain and help me to serve You and others for love alone. Amen.

November 17   Luke 10:25:37; Ephesians 4:15;
                           1 John 3:17

GROWING IN SOCIAL LOVE

The real test of spiritual love is whether we are growing in love. And this test applies to society as well as to individuals. Our Christian influence in any society is measured by the love we bring into the society. The evidence of which is – social justice and the abundant life of all. There are two great driving forces in human life – hunger and love: Hunger being our passionate desire for life, and love being our desire for life for others. We have organized our entire life largely around the hunger drive (our desire for life), with love (desire for life for others), coming in last. This puts disruption and conflict at the very center of our life. If we would change the center from our hunger for life, to love, then life would be co-operatively organized. Then the center of our life would be the driving force and hunger would be at the outer edge. This would not only be good Christianity but good economics, for we have now discovered the means of supplying everyone's economic needs, provided we can co-operate to do it. To have co-operation life must be organized on the basis of love. Sound economics pushes us to the Christian solution. Supplying our economic needs should just be a regular event in our life not an absorbing passion. We should not live for our hunger, but hunger because we live. When Jesus was hanging on the cross, (John 19:28) says, *"Later, knowing that all was now completed, and so that the scripture would be fulfilled, Jesus said, 'I am thirsty.'"* After He had done all He could for others He thought of His own needs – *"I am thirsty."* We have put our thirst first far too long. This is not cool, it is chaos. Love must dominate and our individual thirsts must be ranked lower, if we are to be Christian.

Prayer for today: O Christ, we pray that we will grow in Your way of love. For only as we love do we live and grow. Amen.

(Please read next page)

Read again Luke 10:25-37.

(Verse 30) In reply Jesus said: and.....

(MaryAnn's version) —

SOCIAL LOVE

A person was going across life's highway. He was confronted by the World's Social Church bandits. They stripped him of all this life's worth – his dignity, his faith in fellowman, his everything. They left him broken hearted, dirty, ragged and alone with no sense of direction, spiritually dying beside life's road.

By chance a "regular" church member came along and when they discovered this man sitting in <u>THEIR</u> church pew this Sunday morning, they quickly passed him by and crossed over to the other side of the church. A "professing" Christian walked over and looked at the man sitting there alone and he too crossed over to the other side of the church to be seated. A "known neighborhood drunk" came to church this morning, as he often does when he is sober enough, and when he saw the lonely man, he felt deep pity for him. He went over to him, sat down beside the man, smiled a broad friendly smile, and offered him a few kind words of welcome and a firm handshake. After the service he took the man home with him for a hot meal and soothed his hurts with words of understanding.

In your opinion, which one of these three acted like a "Christian neighbor" toward this man who had been brutally attacked by "Social Church Bandits?" *The teacher of the law answered, "The one who had mercy on him." Jesus replied, "Go and do likewise."*

November 18   1 Corinthians 12:5,12,13,26,27;
                Ephesians 4:25; 5:30

GROWING THROUGH FELLOWSHIP WITH OTHER CHRISTIANS

We grow when we fellowship with others who are also pursuing a life with Christ - Hence the Church. How can we get the most out of that collective fellowship? Simeon came into the Temple and saw the Lord's Christ. How did it happen? Simeon brought something with him, and seeing the Lord's Christ was the result of what he brought. We see in (Luke 2:27) – *"Moved by the Spirit, he went into the temple courts."* Go to church – *"moved by the Spirit"* – and you will see something. But many go to church "moved by the flesh." Maybe to show-off beautiful clothes or to hear myself speak, maybe to visit with my friends. Or just to listen to some new attractive music. But the Lord's Christ does not appear. We were not *"moved by the Spirit"*. What does it mean to be *"moved by the Spirit"*? The account tells us there were four foundational things: *"Simeon was righteous and devout. He was waiting for the consolation of Israel, and the Holy Spirit was upon him."* (Luke 2:25). He had: (1) Rightness toward people – *"righteous."* (2) Rightness toward God – *"devout"*. (3) Rightness toward the nation – *"waiting for the consolation of Israel.* (4) Rightness toward himself – *"the Holy Spirit was upon him."* Waiting and watching for the consolation of his own people did not keep him from seeing the possibilities in other people: *"A light for revelation to the Gentiles."* (Verse 32a). He saw that Christ would not only bring consolation to Israel, his own nation, but would reveal possibilities in others, the Gentiles. This is Christianity – narrow nationalism is not. Bring these four basic things with you into the Temple, and then you will see amazing possibilities in yourself, in others, in nations, all through Christ.

Prayer for today: O Christ, as we prepare to go into Your Temple, help us to take this fourfold rightness with us, and then we shall see

You. And then when we go out into the world we can stand four-square to life. Amen.

November 19   Ephesians 1:9-10; 4:4-6,12,13,16;
                     Colossians 3:15

GROWING THROUGH UNITY

The next big step in Christianity is Christian unity. **In a world seeking unity, Christians have little moral authority unless they can demonstrate unity.** **It seems that more often we demonstrate disunity rather than unity. This hinders the acceptance of Christianity and hinders the growth of Christians themselves.** We have gone as far as we can in spiritual growth under separate denominationalism. We may advance here and there, but with no great burst of collective spirituality until we come together. But you ask, "How can we come together unless we agree in everything?" We do not make that a requirement of fellowship in our home. The home can be a unity in spite of differences in temperament and belief. **The one thing that binds us together is that we are children of the same parent**. So in the family of God the thing that binds us together is not that we all have the same spiritual temperament, or even the same shades of belief, but **the fact that we are all children of the same Father**. Let that be enough for us. We can use our differences as growing points. Some music is based on melody and not on harmony. Some traditional songs are sung in parts bringing out marvelous harmony. Anyone not familiar with this style of singing would obviously think, "What a pity, they can't all sing the same tune." But doing so wouldn't be harmony. The very differences make strong and beautiful harmony. We will never get "melody-unity", in church unity, for we cannot all sing the same part, but we can have "harmony-unity", and that will be far stronger and more beautiful. Each denomination will sing its part, and out of it will come the full strength and beauty of our gospel. We will grow individually and collectively only as we appropriate from each other the distinctive contribution of each. We must grow in unity.

Prayer for today: O Christ, You are bringing together many different parts to make one great harmony. Help us to sing our part and to appreciate and appropriate the parts of others. Amen.

November 20   Psalm 84:7; Proverbs 4:18;
                               Philippians 1:6; 2 Thessalonians 1:3;
                               2 Peter 3:18

GROW IN GRACE

Perhaps the most distinctive fact in the gospel is grace, so the most distinctive fact in our spiritual growth must be growth in grace. The grace of God is LOVE: - Judging our sins, suffering for our sins, forgiving our sins, removing our sins, and then abiding in our unworthy heart. That is grace. To grow in acceptance, in living by that very same grace, is to grow in the most distinctive and deepest fact of our gospel. However, the modern mind is afraid of the doctrine of grace, but the deepest instincts long for it. We are afraid that to depend on Christ will destroy our initiative, weaken our very fiber, and turn us from upstanding into clinging personalities. If this were the result of grace, I would reject it too. But His gifts of grace do not weaken our personality, they strengthen it. Jesus says, *"Indeed, the water I give him will become in him a spring of water welling up to eternal life."* (John 4:14). Now, note the gift of water becomes within us a well of water welling up. The gift produces spontaneity! Many gifts do not. They weaken. It is hard to give to people and not weaken them, especially those who are always looking for something for nothing. But here is a gift that strengthens in the very act of giving. It is not a gift that demands nothing from us. It is the most expensive gift we will ever receive – expensive to us. For when we take that gift of water and it wells up within us, EVERYTHING we have goes out in exchange. Now, having given to God mutual sharing, we are a co-operating person. **The lower we bend the straighter we stand**. Those who depend on the grace of God develop the strongest personalities. So when we grow in grace, we grow in personal initiative and energy.

Prayer for today: O Christ, may this well of spontaneous life forever well up within us, since we depend upon Your life. Amen.

November 21   John 13:3-5; Romans 12:3, 10, 16;
                            1 Corinthians 15:10; 1 Timothy 1:15

GROW IN HUMILITY

Yesterday we learned that grace strengthens personality. But the very strengthening of the personality will bring danger. As we grow spiritually **pride** becomes a real danger. Many fall because of it. After a storm you may have seen a beautiful branch of a tree broken and lying on the ground. Parasites may have caused it. Large bunches of a parasite, like mistletoe, (yes, our Christmas decorating mistletoe grows parasitically on trees). Anyway, parasites weaken trees and when the storm comes, it breaks and falls. **Our most dangerous parasite is spiritual pride – many are weakened by it and when the storm comes they fall.** The true way to be humble is to stand tall against something bigger than we are and that will show us the smallness of our greatness. Stand at your very highest, and then look at Christ, and go away and be forever humble! When we lose sight of Christ, we ourselves begin to loom large. When we lose God, we lose our source of humility.

(John 13:3-5) – "*Jesus knew that the Father had put all things under his power, and that he had come from God and was returning to God;…He wrapped a towel around his waist. After that he poured water into a basin and began to wash his disciples' feet…*" The consciousness of greatness was the secret of humility. Jesus' greatness was rooted in God. Being in God made Him great – and humble. Great became humble and humble became great.

Remember, only the humble can lead. "**People who parade their greatness seldom lead the parade**." They cannot lead, because we simply cannot inwardly respond to the proud however "spiritual" they may seem to be.

Prayer for today: O Christ, give me a mind like Yours, for You are meek and lowly in heart, and I want to be like You! Amen.

November 22   John 15:10, 14, 16; Ephesians 2:10;
                               1 Peter 2:9; 1 John 2:17

GROWING IN OBEDIENCE

When the disciples came in from a night-long, but fruitless, effort at fishing, *Jesus said, "Put out into deep water, and let down the nets for a catch."* Peter in half-doubt, even less faith said, *"Master, we've worked hard all night and haven't caught anything. But __because you say so, I will__ let down the nets."* (Luke 5:4-5). *"__Because you say so, I will__"* – do these words not sum up the Christian attitude? *"__Because you say so__!"* His **"word"** speaking through the ages has never let us down. Whenever people have obeyed it, they have found themselves on an open road; when we have disobeyed it, we find ourselves on roads with dead ends. His **"word"** has been energy to the living and grace to the dying. People's words may let you down – God's WORD will not. Nothing has been so tested in history as Jesus' righteousness, and nothing proven itself more right as His righteousness. So – there is only one thing left: **"Because You say so, I will!"** But many of us do not say that. We say – "Because You say so, I'll think about it." Our mind is stirred by Him, but not controlled by Him at the place of "the will". Or some of us say, "Because You say so, let me see how I feel about it." We are moved by strong emotional responses to Him – sermons stir us, the reading of the Bible brings a thrill to our heart, but it does not go beyond that, it does not work itself into our "wills". But there are those who say, **"Because You say so – I will."** __These are the Growing Christians__. We truly are growing as we grow at this point. This is the test as to whether the gospel is functioning within us. Many of us are willing to do God's **work** but not God's **will**. If this is so with us, then our center remains unchristian. We are Christian to the degree that Christ has our will. When we can say, **"Because You say so. I will,"** then we really are growing toward Living Victoriously.

Prayer for today: O Christ, I know I can trust Your will for my life. Help me to show that I do, by the way I live. Amen.

November 23 Proverbs 28:1; Ezekiel 3:9;
Philippians 1:27; 2 Timothy 1:7

GROWING IN COURAGE

To break with your present way of life, to put into operation your vision for Living Victoriously demands COURAGAE.

We can all think of incidents of courage, our own or those we have seen or heard about recently. However, these two incidents happened early in the twentieth century: An afghan convert felt the call of Christ to witness for Him in the closed country of Afghanistan. He no sooner began witnessing in Khandhar than he was captured and driven to Kabul. Literally "driven", for they put a bridle in his mouth and drove him like a donkey the two hundred miles, and along the way men were invited to pluck his beard and spit in his face. Arriving at Kabul, he was asked by authorities if he would renounce his faith. He refused. One arm came off. He was offered everything. Again he refused and the other arm came off. When even then he still refused to deny his Master, his head went off. **Courage**! A lamp burns continuously before the "Martyr's Shrine" at Peshawar, and high up on the list is this man's name. We should feed upon such courage as that.

Look at these two pictures: The Christian Commissioner of Peshawar was asked if mission work could be started on that wild frontier. His reply: "What do you want, all of us to be killed in our beds?" He wasn't killed in his bed, but a Moslem fanatic did stab him to death. What he feared came true. Mr. Edwards, the next Commissioner, when asked the same question, replied, "It is not a matter of our safety, it is the matter of the will of God. Of course we will do it, for us Christians have no other choice." He called the Christian people of his station together, took a collection of three thousand rupees (dollars) on the spot and invited the missionaries in. Mr. Edwards name is loved and revered by Christians and non-Christians alike. **Courage, creative courage**! Grow in that and you really grow!

Prayer for today: O Christ, give me this gift of courage, for You have it and I need it – today. Amen.

November 24   1 Corinthians 6:20; Ephesians 2:15;
                               1 Peter 2:21-25; 3:8-9

GROWTH IN RECONCILIATION

"Be reconciled to God!" How familiar that sounds as a text for
the unsaved! The text was **not** written for the unsaved, but for the
saved: *"We are therefore Christ's ambassadors, as though God were
making his appeal through us. We implore you on Christ's behalf:
Be reconciled to God."* (2 Corinthians 5:20).

(2 Corinthians 6:1)— *"As God's fellow workers we urge you
not to receive God's grace in vain."* The message was to "fellow
workers" who had received the grace of God that the plea to be
reconciled was given. It was not for initial reconciliation, but for a
continuous reconciliation that the demand was made. Otherwise the
grace of God will be received in vain.

Christ is calling to the Church today to be reconciled to God.

(1) In regard to our message **OUR** message has not been **HIS**
message: "The Kingdom of God". We have not preached the
Kingdom "as a head-on sweeping answer to the world's needs." We
preach a doctrine here and a doctrine there for individuals, but this
full answer to our total needs, individual and social, has not been
single-pointedly proclaimed with any firm conviction. We need to
be reconciled to God at the place of our message. (2) We need to be
reconciled to God at the place where we contact society and make
the Kingdom of God believable, attractive, acceptable and real.
Concerning Christ we have too often given the wrong impression to
society, we have been antagonistic, argumentative, and untouchable.
Who wants to join up with that? We need to suffer in the sufferings
of those who suffer, to be hungry in the hunger of the hungry.

(3) We need to go over our lives and see where there are any
points not reconciled to God. Has our self-will slipped in and taken
the place of the will of God? ere is scarcely anything needed in the
**world today so much as that the Church be reconciled to God in
its total life to the total will of God.**

Prayer for today: God, Your everlasting love flows free,
Help my declining self subside;
My empty heart hungers to be
Reconciled to Your even flowing tide. Amen.

November 25   Genesis 18:19; Deuteronomy 11:19;
                               Joshua 24:15

GROW SPIRITUALLY WHILE MAKING A CHRISTIAN HOME

Jesus finally won His whole family to His cause. There was a time when His family thought, *"He is out of his mind."* (Mark 3:21). But at Pentecost they were all there – "His Mother and his brothers," waiting for the gifts of the Holy Spirit. Apparently, they all were now believers. One of the great proofs of the resurrection can be found in that simple fact. Something had happened to change them.

Jesus did not win His family by compromising with them. He won them by making sacrifices that cost both He and His family. Many are willing to sacrifice for the Kingdom, but not if it causes suffering to their loved ones. This is a mistake. Our decisions will involve our loved ones in common suffering with us. It is part of the price of being family. However, it works both ways – as we sacrifice for the cause of Christ, it **will not only lift us, but will lift our family as well.**

We do not win our family by some spectacular sacrifice, but by consistent Christian example. In (Luke 1:66) – When John the Baptist was born the question was, *"What then is this child going to be? For the Lord's hand was with him."* Ask the question this way – "What will this child be, for the hand of national propaganda is with him?" **ANSWER:** A narrow-minded partisan who hates and is ready to fight! And "what will this child be, for the hand of ruthless society is with him?" **ANSWER:** Either a destroyer of others or a man who turns out beaten down by such society as this. And again, "What will this child be, for the hand of a sex-saturated world is with him?" **ANSWER:** A dissolute person who is morally and sexually unrestrained.

And "**What will this child be, seeing that the hand of a consistent and contagious Christian is with him?**" **ANSWER: Infinite possibilities of development are open to such a child. Are you that kind of father or mother or will you be?**

393

Prayer for today: Christ, thank You that You did win Your family. Help me to do the same. Amen.

November 26   Leviticus 19:18; 1 Corinthians 13:4-7;
                  Colossians 3:20-21; 1 Thessalonians 4:9;
                  Hebrews 10:24

GROWTH IN APPRECIATION

We cannot change our loved ones or anyone else with continual nagging. The Pharisees thought the only way to change people was by disapproval of them. They tried it, it backfired, and they themselves were disapproved of. One time they traveled all the way from Jerusalem to Galilee, and what did they see? Did they see the glorious coming of the long-looked for Kingdom? NO! Did they see the wonder of the love of the man with the Healing Hands? NO! Did they see the gates of life being opened to wounded souls? Oh NO! They saw only that the disciples ate *"with unwashed hands"*! (Matthew 15). They looked right over the great and saw the trivial. And they became very small by what they saw.

The little boy, who said his name was "Johnny Don't" for that was what he was called at home, probably had an attitude of resistance and rebellion. On the other hand, when a hungry little boy sat down to eat and began obeying his appetite instead of waiting for the blessing, which now had to be said with his mouth full, replied in response to his Mother's inquiry, "Well, anyway I didn't chew." His wise Mother commended him for that much restraint, then appealed for full restraint next time. The little fellow evidently caught the spirit of appreciation for others, for when asked by an evangelist if he would like to travel with him in his work, he replied, "Take my baby brother, he's a good Christian."

Bring into the home a lot of appreciation and you will fine that the little ones will open to its comfortable warmth.

Prayer for today: Christ, help me to appreciate people not only for what they are, but for what they may become – in You. Amen.

November 27   Proverbs 31:28; Ephesians 6:4;
                               1 Thessalonians 2:11

"PROMPTED BY HER MOTHER"

It is a serious fact that children in the home take the attitudes of the parents, rather than what the parents say. You may have heard your parent say it or at least heard it said, "Don't do as I do, do as I say do." It doesn't work that way, because action speaks louder than words. **A child learns by what you do, not by what you say**.

The daughter of Herodias dancing before Herod, it says in (Matthew 14:9): "<u>Prompted by</u> her Mother, she said, *'Give me'*..." What did the daughter desire? Well, that depended on what her Mother desired. She wanted what her Mother wanted.

We wonder at the undisciplined youth of this generation. Do we not need to look back to the previous generation upon who rests a great deal of the responsibility? This generation has been <u>prompted</u> by the parents of today. Parents should not be astonished at present-day youth, for did not today's parents repeat the same old claims of morality and religion? Why didn't youth listen? Well, because this generation of parents repeated the sanctions of morality and religion with <u>less</u> and <u>less</u> conviction and certainty. The great grandparents of today's generation, having undergone conversion in the evangelical revivals at the beginning of their century had some personal living convictions. The next generation lived on that afterglow with little PERSONAL experience and the next generation a lot less personal convictions and therefore far less personal experience with God. <u>This generation of youth learned not what their parents said, which was very distant and weak, but what they did, which was not distant or weak</u>. The actions of the generation of parents now living <u>prompted</u> this generation – and this is the result.

The story of the daughter of Herodias is the story of "the prodigal daughter," the counterpart of the story of "the prodigal son." They both said, **"Give me" – always the first step down**. The prodigal son came back because he had a good father. The prodigal daughter never came back because she had a bad mother.

Prayer for today: God, Our Father, help us so live that we may prompt this generation of youth in desiring the best because they see You in us. Amen.

November 28   Deuteronomy 6:7; Malachi 4:6;
                               Luke 11:11-13

POINTS OF LIGHT

An old but true story is told about an ancient Syrian church in India. This church had a wonderful old brass lamp, with a hundred arms hanging from the ceiling. At the end of each arm was a cup with oil and a wick. At the close of the service the young people came up and took one of the wicks from the lamp to guide them home through the dark night. If you stood on a hill overlooking the village you could see the points of light moving in the darkness.

That is what a Christian home should be – a place where points of light are put into the hands of youth to go out into the dark world. There are many such points of light our youth can take from the home – **the light of basic honesty, of good will to others, co- operation, respect for all people, the spirit of giving,** that's to name only a few, **but first and foremost – a rich personal experience of Christ.**

In your time of devotion today write down any points of light you were able to take from your parents home. If possible thank them for those points of light that helped light your way as you grew into an adult. And then make sure you keep those lights burning bright in your own home.

The saddest thing on earth is a spiritually poverty-stricken home, where there is no central lamp from which youth can get light. **Be victorious in the home and you will be victorious everywhere.**

Prayer for today: Christ, I pray that this book will bring into the home such a flame of spiritual living that youth, and all who study it, may grasp a light that will never go out, **an eternal flame.** Amen.

November 29   Malachi 2:8; Matthew 18:5,6,10;
                               Hebrews 12:12-15

IN SOCIETY AND IN THE HOME

Yesterday we said that the light from a personal experience of
God is the greatest thing we can put into the hand of youth. Many
youth stay steady when faced with by modern doubt because of the
clean living faith of parents, or someone close to them. Then some
are wrecked because weakening of their parent's faith and the way
in which the parent or parents live or lived their life before them.
Hear the cry of this distressed and disillusioned youth:

> *Because I believed God brought you to me,
> And because I believed you were a Christian,
> With honor, truth, and love for all that is right,
> I believed in God and worshiped Him;
> Then when I found you were just a <u>pretender</u>,
> Full of unfaithful, dishonest, prejudices, and hate,
> All for wealth, fame, and power,
> The ruin of you, ruined by belief in God;
> So I fell beside the ruin,
> And sat in the stillness
> That followed the fallen image of God.

**If a person looks on you as "the image of God" do not let
them down, for the ruin of you, may be the ruin of God for them.**
If you are in danger of slipping, remember this – Living Victoriously
<u>is possible</u> in society and in the home. We blame society and say
Living Victoriously cannot be lived in such a society, with its temptations, its pressure and stress, its greed, its injustices – but right
there is where Christ will make us strong and victorious. And also
in the home! Pentecost took place in a home – upstairs in a common
home, not in a church, not in a temple.

Prayer for today: Christ, who gives power in the very place where we fail, give me power, today, any place the day takes me and especially in my home. Amen.

November 30   Matthew 5:13-16, 45; 19:3-15

HOLDING THE HOME TOGETHER

We have heard it said, "Christians hold the world together." They do, and they also hold the home together. Godliness in a marriage becomes the power that holds the home together. That power has never been more needed than in our homes today. For the home is being attacked from all directions. **If the home survives – the Christian will most definitely have to save it.**

Divorce "should" seldom be seen among sincere members of the Christian church. The Christian should not go to pieces under trouble and misunderstanding, and should know how <u>to give forgiveness</u> when wronged – and <u>how to sincerely apologize</u> when we have done wrong to another. A sincere apology often saves a situation from turning bad. Some one has said: A sincere apology – <u>Is a friendship preserver</u>, <u>Is often a debt of honor,</u> <u>Is never a sign of weakness</u>, <u>Is an antidote for hatred</u>, <u>Costs nothing</u> but one's pride, <u>Always saves more than it cost</u>, <u>Is a device needed in every home.</u>

Jesus says, "*You (we) are the salt of the earth.*" (Matthew 5:13). And in (Matthew 5:14) – "*You (we) are the light of the world.*" Also in (2 Thessalonians 5:13b) – "*Live in peace with each other.*" We are the salt of the earth – don't be dependent on your environment for life's taste. Shine light from within. Then the rough places at home will not mean all of life is rough. We are fed from within. That self-contained sense of taste will help us be at peace with one another. The main cause of not having peace with others is the sense of tastelessness within us. We feel frustrated with ourselves and take it out on others. The Christian holds the world together; we hold the home together, for we hold ourselves together by the fact that life has inward taste no matter what happens on the outside.

Prayer for today: Christ, give us inward salt that we may give outward peace. Hold us together, that we may hold our home and all situations together. Amen.

December 1   1 Peter 1:22; 2:9-10; 4:8-10

A DIFFERENT PEOPLE

The Christian is meant to be a new type of individual as different from ordinary humanity, as ordinary humanity is different from the animal.

Christians know and love God...

They do good to their enemies and make them their friends.

They abstain from sexual immorality and all impurity.

They love one another.

They help those in need.

They obey the commands of God.

They continually thank and praise God for His loving kindness to them...

Because of the Christians there flows forth the beauty of life.

And the good they do is not for their glory, but for the glory of God.

So – they labor to become righteous...Truly they are a different people

And there is something divine in them.

"A different people...something divine in them." This is the spirit that will create a new and better world. We must rediscover it and embrace it for this generation and any future generations.

Prayer for today: Christ, we pray that we may be worthy of this inheritance and give of it to this generation so desperately in need of just this. Amen.

December 2   Romans 15:4, 13; 1 Timothy 1:1;
                              Hebrews 6:11, 18-19; 1 Peter 1:3

SOLID FOUNDATION

We began this study and search for Living Victoriously by asking the question: Is life a bubble or an egg? I trust that now you have a firm belief that life is an egg, with infinite possibilities **IF** we hold on to the redemptive energies of Jesus Christ. Would you say: (1) Life is all bad, so get high on drugs or get drunk to evade and forget it? (2) Life is bad, but struggle against it with an impassive attitude? (3) Life is bad, so do the logical thing, just kill yourself? (4) Life is bad, but live illogical, accepting life as it comes? Obviously, the first three are absolutely not what we should say or even think. And number four is not the complete Christian statement, for <u>in Christ we do not merely accept life as it comes, we make life what it ought to be, by that redemptive energy available to us through Jesus Christ, the quality of life can be changed and the course of life can be turned to give it a moral mastery</u>. It is true that the Christian life has its limitations under present conditions, for there are those who successfully oppose us and then there is our recalcitrant nature. *"Jesus returned to Galilee in the power of the spirit"* (Luke 4:14), but He confessed that, *"only in his hometown and in his own house is a prophet without honor."* (Matthew 13:57). He was successfully opposed. The seed may be good, but a lot depends on the soil and other conditions if it is to be fruitful. So there are limitations. But, hang in there, in the finality we are not limited by those limitations. **We can turn limitations into contributions**. When the invited guests in the parable of the wedding banquet (Matthew 22) refused their invitations to the banquet, the servants were told to go to the street corners and invite anyone they could find. Successfully opposed at one point, successfully unopposed where it counted. Christianity has been described as for those who are "weak" or those who need a "crutch". Is it??

Prayer for today: Christ, Thank You that we can now face life with You as our hope and You as our solid foundation. Amen

This poem was written October 1978 to encourage a group of college students to stand firm while experiencing a time of struggle and confusion.

SOLID FOUNDATION

If we have a solid foundation
It is difficult to dent
It will stagger Satan's imagination
When on our destruction he's bent.

God said, "On this rock I will build"
Christ expects us to do the same
To build on anything else is self-willed
And will not hold through wind and rain.

This is made very clear
In Matthew chapter seven
Build on the Solid Rock
And have a home in heaven.

When Satan tries his tricks on you
Be steady, strong, and true
God is with you through any situation
As you firmly build on a solid foundation.

So – build on a solid foundation
And on God fully depend
Rejoice, for Satan's reputation
We do not defend.

Written by- MaryAnn Moore

December 3   Lamentations 3:21, 24, 26; Romans 5:2-5;
                    Colossians 1:5, 23, 27; 1 John 3:3

TIMELESS OPTIMISM

Christianity is "timeless optimism". As we listen to what others say about life, we find that the Christian is the only one – the only one who seems to have hope and an open road. We may be smeared and seem like poor material at times, but we know that we have grasp the ultimate reality in Christ.

True, there are failures among Christians and among well established Christians as well.

The reason is like this illustration: A vine reaches its delicate fingers up and across the void until it grasps the branch of a tree. It now has a grip on something. But a storm causes the vine to lose its grip and now it hangs loosely to the earth below – the branch of the tree upon which it was clinging had broken in the storm. The vine had fastened itself to a rotten branch instead of the strong healthy trunk. Many Christians are like that – they fasten themselves to some dead branch of Christianity, a special custom, or doctrine, or person, but not to <u>the central trunk</u>, **Christ**. The storm comes and they go down with the dead branch. This can happen when we fasten ourselves to the culture surrounding our Christian Church, but with no living contact with **Christ,** <u>the central trunk</u>. But when we have a firm grasp on <u>the central reality</u>, **CHRIST,** we can stand up against things victoriously and grow strong under adversity. In (Acts 13:17) it says, *"the people were made to prosper during their stay in Egypt."* They prospered in more ways than one. In adversity we "prosper" – provided we firmly grasp the central trunk, CHRIST. So Christianity is a "timeless optimism" only if it is Christ-optimism.

Prayer for today: Christ, my LORD, You have become my one steady place in a world of movement and change. Help me be dependable like You, so if people should fasten upon me I will not let them down. Amen.

December 4   Psalm 43:3-5; 71:5; Hosea 2:15;
                              Zechariah 9:12

LIVING IN TOMBS

Scripture tells us that a certain man *"Lived in the tombs."* (Mark 5:3). The fact is we all Live in a tomb – the earth is one vast tomb largely made up of dead bodies shortly after the beginning of time. We are on our way to becoming part of that cosmic dust. That is of course a pessimistic truth. But there are two ways to live in tombs – one way is the way of the man who had an evil spirit within him that caused him to cut himself with stones. On his way to death he deals death to himself. The other way to live in a tomb is to transform earth into a temple. Here we live in joyous fellowship and service. We live a deathless life among the dead.

This man living in the tombs was a man <u>out</u> of modern society. Modern society with its problems and oppressions had driven him mad. Modern society is doing that to many people today, for it is the focal point of our problems. It gets on our nerves and defeats us, so we retreat to tombs of our inner self and live there tormented by devils of depression and gloom and fear. It all depends on what is on the inside – unholy demoniac fears or the Holy Spirit.

When we have learned the secret of the Holy Spirit's indwelling, then the tomb becomes a temple. Our bodies, God's temple. *"Do you not know that your body is a temple of the Holy Spirit, who is in you…?"* (1 Corinthians 6:19).

Prayer for today: We thank You, O Christ, that Your tomb was a gateway to true life. Help me to keep my body a temple for Your indwelling. Amen.

December 5   Acts 23:6; 24:15; Romans 4:18;
                                    1 Corinthians 15:19;
                                    Thessalonians 2:16

SAY "NO" TO DENIAL

The Sadducees were the people who said, *"There is no resurrection."* (Acts 23:8). All they could say was "there is no." They lived on a diet of denial – poor diet! There are many who are living on denials. They get more spiritually lean every day. The whole thing seems so deviating – denying the fact of God and the world around us that radiates His power and His handiwork. We are His handiwork, too, and yet, our very faculties that God made can weigh values and meaning, even when deciding against those very values and meaning. It's like looking for your glasses with the very aid of the glasses you are looking for. You already have them on! So – do we deny God by the very God-given life within us?

The Christian does not deny death. He lives in it and then says: "There is a resurrection, because I am resurrected. I live now in victory over all denial." We do not deny death.

Satan's first supreme lie, *"you will not surely die."* (Genesis 3:4). Many try to deny death. Christians do not, we acknowledge death then proceed to overcome it and use it for Christ glory.

The Christian lives in perpetual springtime. There is a renewing taking place at every moment of our lives. For when we look at Christ we can say, "Nothing is too great to be believed and nothing is too great to be true."

Prayer for today: O Christ, save me and my world. I thank You. Amen.

December 6   Matthew 7:24-27; 2 Timothy 2:19;
                              Peter 2:6

SUFFICIENT OR INSUFFICIENT?

We have all seen that deep spiritual person lose a close family member - spouse, child, mother, father, etc. And we have watched as they go on with life unperturbed and radiant. They never go to pieces under the strain of their grief and sorrow. And you ask, "Are all Christians like that?" Maybe not, but it certainly is the central distinction of a Christian – solid, strong, sufficient. All other ways of life are lacking solidity, strength, sufficiency. The Christian way stands up under life. It has wearing qualities. It will outlast all other things.

Recently we watched as hurricanes ripped away entire cities, towns, shorelines, flattening everything in its path by the wind, rain, fire, and flood, it all became part of the devastating destruction. Only the "**solid**" stood up under such devastating conditions.

We find people everywhere being flattened by the pressures and devastation of life. Life becomes too much for them. But the Christian has beneath them a **Solid Foundation** –

And that **SOLID FOUNDATION** is **CHRIST** – our **SOLID ROCK**! That Rock being fused in the fires of the cross is igneous, the ultimate granite upon which the world is built.

The Christian finding the Central Solid Foundation beneath their feet dances with great joy. The Christian deals in ideas which become facts – the Word made flesh. It is all very solid, strong, and sufficient!

Prayer for today: O Christ, the Solid Rock beneath my feet, help me today to help someone who is on sinking sand to get their feet on the Rock. Amen.

December 7   Acts 7:54-60; 2 Timothy 4:6-8, 16-18

IN THE FUTURE

We have been asserting that Christianity is "basic optimism." It is. And it asserts that optimism about people and things when life is darkest. Christianity combines pessimism concerning our own limited ability with an exciting optimism as to what we may become when in God's hands. Pessimism – optimism, the last word is optimism. If there was ever a time when Jesus should have asserted pessimism, it was when standing before the council. *"They spit in His face, struck Him with their fists, slapped Him,"* (Matthew 26:67), *"they mocked Him, beat Him, and blindfolded Him"* (Luke 22:63-64). And through it all He said to them, *"In the future you will see the Son of Man sitting at the right hand of the Mighty One and coming on the clouds of heaven."* (Matthew 26:64).What a victorious soul! With the worst opposition in His face, He talks about sitting at the right hand of God. (Matthew 26:64) - With swollen lips and bloody face He basically says, "Final power is mine!" And it is! The ages have confirmed it. But the amazing thing is that <u>He asserted it while in despicable subjection to brutal authority</u> – *"<u>In the future</u>."* This is an important element in Living Victoriously. He did not say, "I <u>hope</u> that victory will be mine some day." But the (KJV) says – *"<u>Henceforth</u>"* meaning, <u>from now on, from this time forward, in the future</u>. He brought it into the here and now. And bringing it into the present is a part of the victory, a very large part. When the shadow of the cross fell upon Jesus, He saw in the shadow His Father's face, and knew "in the immediate future everything would change." We too must catch and assert the immediacy of the victory. Then we will be close to –

"The pierced side of the One
Who died upon an ancient hill
And left a singing in our heart
A song of victory from His asserted will."

Prayer for today: O Christ, You have put within me a song. Help me to sing it with immediacy in it. Amen.

December 8   John 15:3; Ephesians 5:25-27;
                             Hebrews 12:8; 1 Peter 4:17

INNER CORRECTIVE

As we talk about holding a basic optimism there rises up before us the many, many frivolous and foolish, immature situations within the Christian church, and this dampens and sometimes destroys, that optimism. Even now these irrelevances stand out and weaken the Church reputation against the world's need. We have built up things about Christ which have become and embarrassment to Him – and to us, weakening everything Christian. The story is told of a dutiful monk finding a little mouse disturbing his devotions, tied a cat near by, so it would frighten away the mouse. After the monk died, his followers wanted to do everything just as their master did, so they tied cats all over the rooms where they meditated. In the course of time the original reason for tying the cat wasn't even known, and so they had long discussions on what kind and color of cat should be used, how far from the worshiper, and so on. Many things which occupy our attention in Christianity are as meaningless as tying cats in devotional rooms for worship. This tendency toward irrelevancies within Christianity drives one almost to despair. Except for one fact — There is within the Christian system a corrective and regenerative principle and power in the person of Christ. He has an aseptic influence on the Christian system. He exerts a constant cleansing from within us. This inner corrective is our hope. Even today He confronts us with the question He asked His disciples, *"Do you still not understand?"*

(Matthew 16:9). And we are silent, as they were, for we too have disputed about irrelevancies. But as He corrected them so will He correct us. His Spirit is even now pleading through voices both within and without the Christian Church. And, above all it is pleading through the need of the world itself. Those that hear His voice shall live; those who do not shall perish.

Prayer for today: O Christ, we pray that Your call to us will lead us to complete repentance and obedience. Amen.

December 9   Matthew 16:18; 21:44; Romans 9:33;
                             1 Peter 2:4-5

STONES WHICH THE BUILDER REJECTED

As we look at the world situation the thing that hits us with the greatest force is the fact every place in the world needs the mind of Christ to become relevant, and not only relevant, but imperative, if the need of the world is to be met. George Bernard Shaw, (1856-1950, an Irish writer), wrote the truth when he wrote, "The only man who came out of the world war with an enhanced reputation for common sense was Jesus Christ. Though we crucified Christ on a stick, yet He some how managed to get hold of the right end of that stick...and if we were better men, we might try His plan."

Never have so many people realized this until now. And yet never have we seemed so desperately near abandoning His plan altogether as now. The world situation is dangerously unbalanced. It could go one way or the other. But those of us in this world who see clearly, see that what Jesus said is true, *"The stone the builders rejected has become the cornerstone."* (Matthew 21:42). The builders of civilization have tried to build a civilization without Christ. True, we thought we could put Christ in a decorative position to make our building more religiously respectable. But we <u>did</u> <u>not</u> put Him in the foundation and build upon Him. We thought He wasn't practicable. And now the structure of civilization is crumbling around us. The foundations are wrong – they are Christ-less, hence crumbling. <u>"The builders" rejected the very stone that would hold it all together</u>. All their attempts at diplomacy, balances of power, security through armies, selfish nationalism have broken down. The bankruptcy of these methods is laid bare before us. We must start again. This time Christ must not be merely decorative, but He must be in the foundation itself.

<u>Christ must be</u> "<u>The Cornerstone</u>." It is our only hope.

Prayer for today: O Christ, Your patience, astounds us. You have waited while we messed up the world with our Christ-less planning and now we are in confusion. Save us, we pray. Amen.

December 10   Galatians 5:13; 1 Thessalonians 3:12;
                               James 2:8; 1 John 3:11, 14, 16-18, 23

SOME REJECTED STONES

Yesterday we said that if civilization is not to crumble, Christ must be put into the foundation. The world demand, rightly interpreted, means that Christ must become the corner stone in the structure of our entire life. We have not put Him there. The builders rejected Him, and instead they put within the foundation something that was anti-Christ, namely, ruthless competition. Can you see how these two things cannot be compatible? In our scripture for today: Each scripture spoke of love – *"Serve one another in love."*

(Galatians 5:13). "May the Lord make your love increase and overflow for each other

And for everyone else." (1Thessalonians 3:12). "If you really keep the royal law found in scripture, 'love your neighbor as yourself.' You are doing right." (James 2:8). And the scripture in (1 John) everyone speaks of love. So, the picture here is Christ wants us to love others, not always trying to outdo them. Competition in life is selfish; it is always for the betterment of ME, not others.

We must change from competition to co-operation. If we do, then Christ would be our Foundation. His principles would spread through all society by a conforming LOVE.

Prayer for today: O Christ, this stone of LOVE rejected by the builders is so desperately needed in our lives today. Help us to find the love You have so faithfully revealed to us again and again in Your Word. Amen.

December 11   1 Corinthians 13:1-3; James 1:2;
                                1 John 4:7,11,12,20,21

LOVE MOTIVE – A REJECTED STONE

Present-day life demands that love be built into the social structure, for living demands love. The suggestion is that society organize itself around one to two motives – the greed motive or the love
motive. We have organized life around the greed motive; largely
it benefits a few at the exploitation of many. This has brought us
discontent, disruption, and disaster.

Look at Communism for example – life in Russia was organized
on the greed motive, not on behalf of a few, but on behalf of all who
would co-operate. This is even a higher step than organizing life
around the greed motive on behalf of a few, for they went far beyond
the limits of co-operation. But note that it is still the greed motive.
The entire Communist interpretation was about greed and excluded
the love motive. This meant that ultimately Communism would be
disrupted, it is not dead but disrupted, for greed is disruptive. When
a dominant greed is practiced it may co-operate with the love-prin-
ciple which is secondary to it, but in the long run it will inevitably
break into open struggle, between individuals and groups. Only love
can provide the ultimate motive for society.

People who love one another, with sincere love – will be moti-
vated by that love to co-operate for the satisfaction of one another's
individual needs and happiness.

Now, this love motive rejected by the builders has become the
capstone.

Prayer for today: O Father, we come to You asking for courage to
believe that this love-motive is the only way to live, and help us to
act on it. Amen.

December 12   Matthew 6:33; 21:43-44; Luke 4:43;
                               Acts 1:3

THE KINGDOM OF GOD – ANOTHER REJECTED STONE

When we study the recording of the New Testament, we find that the message of Jesus was the Kingdom of God. When we study "church history," (a significant phrase, for the history of the centuries of Christianity is "church history," rather than "Kingdom history"), we find that the message was the Church. Why did we let the Church take the place of the Kingdom of God? Jesus intended that the Church should be subordinated to and a servant of the Kingdom. But we have reversed that. Church first, Kingdom of God second. Jesus said, in (Luke 17:20-21), *"The Kingdom of God does not come with careful observation, nor will people say, 'Here it is,' or ' There it is,' because the kingdom of God is within you."* But we observe the Church from without. We observe the Church as in counting statistics, buildings, and other outer forms. The Kingdom concept is to be like Christ, it obeys the fundamental Christian law of losing oneself and finding oneself again. Hence – the Kingdom is much more Christian in than the Church, for the Christian obeys the fundamental Christian law of losing oneself and finding it again. Hence the Kingdom as gone further than the Church. If you doubt this, ask yourself this question: Is the <u>Church</u> a sufficient foundation upon which to build a new society? To ask is to answer. It was tried in the middle Ages and failed. But ask <u>is the Kingdom of God</u> a sufficient basis upon which to build a new society? The answer is that it is the <u>only</u> foundation on which to build. This stone which the builders, both Secular and Sacred, rejected has now become the only solid foundation of human society. The Church must become the servant of the Kingdom, which is far larger than the Church. For the need of the world cries out for the Kingdom of God.

Prayer for today: O God, our Father, in rejecting the Kingdom we have rejected You. Thank You for Your patience. We now see Your Kingdom as our only light. Amen.

December 13   Mark 1:14-15; 13:28-29; Luke 21:28-31;
                     1 Corinthians 1:30

THE KINGDOM OF GOD IS NEAR

When Jesus described the coming of the Kingdom, He used four different phrases all connected with the word, "near".

He said, "A*s soon as the fig tree has tender twigs and its leaves come out, you know that summer is near*". (Mark 13:28). When our life becomes sensitive, "tender", and the urge is there for a fuller life, we are ready to branch out (reach out), then we know that summer is near, the Kingdom is near within us. Has our world situation ever been; more tender and sensitive, tired of the old and longing for a new, fuller and better life than now? We have wanted fuller spiritual life for ourselves and other individuals, but we have never longed like this for a more victorious life for everybody, in everything. Does this not mean that the Kingdom is at our hearts door?

Jesus said, "*When you see these things happening, you know that it is near, right at the door.*" (Mark 13:29). The Kingdom is not impersonal. It is a personal Presence – universalized. It is breathtaking to assume His description of the coming of His Kingdom within us and His own second coming is synonymous!

In a parallel passage Luke says, "*When you see these things happening, you know that the Kingdom of God is near.*" (Luke 21:31). So the kingdom is redemption! We have seen that the "Kingdom" and "redemption" are also used synonymously. The Kingdom is His life within us, but it is the redeeming of all life as well. The Kingdom covers both.

The Kingdom, therefore, is the one open door before a confused and morally collapsed world. It is the stone which the builders rejected, but is now the cornerstone.

Prayer for today: O Father, Your Kingdom is near. It is now within us yet we long for it to burst upon the world with redemptive power. Help us bring it near to others. Amen.

December 14 Psalm 130:7; Colossians 1:14;
Titus 2:13-14; Revelation 5:9-10

REDEMPTION – A REJECTED STONE

Of all the stones which the builders of civilization have rejected, none has been more tragic in its effects than the rejection of redemption. Of course, individuals here and there have known redemption, but we have not used its resources for the remaking of the world. We thought we could make a changed world without changed men and women and now we know that didn't work. **Human sin is the real destruction of any world – our individual world or the world at large.** The Church must also take responsibility for rejecting this stone of redemption by confining that redemption to a restricted area. We rejected it by reducing it. We entered into a compromise with the world in which we said we will confine ourselves to saving souls while turning over the economic and social life to the forces of the world to manage

In this we betrayed Christ. We have lovingly preserved and confined Christ to our places of worship. We have confined Him to the personal, and have turned over the rest of life to other lords and masters – to our ruin. Now we see where the issues of life must be joined: One is the issue of economics (human welfare). For this part of life belongs to Him as does all other. Someone has said, "Christianity is the only religion that takes economics seriously. The material basis of human life is of the utmost importance to it." For, "if I do not master economics, then economics will master me." Christ must Master and redeem both.

This stone of redemption of the whole of life is now becoming the cornerstone. We perish without it.

Prayer for today: O Christ, our Redeemer of all of life, redeem us completely. And help us not to fear to claim all of life for You. Amen.

December 15   Matthew 7:28-29; 11:4-6; Mark 1:27;
                               John 6:63

THE REALISM OF JESUS – A REJECTED STONE

Of all the strange happenings in history the strangest may be: The Man who was the greatest realist in history has been turned into the greatest idealist. Jesus realism was so astonishing, so different that people did not know what to do with that reality. They had to accept it and act accordingly or reject it. But they couldn't seem to do either, so they found a way to hold onto Jesus and also hold onto their old way of life – they made Him an ideal – a person with good ideas to be followed later – but not right now. This satisfied their sense of loyalty to what they know was the higher road while still staying on the low road of life. Christ was crucified on the cross as being irrelevant. So we adopted Christianity as an idealism, lifted high above life, but inoperative except here and there in small things. Because we held high ideals we thought we were spiritual. Idealism is just concealed materialism, for it separates body and spirit, it refers religion to the spirit, while other ways of life control the materialistic. Hence – idealism becomes materialism, for materialism is what we act on. Jesus was astonishingly realistic. So realistic that people thought it idealism. When He said we must love our neighbor as ourselves, that is not idealism – it is realism, and we have now discovered that is the only realism that will work, nothing else will. Unless we give an equal and fair chance to everyone, we will have nothing for ourselves. Selfishness is suicide, collectively and individually.

When Jesus said we must lose ourselves to find ourselves, this is not idealism, it is realism. It is obeying a fundamental law of life. Nothing else will work. The demand that religion be realistic is with us **now.** The world is dying for this very need. So the realism of Jesus, rejected by the builders, is made the cornerstone.

Prayer for today: O Our Realistic Christ, make us realistic. Save us from those ideals that have become dangerous to us. Amen.

December 16   Matthew 9:8; 28:18; Luke 4:32;
                               Romans 1:4

OUR GREATEST NEED MET

"She will give birth to a son, and you are to give him the name Jesus, because he will save his people from their sins." (Matthew 1:21). A message to the world! In these words, and the fact of their meaning, our greatest need is met.

We said that people need two things: **Light** (understanding) on how to live this mysterious life of ours and **Power** to master this life we live. Christ gives us understanding on how to live this life by the way He Himself lived. His life becomes a focal point for our life's problems – in Him all our problems of life find their solutions. He is light. But He is more – He is Power – our power - to master this life and whatever it brings us. He saves His people from their sins.

Have you met Christ as a man – His humanity brings Him so near to us we can sense His presence, struggling with our struggles. We have found an example of life. In Jesus we have two things: One who is like us, meeting life as we meet it, **Jesus called on power from God to meet His moral battles, and we can call on that same power today**. Jesus met life, not as God, but as man. He experienced life as a human being like us. He showed us how we should live. Therefore He is our example. But I find something else in Him. He confronts me from the side of God with offer of redemption. Therefore unlike us, He is both our example and our Redeemer. But He was both, like and unlike us, therefore meeting both our need – for we need **light** and we need **power.**

Prayer for today: O Christ, help me to not stop half way, but continue until I find complete victory in life. Amen.

December 17   Deuteronomy 28:65-67; Job 17:13;
                               Luke 23:29-30

WHY THE MOOD OF DESPAIR?

If anyone would describe our <u>modern scientific humanism</u> in a very few words, these words would fit perfectly: **"Put your trust in modern society and have confidence only in yourself."** And a statement modern society has embraced, **"If it feels good, do it."** This is modern philosophy. This is the attitude and belief of our modern world today. They are so sure of this that they have become dogmatic.

This may be accepted as a modern gospel, but it is a gospel with no music at its heart. It doesn't sing. The fact is that modern society is growing very weary and its soul is confused and dismayed, <u>this kind of world is an illusion; it consists of short, small, and haphazard events, nothing permanent.</u> <u>No order, no unity, no quality of life.</u>

<u>Modern society's thinking is that it needs no savior except **itself**,</u> <u>now it finds itself</u> <u>disillusioned and full of despair.</u> Whether we want to admit it or not – modern society is fundamentally bankrupt. It can sustain neither faith in its philosophy, or hopes for humankind. If only it could see the necessity of humanity having a savior. We should not look at the drug scene, the sexual exploits so evident all around us, or the disorder of people, but look at the finest flower that ever bloomed – He was more than human and therefore is able and willing to meet our every need. Christ is necessary for humanity – <u>ALL humanity.</u>

Jesus Christ saves His people from the sins that cause despair, gloom, discouragement, and more, because He saves us from ourselves. **Jesus Christ is enough for anything that can confront us through this life!**

Prayer for today: O Christ, You are my remedy from gloom, discouragement, and despair. For in You I find happiness. I thank You and I love You! Amen.

THE GREAT EXPERIENCE

The greatest experience
You can ever try
Has no price tag
For this experience you cannot buy.

It was bought long ago
With Christ blood on Calvary
So enjoy it to the fullest
This great experience is free.

If you will try it
You will never let it go
You will keep it forever
Burning deep within your soul.

When you have experienced this joy
And know such peace within
You will want to share it with others
So their joy can begin.

If you are living this salvation experience
There is revelation in your heart
For God is Author and Finisher of this experience
And He has been from the very exciting start.

Written by – MaryAnn Moore
October, 1978

December 18   Matthew 7:13-14; 1 Corinthians 3:21-25;
                     2 Corinthians 5:14

"NARROW" AND "BROAD" – "WEAK" AND "STRONG"

In the course of our study together we have mentioned many things from which we are saved by the power of Christ. As we near the end of our study, we need to begin tying together any loose ends – so let's look at a great fear of many people – the fear of being considered "narrow-minded" or "weak." To be called either is terrifying in today's society. This stops many people from complete commitment and freedom in Christ.

It is true that living for Christ narrows our actions from that of the world. There is a sense in which Christians refrain from certain relationships and situations, and to those who do not know Christ; this may appear to be narrow-minded. Christ does narrow us in that regard and keeps us from doing many things we might otherwise do. But this is only one phase of the truth. Christ within us continually expands us. So as Christians we are at once the "narrowest" and "broadest" of all people! We are a people of – One Book and One Person. And yet, with Christ we can break all strongholds and barriers. We are people Of – One Book, and yet all books;

Of - One Faith, and yet all faiths;
Of – One Person, and yet all persons;
Of – One Interest, and yet all interest;
Of – One Kingdom, and yet all kingdoms.

Our main focal point is on Christ and with the other we sweep the horizon of all the above just mentioned. To sweep the horizon without our main focus on Christ would be Theosophy.

(Theosophy is any of various forms of philosophical or religious thought based on a mystical insight into the divine nature).

To have a focus on Christ without sweeping the horizon would be narrow-conservatism.

To have both – our main focus on Christ and an all-inclusive view of everything else is to be Christian. *"When we belong to Christ then the Spirit of truth will guide us into all truth."* (John 16:13). We are at once the "narrowest" and the "broadest" people in the world!

In Jesus prayer for His disciples, (John 17:20), He says, *"My prayer is not for them alone. I pray also for those who will believe in me through their message,....."* <u>That includes <u>you and me</u></u>! *In (John 15:5) Jesus says, He is the vine and we are the branches. If we remain in Him, we will bear much fruit; but <u>apart</u> from Him we can do nothing.* (Philippians 4:13) Reminds us that, "I can *do everything through Christ who gives me strength."* So as Christians we are at once the "weakest" and the "strongest" people in the world!

Prayer for today: O Christ, Thank You for Your freedom. Amen.

December 19   John 15:3; Romans 8:14-16; 1 John 1:4

EXPERIENCE – REVELATION

We have talked about experience during our study, however we need to address the issue that there are those who will say, "experience is an unsure foundation, it is too subjective, (exist only in the mind); too mysterious, (no explanation); too much like the historical process, (religious happenings of the far past). They believe we must depend entirely upon the objective Word of God, which speaks to us through the written Word. Experience from anything else would depend on emotion, but a religious experience through the written Word is steadfast and sure.

The full truth is in both experience and revelation. Read (Luke 24:35), this puts experience and revelation together. "*The two told what had happened on the way*," (Experience), and "*how Jesus was recognized by them when he broke bread,*" (Revelation).

In that experience they told of how the living Christ was with them and how their hearts burned within them as He spoke to them on the road (verse 32). To discount this experience is to discount an authentic meeting with Christ which is individual, personal, intimate, and life-changing. Therefore make no apology for religious experience, for Christ is in that experience just as definitely as He is in the Revelation. To deny experience, or to minimize it, is to minimize and in this way deny the living Christ of experience.

At the same time we must not minimize that this story's Revelation pertains to Christ. He revealed Himself in the breaking of the bread. He does speak through the Word. And that revelation of Himself is redemptive. Experience is always followed by Christ revealing Himself to us. To take one away from the other is to decrease each. We need both. They go together.

Prayer for today: O God, live within me each day in intimate experience, and then help me to listen to Your voice through Your Word in humble obedience. Amen.

December 20   1 Corinthians 4:12; Colossians 1:29;
                                2 Thessalonians 3:10;
                                Proverbs 26:13-16

CHRIST SAVES US FROM LAZINESS

We need to be saved from laziness, sluggishness, lack of ambition, lacking creativity, etc. The soul must be re-energized, made
alive and fruitful.

Christ does that for us. With Christ in our life our soul is made
more energetic. By our energy and happiness we know we have
found God. The soul now has a joy that is pure -a joy with a sense
of rhythm and harmony that produces fruitful energy. It does not
produce discomfort and disturb the flow of our energy, as some joys
do. The soul is not wasted on the lesser issues of life.

When the disciples said to Jesus, *"Rabbi, a short time ago the
Jews tried to stone you, and yet you are going back there?" Jesus
answered, "Are there not twelve hours of daylight?"* (John 11:8-9).
It is not a question of what they will do, or not do – there are twelve
hours of daylight. I must complete my task.

Look at the inward drive found in those words! The redemptive life within Him must express itself in spite of threats or obstacles. The life of Christ within us breaks up inactivity. Jesus disturbs
our complacency. He becomes the conscience of our conscience.
And because of this we do not waste time in needless rest. When
Christ comes into our life we have ambition, freshness, and energy.
No laziness. There is a sense of abounding energy when we are in
fellowship with this renewing, life-giving Christ.

Prayer for today: O Christ, I pray that today I may be saved from
all lethargy, all evading of responsibility. May I be alive and full of
energy for anything worth-while? Amen.

December 21   Romans 8:2: Galatians 1:3-4;
                               Colossians 1:13, 28: 2:10

CHRIST WILL SAVE HIS PEOPLE

As a Christian it is difficult to be pessimistic. There are enough hard, brutal facts of life to cause pessimism if we take our eyes off Christ. But with our eyes on Him our pessimism is cured. He is sufficient – He is power. Of course that power can only be released if we tap into it by completely surrendering to His will for us. But doing this, anything can happen. "*He will save His people from their sins.*" (2 Corinthians 12:9). That covers our every need.

We can hope with hopelessness all around us. For as we discover the larger meaning of sin – we discover that one central issue is selfishness. When we organize our life around personal gain instead of working for the greater cause of Christ, then we have organized our life around the un-Christian principle of selfishness. We find ourselves being disloyal to Christ as we are involved in the production of our own personal gain and ignore the need of the world around us. In (Galatians 5:19) selfish ambition is listed as one of the acts of a sinful nature. And in (Philippians 2:3-4) – "*Do nothing out of selfish ambition or vain conceit, but in humility consider others better than yourself. Each of you should look not only to your own interest, but to the interest of others.*" And (James 3:16) "*For where you have envy and selfish ambition, there you find disorder and every evil practice. "He is able to save completely…*" (Hebrews 7:25). That "completely" we have only started to explore. In that word we see provision for **every one** of our personal sins and **every one** of the social sins of the present and future. **Christ power is limited only as we limit it. When we allow Him complete control of our life His full power can be let loose**. He can save us "completely" because we will allow Him complete control. And that salvation will not be completely "**in** our sins" but completely "**from** our sins." There is a profound difference.

Prayer for today: O Christ, work today in my life saving me from my sins, help me to help others to be saved from their sins. Amen.

December 22   John 16:33; Colossians 1:13-20;
                     Hebrews 13:8

"YOUR HOUR"... "MY TIME"

We find conspicuous discouragement in our present society, this is characteristic of a civilization dominated by exhausted humanism. An exhausted humanism! <u>We have put **people** on the throne and worshiped them far too long</u>! We should rethink our object of worship. The people we worship have had their day and they have turned it into darkness. Jesus said, *"This is your hour – when darkness reigns."* (Luke 22:53b) – You have had "<u>your hour</u>," and the best you could do with it was turn it into darkness. These words certainly fit this day of humanism. Humanism has exhausted itself and us. Jesus uses another phrase to the people of His day: "<u>My time</u>." (Matthew 26:18, John 7:6 & 8). He was speaking of His appointed time to die. "<u>Your hour</u>" and you reveal darkness! "<u>My time</u>" – and I reveal light through that very darkness! I reveal hurt through your very hate, I heal through the wounds you inflicted; I sacrificed myself through your selfishness; I am characterized as a scoundrel universally because of your narrow mind. I create a universal fellowship through your national rejection; through the death you inflict I bring life to you and to all people. "<u>My time</u>" – I am Master even when most passive. I conquer even when most conquered. I save even when I cannot save myself. Then and now He is the unexhausted Christ. His "<u>time</u>" will yet come. The "<u>hour</u>" of exhausted people is drawing to a close – the "time" of the unexhausted God-man will dawn. He is here – at our doors. Some have taken Him in, know His power, but exhausted humanity as such must turn to Him or perish.

<u>Our "hour" is brief</u>. <u>The "time" of God is eternal</u>. We belong to that eternal and we will not be discouraged at this "hour." <u>This "hour" may belong to humanity – but the next is HIS</u>! So we rejoice in a victory that is, and that is to come. His touch is our victory – His "time" is our complete victory.

Prayer for today: O Christ, we thank You that we belong to the inexhaustible – help us to draw heavily upon it today. Amen.

December 23   John 17:10, 15-18; Acts 26:28-29;
                     Philippians 4:11-13

"IN ALL THESE THINGS"

To choose a verse that would sum up our entire study, it would be (Romans 8:37), "*In all these things we are more than conquerors through him who loves us.*" This statement combines an intense realism with an amazing positive affirmation of victorious optimism. The word "realism" defines real difficulties confronting such living. Look at the context. This is not a glossy painted picture which says that all is well for there are no problems, but an opened eyed frankness that says, "Yes, I see the difficulties that come from distress, persecution, hunger, godlessness, danger of death, of life, of things present and future – and yet – in all these things we are more than conquerors." It takes in all the facts of life, but it also asserts the central fact "VICTORY."

The word "in" depicts relations to, and yet it does not identify with all these things. It shows realistic <u>contact</u>, and yet inwardly beyond that contact, and that is the relationship we need. <u>To live **in** the world we will come **in contact** with many things, but we do not have to attach ourselves to them, "through Christ we can do anything,"</u> <u>that includes all the things we come **in** contact with day-in and day-out that we need to live beyond</u>. We may see these things, but we are not to be blinded by them. **"In all these things we are more than conquerors."**

Prayer for today: O Christ, make me more than a conqueror in all these things. May I learn to be at home <u>in</u> the world and yet not <u>at</u> home – as You were not. Amen.

December 24   2 Corinthians 6:4-10;
                                               Ephesians 6:13-20

"CONQUERORS"

Our battle is an embodied battle so the victory must be an embodied victory. If our spirituality is not shown in relationship to material things, then we fail spiritually. A person grows spiritually as they apply their spirituality to all life's situations. So "in all these things" we must be conquerors. But how can we be conquerors when so many of our social problems are not yet solved and we cannot solve them personally? We can acknowledge that complete victory is not here, **but it is as far as we are concerned,** for we and any power we might have is set in direction of solving them and we are dedicated to that end.

In the meantime set in motion a counteraction of any evil you encounter. When evils came at Jesus, He did not dodge them, or bear them, but He used counteraction. Through His crucifixion His counteraction was redemption. When evil came at Him, He had power to destroy that evil. When hate turns ugly against us, we can counteract it with reconciling love. If poverty is our station in life, we can start counteracting that with a Godly spirit among that poverty. When death takes our loved ones, we can counteract that deathless joy and began to hope through it all. In that way we help to conqueror death in ourselves and the world. If we live in turmoil and conflict, we can counteract with a peace and an undisturbed calm. If we live in an unfriendly world, we can counteract by being friendly. Christians love one another even before they are acquainted. Why? Because Christians started the counter-good of class-transcending reconciling love. So – every evil that comes upon the Christian can then make him produce a counter-offensive of victorious love.

Prayer for today: O Christ, Help us today in every situation to whisper to ourselves and to You, "more than conquerors." Amen.

December 25   Luke 2:1-20; John 1:14

THE SIGN IS A BABY

On the first Christmas morning the announcement was made: *"This will be a sign to you; you will find a baby..."* (Luke 1:12). The sign was a Baby – a fact; an embodied fact. This is the key to all of Christianity: it began as an embodied fact, it must continue as an embodied fact.

One country would have said, "You will find a mystic light – that will be your sign." Another country would have said, "You will find a correct code of morality." And yet another, "You will find a philosophical conception." <u>But the gospel said</u>, "*You will find a Baby*." The mystic light, the correct code, the philosophical conception, and much, much more, have come together in an embodied Person. Religion was now realization.

Christ became the reconciling place where opposites met. He was the meeting place of God and man. Man the aspiring and God the inspiring meet in Him. Heaven and earth came together and are forever reconciled. The natural and the supernatural blend into one when we are living a Christian life – you cannot tell where one ends and the other begins. The passive and the aggressive are so one in Him that He is aggressively passive and passively aggressive. The gentle qualities of woman and the sterner qualities of man so mingle that both men and women see in Him their ideal. The new Individual, born from above, and the Kingdom of God on earth are both offered to us in Him. The sign is a fact. <u>The weeping child cannot be satisfied with just the idea of a mother</u> – it needs a Mother! <u>We cannot be satisfied with just the idea of salvation</u> – **we need a Savior**!

Prayer for today: O Christ, since the sign must be an embodied fact, help me today to embody Living Victoriously and may this be in <u>all</u> of my life. Amen.

December 26 Matthew 5:44-47; Luke 11:10-13;
Philemon 16 & 17

"MORE"

Let's go back to (Romans 8:37) – *"In all these things we are* ***more*** *than conquerors through him who loved us."* The word **more** stands out with peculiar force: "**more** than conquerors." That word is a window-word that let's us see into the inexhaustible nature of our resources and the unlimited development before us. It is the **more** that really counts. It is the **more** that turns the tide toward victory. This **more** is the characteristic of the gospel. It allows us to go beyond the ordinary level in goodness, in achievement, in joy, in radiant living. It's that which gives "survival value" to the Christian. In the struggle of life in our lower nature it is that extra ounce of strength, the extra power of endurance that helps us survive when others fall, <u>beaten</u> by the struggle. It is this extra power that the Christian has at their disposal that keeps us from breaking when everything is breaking around us. It keeps us hopeful among hope-lessness, radiant among the shadows, morally able when surrounded by moral collapse. In the race of life the extra resources that the Christian finds in Christ makes us a moral winner. Since these extra resources are at our disposal, Jesus expects His followers **to do more** – He expects us **to do more because we have more.** There is only one thing better than Christian religion, **more** Christian religion, and you <u>will</u> want **more.** One touch from Christ and your soul will long for **more.** That inward passion for **more** of Christ should be an eternal thing, not dissatisfied, but forever satisfied! And when our inward cry for **more** is met by God's offer of perpetual **more** there is no limit as to what the Christian might be and do. Our potentiali-ties are limitless. They are if we are in contact with UNLIMITED RESOURCES.

Prayer for today: O Christ of the unlimited love, take away the limitations of my love. Put me under the umbrella of **more.** Amen.

December 27   John 15:5; Galatians 5:22-23;
                Philippians 1:9-11;
                Thessalonians 1:5;
                2 Thessalonians 1:3-5

PERPETUAL PARENTAGE

Christian religion "has had a perpetual parentage." It has been "the Mother of the arts."

All the arts as we know them owe their life to the historic body of religion; there is little that we call culture which was not at some time a purely religious function.

Christianity has given birth to one after another of the arts – not only music, painting, sculpture, drama, architecture, but also dancing, legislation, science, philosophy, morality. Christianity has given birth and nurtured them through their critical infancy. Then as they attained maturity and sufficient strength to exist independently, they continued their development as secular enterprises – often NOT without struggle. Hospitals, schools, universities, institutions for the unfortunate and the outcast, general philanthropy – all had their birth within the life of the Church. These and many other things, such as prison reform, abolition of slavery, improved labor conditions, organizations for world peace, were the results of that perpetual parentage characteristic of Christianity. The Gospel of Christ is very capable of producing spiritual offspring. And now Living Victoriously is under a new test. Has it enough power to give birth to a better world? This is the demand for parentage that is now laid on Christian religion. If we can show that the Gospel of Christ is capable of producing spiritual offspring here, Christianity can become the Mother of a better world.

We who are launching out into Living Victoriously must be so alive that new movements, new initiatives, new impulses, new lives will follow as evidence of the spirit of perpetual parentage within us. We are more than conquerors because we not only conquer our own battle, but we establish other organizations which help other people to conquer. We are more than conquerors because we are conqueror-producing.

Prayer for today: O Christ, may Your power produce in me some life-giving organization, however small. Amen.

December 28   2 Corinthians 9:15; Ephesians 6:1;
                               Philippians 3:6-7; Revelation 21:7

MORE THAN CONQUERORS

It would have been sufficient if Paul had said we are conquerors through Him that loved us, but he put in the added emphasis, "**More than conquerors**." Exaggeration? No, plain statement of fact. It is interesting to see how Jesus coming into the world gave language a whole new meaning. The language had expressed human meaning sufficiently, but now it had to express Divine-human meanings. The Divine was breaking through into the human; and language, called on to express that fact, sometimes breaks down. The early Christians had to come up with superlatives, coin new phrases, find more words, and often it became so overwhelming that the "Holy Spirit disorganized their grammar." The rules couldn't handle the pressure of this new, glorious, exciting life. The new wine had not only to be put into new wine-skins of new organizations and institutions, but also into new wine-skins of a new vocabulary. For here was a fresh new set of facts.

"**More than conquerors**" – what does it mean? In Africa, some of the tribes believe that when a man conquerors another, the strength of the conquered passes into the conqueror. That is what happens spiritually. When you conquer an evil through the power of Christ, the strength of the conquered evil effects you in two ways. First, it establishes the habit of victory within you and makes the next battle easier. This means that <u>the more we conquer, the more we **can** conquer</u>. Goodness becomes habitual and hence the normal attitude toward life. The grooves are cut within our nerve tissues so that life flows naturally in the direction of victory. Second, by conquering we are able to pass on to others the victory. And while sharing our victory it becomes more fixed within us. So in a double way we are **more** **than conquerors**.

Prayer for today: O Christ, thank You for freedom – freedom from fear of failure and from fear of future uncertainties. Amen.

December 29   Matthew 22:37; Ephesians 3:14-19;
                     Colossians 2:10; 1 John 5:4-5

THE BASIS OF BEING MORE THAN CONQUERORS

The basis of conquering life through Christ must be examined to see if it is sound and sure. For this purpose (2 Timothy 1:7) makes it very clear. *"For God hath not given us the spirit of fear; but of power, and of love, and of a sound mind."* (KJV) Here is the basis for the conquering – the entire being is strengthened. The personality made up of will, emotion, and mind is renewed – there is "**power**" for the will, "**love**" for the emotion, and "a sound mind. By the renewing of the total life the spirit of fear is gone. You cannot get rid of fear by wishing the fears away. They will not go away. They will go away only as they are forced away by some positive influence that takes the place of those fears. This positive influence is the spirit of <u>power</u>, of <u>love</u>, and <u>of sound mind,</u> – in other words, the Spirit of Christ working in the depths of your very being. The reasons for fear are rooted on one or more of these roots: (1) A sense of being weak, a feeling that we are inadequate. Life is too much for us. It demands more than we have to give. (2) A lack of love. We do not love people, so we are afraid of what they can do to us; we do not love God supremely, so we are uncomfortable at the thought of Him; we do not love His will for our life, afraid of what He will ask to do; we do not love life, so we are afraid of it. (3) We feel helpless and confused, for our minds lack self-discipline. We have no solution in our hands that can take care of the problem of human living – so we fear because of intellectual inadequacy. But now our whole being is brought under a unified control – **the Spirit of Christ**. That <u>means</u> **power** <u>for our will</u>, **love** <u>for our emotions</u>, and **self-discipline** <u>for our mind, to make it a sound (healthy) mind</u>. Christ is the answer for our life!

Prayer for today: O Christ, I can overcome anything outside of me as long as You possess everything inside of me. I am Yours. Amen

December 30   Isaiah 12:2-3; Luke 1:1-4;
                                2 Timothy 2:19; 1 John 3:24

THE BASIS OF OUR CERTAINTY

Have you grown a deeper certainty as we have studied day
after day? Now – a final word about that certainty and its basis. In
(Hebrews 2:3-4) we read, *"How shall we escape if we ignore such
a great salvation? This salvation, which was first announced by the
Lord, was confirmed to us by those who heard Him. God also testi-
fied to it by signs, wonders and various miracles, and gifts of the
Holy Spirit distributed according to His will."* There are three things
in this message: (1) the historic – "announced by the Lord Himself";
(2) the experimental – "confirmed by the gifts of the Holy Spirit";
(3) the collective witness – "confirmed to us by those who heard." It
is interesting that the Christian Church has taken one or the other of
these factors as the basis of certainty, and placed it as the authority in
Christianity. Many Protestants have said the place of authority is the
infallible Word of God – the Bible – the historical. Other Protestants
have made the basis of authority an infallible Christian experience – the experimental. Roman Catholics have made the infallible
Church the basis of authority – the collective witness. Each of these
taken alone is inadequate. But together they contribute to the final
certainty. The basis of authority is where the three come together. (1)
The historical. In Jesus a norm has been established in history which
becomes the touchstone of all life. We have seen Life revealed in a
life. (2) But that Life passes from the historical into the experimental
– the Jesus of history becomes the Christ of experience. We do not
simply remember Christ, we experience Him.

(3) But that personal experience may be a hallucination if alone.
It must be confirmed by the collective witness. It must be tried on
a wide spread scale and confirmed. **It is!** People of all ages agree
unanimously that it works. **Together <u>the historical</u>, <u>the experi-
mental</u> and <u>the collective witness</u>, all saying the same thing,
gives a certainty far beyond the certainty of one taken alone.**

The highest certainty the human mind is capable of knowing on any subject is ours!

Prayer for today: O Christ, I rejoice in this certainty. Help me to live worthy of such certainty. Amen.

December 31   1 Corinthians 12:4-27;
                                       2 Corinthians 3:17-18

A DWELLING IN WHICH GOD LIVES

(Ephesians 2:22) sums up our complete study: *"And in him you too are being built together to become a dwelling in which God lives by his Spirit."* A dwelling! **GOD,** not the dim, fugitive unknown, but **GOD** <u>the real</u>, <u>the intimate,</u> <u>the</u> <u>permanent</u>. And how can this be? By being "built together". Finding God, the Spirit, is an individual thing, but it is also deeply collective. We cannot expect the permanent abiding of God unless we "are built together". **Only a fellowship transcending race, class, and color can be the dwelling place of God.** But we have asked Him to dwell in a compartmentalized society and in a divided heart. It doesn't work that way. When Moses was about to build the Tabernacle, the Lord said to Moses, *"Make this tabernacle and all its furnishings <u>exactly</u> <u>like the pattern I will show you</u>."* (Exodus 25:9). Moses did. Then the story says, *"And so Moses finished the work." "<u>Then...the glory of</u> <u>the Lord filled the tabernacle</u>."* (Exodus 33b-34). <u>When</u>? <u>When Moses made everything</u> **exactly** <u>like the pattern</u>. **We have seen the pattern – the Kingdom of God on earth.** We do not need any other pattern. This is it. For it we will live and for it we will bleed – and if necessary, die. We will go out and make all things according to that pattern both within ourselves and in society. And <u>God will dwell in us as we are built together</u>. We cannot ask Him again to dwell in the ramshackle thing we call society, where so much is wrong and injustice grows deep. No, we will be "built together," where the sufferings of one are the sufferings of all, and where the gifts of God are shared by all. Into the holy tabernacle of humanity we can ask Him to dwell – and He will!

Prayer for today: O God, our Father, we cease our divisions within ourselves and in society and ask You to dwell with us. We will do our part. We say it with our life. Amen.

Printed in the United States
122105LV00003B/1-3/P